Leisure and Power in Urban China

Leisure and Power in Urban China is the first comprehensive study of leisure activities in a medium-sized Chinese city. Hitherto, studies of Chinese leisure have focused on holidays, festivals and tourism. This, however, is a study of the kinds of leisure that take place on regular workdays in the local environment of Quanzhou city. In doing so, *Leisure and Power* introduces leisure studies to Chinese studies, and data from China to the field of leisure studies.

Based on interviews with people from all walks of life and case studies from bookshops, internet bars, karaoke parlours, streets and public squares, Rolandsen brings to attention the importance of fun and socializing in the lives of Chinese urbanites. Central to the study is the contrast between popular practices and official discourse. Rolandsen provides in-depth analyses of the moralist 'PRC leisure ethic' so characteristic of official Chinese publications and news media. Using examples from everyday life as a contrast, this study demonstrates that official propaganda has but little influence on how Chinese individuals lead their lives. Taking leisure as a point of departure, this book describes the new kinds of interaction between the local party-state and the population it seeks to govern.

This book will be of interest to students and scholars of Chinese Studies, Leisure Studies, Urban Studies and Asian Studies in general.

Unn Målfrid H. Rolandsen is a postdoctoral research fellow at the University of Oslo, Norway.

Routledge contemporary China series

1 **Nationalism, Democracy and National Integration in China**
Leong Liew and Wang Shaoguang

2 **Hong Kong's Tortuous Democratization**
A comparative analysis
Ming Sing

3 **China's Business Reforms**
Institutional challenges in a globalised economy
Edited by Russell Smyth and Cherrie Zhu

4 **Challenges for China's Development**
An enterprise perspective
Edited by David H. Brown and Alasdair MacBean

5 **New Crime in China**
Public order and human rights
Ron Keith and Zhiqiu Lin

6 **Non-Governmental Organizations in Contemporary China**
Paving the way to civil society?
Qiusha Ma

7 **Globalization and the Chinese City**
Fulong Wu

8 **The Politics of China's Accession to the World Trade Organization**
The dragon goes global
Hui Feng

9 **Narrating China**
Jia Pingwa and his fictional world
Yiyan Wang

10 **Sex, Science and Morality in China**
Joanne McMillan

11 **Politics in China Since 1949**
Legitimizing authoritarian rule
Robert Weatherley

12 **International Human Resource Management in Chinese Multinationals**
Jie Shen and Vincent Edwards

13 **Unemployment in China**
Economy, human resources and labour markets
Edited by Grace Lee and Malcolm Warner

14 **China and Africa**
Engagement and compromise
Ian Taylor

15 **Gender and Education in China**
Gender discourses and women's schooling in the early twentieth century
Paul J. Bailey

16 **SARS**
Reception and interpretation in three Chinese cities
Edited by Deborah Davis and Helen Siu

17 **Human Security and the Chinese State**
Historical transformations and the modern quest for sovereignty
Robert E. Bedeski

18 **Gender and Work in Urban China**
Women workers of the unlucky generation
Liu Jieyu

19 **China's State Enterprise Reform**
From Marx to the market
John Hassard, Jackie Sheehan, Meixiang Zhou, Jane Terpstra-Tong and Jonathan Morris

20 **Cultural Heritage Management in China**
Preserving the cities of the Pearl River Delta
Edited by Hilary du Cros and Yok-shiu F. Lee

21 **Paying for Progress**
Public finance, human welfare and inequality in China
Edited by Vivienne Shue and Christine Wong

22 **China's Foreign Trade Policy**
The new constituencies
Edited by Ka Zeng

23 **Hong Kong, China**
Learning to belong to a nation
Gordon Mathews, Tai-lok Lui and Eric Kit-wai Ma

24 **China Turns to Multilateralism**
Foreign policy and regional security
Edited by Guoguang Wu and Helen Lansdowne

25 **Tourism and Tibetan Culture in Transition**
A place called Shangrila
Åshild Kolås

26 **China's Emerging Cities**
The making of new urbanism
Edited by Fulong Wu

27 **China-US Relations Transformed**
Perceptions and strategic interactions
Edited by Suisheng Zhao

28 **The Chinese Party-State in the 21st Century**
Adaptation and the reinvention of legitimacy
Edited by André Laliberté and Marc Lanteigne

29 **Political Change in Macao**
Sonny Shiu-Hing Lo

30 **China's Energy Geopolitics**
The Shanghai cooperation organization and Central Asia
Thrassy N. Marketos

31 **Regime Legitimacy in Contemporary China**
Institutional change and stability
Edited by Thomas Heberer and Gunter Schubert

32 **U.S.–China Relations**
China policy on Capitol Hill
Tao Xie

33 **Chinese Kinship**
Contemporary anthropological perspectives
Edited by Susanne Brandtstädter and Gonçalo D. Santos

34 **Politics and Government in Hong Kong**
Crisis under Chinese sovereignty
Edited by Ming Sing

35 **Rethinking Chinese Popular Culture**
Cannibalizations of the Canon
Edited by Carlos Rojas and Eileen Cheng-yin Chow

36 **Institutional Balancing in the Asia Pacific**
Economic interdependence and China's rise
Kai He

37 **Rent Seeking in China**
Edited by Tak-Wing Ngo and Yongping Wu

38 **China, Xinjiang and Central Asia**
History, transition and crossborder interaction into the 21st century
Edited by Colin Mackerras and Michael Clarke

39 **Intellectual Property Rights in China**
Politics of piracy, trade and protection
Gordon Cheung

40 **Developing China**
Land, politics and social conditions
George C. S. Lin

41 **State and Society Responses to Social Welfare Needs in China**
Serving the people
Edited by Jonathan Schwartz and Shawn Shieh

42 **Gay and Lesbian Subculture in Urban China**
Loretta Wing Wah Ho

43 **The Politics of Heritage Tourism in China**
A view from Lijiang
Xiaobo Su and Peggy Teo

44 **Suicide and Justice**
A Chinese perspective
Wu Fei

45 **Management Training and Development in China**
Educating managers in a globalized economy
Edited by Malcolm Warner and Keith Goodall

46 **Patron–Client Politics and Elections in Hong Kong**
Bruce Kam-kwan Kwong

47 **Chinese Family Business and the Equal Inheritance System**
Unravelling the myth
Victor Zheng

48 Reconciling State, Market and Civil Society in China
The long march towards prosperity
Paolo Urio

49 Innovation in China
The Chinese software industry
Shang-Ling Jui

50 Mobility, Migration and the Chinese Scientific Research System
Koen Jonkers

51 Chinese Film Stars
Edited by Mary Farquhar and Yingjin Zhang

52 Chinese Male Homosexualities
Memba, Tongzhi and Golden Boy
Travis S. K. Kong

53 Industrialisation and Rural Livelihoods in China
Agricultural processing in Sichuan
Susanne Lingohr-Wolf

54 Law, Policy and Practice on China's Periphery
Selective adaptation and institutional capacity
Pitman B. Potter

55 China–Africa Development Relations
Edited by Christopher M. Dent

56 Neoliberalism and Culture in China and Hong Kong
The countdown of time
Hai Ren

57 China's Higher Education Reform and Internationalisation
Edited by Janette Ryan

58 Law, Wealth and Power in China
Commercial law reforms in context
Edited by John Garrick

59 Religion in Contemporary China
Revitalization and innovation
Edited by Adam Yuet Chau

60 Consumer-Citizens of China
The role of foreign brands in the imagined future china
Kelly Tian and Lily Dong

61 The Chinese Communist Party and China's Capitalist Revolution
The political impact of the market
Lance L. P. Gore

62 China's Homeless Generation
Voices from the veterans of the chinese civil war, 1940s-1990s
Joshua Fan

63 In Search of China's Development Model
Beyond the beijing consensus
Edited by S. Philip Hsu, Suisheng Zhao and Yu-Shan Wu

64 Xinjiang and China's Rise in Central Asia, 1949–2009
A history
Michael E. Clarke

65 Trade Unions in China
The challenge of labour unrest
Tim Pringle

66 **China's Changing Workplace**
Dynamism, diversity and disparity
Edited by Peter Sheldon,
Sunghoon Kim, Yiqiong Li and
Malcolm Warner

67 **Leisure and Power in Urban China**
Everyday life in a Chinese city
Unn Målfrid H. Rolandsen

Leisure and Power in Urban China
Everyday life in a Chinese city

Unn Målfrid H. Rolandsen

LONDON AND NEW YORK

First published 2011
by Routledge
2 Park Square, Milton Park, Abingdon, Oxon OX14 4RN

Simultaneously published in the USA and Canada
by Routledge
711 Third Avenue, New York, NY 10017

Routledge is an imprint of the Taylor & Francis Group, an informa business

First issued in paperback 2014

© 2011 Unn Målfrid H. Rolandsen

The right of Unn Målfrid H. Rolandsen to be identified as author of this work has been asserted by her in accordance with the Copyright, Designs and Patent Act 1988.

All rights reserved. No part of this book may be reprinted or reproduced or utilized in any form or by any electronic, mechanical, or other means, now known or hereafter invented, including photocopying and recording, or in any information storage or retrieval system, without permission in writing from the publishers.

Trademark notice: Product or corporate names may be trademarks or registered trademarks, and are used only for identification and explanation without intent to infringe.

British Library Cataloguing in Publication Data
A catalogue record for this book is available from the British Library

Library of Congress Cataloging in Publication Data
Rolandsen, Unn Målfrid H.
 Leisure and power in urban China : everyday life in a medium-size Chinese city / Unn Målfrid H. Rolandsen.
  p. cm. – (Routledge contemporary China series ; 67)
 Includes bibliographical references and index.
 1. Quanzhou Shi (China)–Social policy. 2. Leisure–China–Quanzhou Shi. 3. City and town life–China–Quanzhou Shi. 4. Sociology, Urban–China–Quanzhou Shi. I. Title.
 HN740.Q35R65 2011
 306.4'8120951245–dc22
                                                                    2010042920

ISBN: 978-0-415-60409-3 (hbk)
ISBN: 978-1-138-01693-4 (pbk)
ISBN: 978-0-203-81877-0 (ebk)

Typeset in Times
by Wearset Ltd, Boldon, Tyne and Wear

Contents

List of figures	xi
Preface	xii
Orthography and reference style	xvii
Abbreviations	xviii

Introduction   1

Lessons from Chinese studies of leisure 3
The organization of the book 16

1 Locating leisure in a medium-sized Chinese city   19

Quanzhou city past and present 21
Gate openers and key informants in the field 27
Strategies for identifying interviewees 29
Data from the field 30
Doing fieldwork in a foreign language 35

2 What is leisure – in China and beyond?   38

What is leisure? 38
Leisure in historical and socio-cultural contexts 44
Leisure in China 48

3 The utility of leisure and the dangers of idleness   54

The Protestant work ethic and popular culture critique 54
The characteristics of the PRC leisure ethic 57
The PRC leisure ethic in academic writing 59

x *Contents*

4 Leisure in the Quanzhou cityscape 69

Envisioning a leisure area 70
The characteristics of a leisure place 73
Changing practices in a changing cityscape 81

5 'Healthy' leisure in transition 85

The decline of the library and the rise of the book café 86
The diminishing role of state-organized leisure 96

6 Bad people in bad places? 108

'Luan': keeping chaos at a distance 109
Internet cafés as chaotic leisure spaces 115
Karaoke rooms as segregated social spaces 126
The importance of first-hand experience 133

7 Consumption as a form of leisure 136

Changes and continuities in Chinese consumption 138
Consumer policy and consumers' agency 143
Shopping as a meaningful leisure activity 148
The cultured middle class's attitude towards consumption 153

8 Contested leisure space 161

Qingyuan Mountain 162
Qingyuan Mountain as a place of leisure 163
Leisure means livelihood at Qingyuan Mountain 167
Qingyuan Mountain from the perspective of the management 168
Confrontation at Qingyuan Mountain 173
Quanzhou people's ways of 'making do' 176

Conclusions 183

Glossary 189
Notes 196
Bibliography 203
Index 216

Figures

I.1	Saturday in Quanzhou's East Lake Park	1
1.1	The skyline of contemporary Quanzhou	19
2.1	Sunday leisure in West Lake Park	39
4.1	Elderly people enjoying a game of *majiang at Tongfo si*	69
4.2	'Leisure square. No parking!'	74
4.3	Kite-flying on a Sunday afternoon at Mintaiyuan Museum Square	77
4.4	Young workers watching the *renao* at Fengze Square	78
5.1	Young and old reading and relaxing in one of Quanzhou's book cafés	85
5.2	Members of the Photographers' Association in action	98
6.1	'Clinging to video games made him a criminal' permission).	113
6.2	Youth in one of Quanzhou's 'black' Internet cafés	120
6.3	Mr Lin, the time-honoured online gamer	121
6.4	Singing – or at least mouthing the words – together at the karaoke parlour	126
7.1	Migrant worker with a taste for middle class-style consumption	136
8.1	A woman making her way up the stone path at Qingyuan Mountain	161
8.2	A lunch of tea and vegetables at Qingyuan Mountain	165
8.3	Climbing the houshan path	174

Preface

'I don't really have any free time.' This statement made by a Chinese middle school student in a small township in Fujian in 2003 was the spark that first ignited my interest in leisure as a social phenomenon. Coming from a Scandinavian background where leisure, in the forms of play, relaxation, and organized activity, is not only taken for granted, but even regarded as one of the most important aspects of everyday life, the notion of having no leisure was almost inconceivable. Moreover, I soon realized that this young student was not the only one who held this opinion. On the contrary, it was the most common answer I got when I interviewed middle school students about their everyday lives. I was in Fujian province trying my hand at field research for the very first time, and my plan was to study leisure activities among rural youth. This endeavour turned out to be rather futile. In the township in question young students' lives revolved around homework and exams, and the prospect of entering a better high-school or college in an urban district. For them, and for their parents, a good score card was considered the ticket to a stable income and a better life for the whole family. As a consequence, Sunday afternoons were the only times when middle school students had any time of their own, and apart from the basketball court or the local underground Internet cafés there were few places for them to meet or take part in activities. The general opinion among both teachers and parents in the township was that leisure activities that did not contribute directly towards the students' exams were a waste of time. Leisure facilitation was clearly not a priority in this community.

When I researched the same topic in a middle school in the more economically developed county town nearby, I found that it was quite common for pupils there to spend weekends engaged in activities such as foreign language tutorials and piano lessons, just like young students in big cities like Shanghai and Beijing. Moreover, parents and teachers regarded these activities as both supplements to regular classroom education and valuable forms of recreation. In the county town, organized leisure was considered educational, and parents were therefore willing to spend money on their child's leisure activities. In the rural township, however, many parents struggled to pay even the regular school fees. The difference in attitudes towards leisure in the two localities rested not only on parents' income level, but also on the leisure facilitation in the community.

By this I mean the access to art schools, language institutes and similar venues – or the lack of such. The only accessible leisure place for youth in the township where I was conducting my field research was the basketball court – a square of concrete where boys and young men gathered in the late afternoon to shoot hoops. This court was brand new when I came to the area. There had been a basketball court earlier as well, but that spot had then been taken over by shops and restaurants. When the local boys lost their playground they went to other places outside the township centre to have fun. Constructing a new basketball court was by many regarded as the best way to 'bring the youth back home'. One of the grown-ups in the township put it like this: it is important to provide youth with 'somewhere to do something, so that they can become grown-ups in a good way, and not become bad people (*huairen*)'. These worries were directed towards young boys in particular, and so was the remedy. Whether the basketball court helped keeping local boys out of trouble, I cannot say.

The idea that the right kinds of activities can produce the right kind of citizen is echoed in Chinese scholars' studies of leisure education (*xiuxian jiaoyu*). This view made me curious about the perceived role of leisure in the building of public morality in China. Was this ethic of leisure in any way related to the Protestant work ethic and its scepticism towards idleness? Or was this a specifically Chinese way of looking at leisure? The questions that arose from my interviews with pupils and parents in a small Chinese township lead me to write this book about the discourse of leisure in the PRC, and the impact of this discourse on the everyday lives of the population in the medium-sized city of Quanzhou.

My first challenge in the preparation for this study was to identify a suitable field for the study of leisure in China. I was looking for a geographic area where I could participate in and observe a variety of leisure activities, and where people do regard leisure as a significant part of their everyday lives. Much had already been written about recreation and leisure consumption in the Chinese metropolises, and I therefore decided to shift the focus of attention to leisure in a smaller city. Discussing this challenge with a Chinese scholar she immediately suggested that I go to Quanzhou, a city on the southeastern coast of Fujian province, just across the strait from Taiwan. She told me that during the last few years the local practice of serving and drinking tea had become a lucrative business in Quanzhou, and that the conspicuous consumption of expensive teas in stylish teahouses was the new leisure craze among both entrepreneurs and the well-educated middle class in the area. We agreed that the commoditization of the local tea culture would be an interesting topic to start off the investigation. As it turned out, tea culture was only one among many leisure activities that caught my interest in Quanzhou, and in the following chapters I use the city as a point of departure for my analysis of how leisure is practised, talked about and managed in contemporary China.

Let us briefly return to the township where I had my first encounter with leisure research and the young student who stated that she had no free time. What do people really mean when they say they don't have any free time? One of the shortcomings of my first attempt at field research was that I paid more attention to my interviewees' statements than to the ways they actually spent their time. I neglected the fact that even if my interviewees spent their days going to classes and doing homework, they also enjoyed short periods of leisure throughout each day. I also overlooked the possibility that the practices that filled these leisurely breaks were perhaps not thought of as 'leisure' (*ziyou shijian, xiuxian* or *xianxia*) by the young students. When interviewees said that they had 'no free time' I simply stopped looking. My field notes from that time reveal that I did observe how local girls often went window-shopping together, and how some of the boys would gather in our neighbour's front yard to talk and just hang out. Could not these practices be regarded as examples of having 'free time'? The truth is that in my first attempt at leisure research I was looking in the wrong direction and asking the wrong questions – or at least asking my questions in the wrong way. Developing the analyses presented in the following pages, it has therefore been important to me to make sure that my understanding of leisure has been guided by the field data, and not the other way around. Consequently, I spent the first three months of fieldwork in 2005 familiarizing myself with local cultural activities – in the broadest sense – in order to get an overview of the kinds of activities men and women in Quanzhou engage in on regular workdays and weekends. I then returned to Quanzhou in 2006 and 2007 for an additional six months of field research, where I observed, and also participated in, a variety of leisure activities, both organized and informal. As will be explained more thoroughly in Chapter 2, my definition of leisure as a practice, rather than as a time period or an experience, is based on observations of actual activities as they took place at different times and in a variety of places in the Quanzhou cityscape.

In addition to participating in various leisure activities and interviewing townspeople about leisure, I also spent quite a lot of time biking around Quanzhou, familiarising myself with different public places. My aim was to better understand how local inhabitants made use of squares and parks, and even the sidewalks, as places of leisure. Biking through alleys and streets made me attentive to the fact that leisure activities were practiced in the most unlikely spots. Some middle-aged women met for morning exercises outside the gates of a large shopping mall, and a group of male day labourers used to play cards on the stairs in front of a local bank, to name just two examples. These observations lead me to study more closely how people are attracted to some areas of town or to certain squares and parks rather than others, and why. Interestingly, designated leisure places built by the local government, such as the Workers Palace or the local museums, were often deserted. What does this tell us about the kinds of leisure that local government planners encourage? Which leisure practices are deemed undesirable by the same authorities? And to what extent does the official discourse of leisure influence the lives of ordinary townspeople? Inspired by Lefebvre's concepts of space and place and my observations and interviews in Quanzhou this book attempts to answer these questions. Based on in-depth analyses of leisure activities and the physical places where they are practiced, this study describes the meeting points between the official leisure discourse of the

Chinese party-state, and the everyday practices of ordinary city dwellers. In other words, this is a book about the characteristics and limits of the social space enjoyed by city populations in contemporary China.

This book has been realized through assistance and encouragement from a number of persons and institutions. I first want to extend my thanks to all the people in Quanzhou who were willing to share their experiences and thoughts with me. Their contributions and generosity have been vital to me and to the development of this study. My field research was funded by the project *The Chinese Individual: negotiations of rights and responsibilities*, an international research project of which this study is also a part. My PhD scholarship and a publication grant for the resulting monograph were generously awarded by the Department of Humanities at the University of Oslo, Norway. I owe much to my supervisor, Mette Halskov Hansen, who knows how to push me in the right direction. I want to thank her for her ceaseless enthusiasm and for believing in me and my research. I am grateful for the criticism and encouragement I received from committee members Yunxiang Yan, Marina Svensson and Andreas Steen. I would also like to thank the anonymous reviewers for valuable input, and the editors and staff at Routledge for their assistance in the publication process.

Special thanks are due to the participants in *The Chinese Individual* project, and Li Minghuan in particular, whose questions, comments, and support have been invaluable throughout the research process. I would also like to thank my colleagues and fellow PhD candidates at the Department of Culture Studies and Oriental Languages in Oslo. In our department I have always felt welcome and appreciated both as a person and for the work I do. Special thanks go to Pang Cuiming for the many fruitful discussions and good laughs, to Marte Kjær Galtung and Ivo Spira who have offered insightful comments on my draft chapters, and to Ann Kunish for her language expertise and her wonderful sense of humour. I am also grateful for the support and care I have received from family and friends and from my husband Øystein in particular. I could never have done this without you! Abundant support and assistance notwithstanding, any shortcomings or errors in the following pages are my responsibility alone. Every effort has been made to contact copyright holders for their permission to reprint material in this book. The publishers would be grateful to hear from any copyright holder who is not here acknowledged and will undertake to rectify any errors or omissions in future editions of this book.

Orthography and reference style

Chinese words and expressions are rendered in *Hanyu pinyin*, and a list of Chinese characters is provided at the back. Unless otherwise noted, quotes stem from participant observation and informal and semi-structured interviews during three periods of fieldwork in Quanzhou during the years 2005–7. In order to protect the anonymity of my interviewees, I have changed the names of all individuals quoted, as well as the names of unofficial groups and associations.

For the sake of clarity, I have chosen to use the full names of authors with Chinese names (e.g. Feng Chongyi), including those names that appear in a Western format in the publication referenced (e.g. Shaoguang Wang, Philip C.C. Huang). In order to distinguish newspaper articles from other sources, I have chosen to retain an abbreviation of the name of each newspaper in the relevant references. Unless otherwise stated, all translations are made by the author. With the exceptions of facsimile from Chinese newspapers and web pages in Chapter 6, illustrations are photos taken in the field by the author. At the time of research, one US dollar was approximately equivalent to eight Chinese *yuan*.[1]

Abbreviations

CNNIC	China Internet Network Information Services
DNZB	*Dongnan zaobao*
FJRB	*Fujian ribao*
HXDSB	*Haixia dushibao*
PRC	People's Republic of China
QZSWHJ	*Quanzhou shi wenhua ju*

Introduction

On the face of it, the title *Leisure and Power in Urban China* contains a curious pairing of concepts. If leisure is the kinds of fun we have after work, in the comfort of our own homes or the lively surroundings of a café or local sports grounds, what has power got to do with it? One answer can be found if we look at leisure from a historical perspective. The question of when and how the ordinary working people should recreate has been a topic for discussion among religious authorities, industrialists and political commentators alike (see Thompson 1967: 86; Roberts 1999: 27; Bauman 1998: 9–10; Bayat 2007). In some respects, contemporary discussions about the dangers of web surfing and the amount of

Figure I.1 Saturday in Quanzhou's East Lake Park.

time we spend in front of the TV is but a contemporary version of this historical moralist critique. Authorities have always been critical of the ways ordinary people spend their time and energy when they are not checked by teachers, employers or other institutional structures.

Governments and different religious and social interest groups – as well as commercial agents – seek to influence the ways we spend our time. One strategy may be to attempt to alter people's attitudes and behaviours through information campaigns, for example by campaigns against video violence or campaigns to inform us about the dangers of obesity. One strategy used to change or influence our leisure practices is the provision of accessible leisure facilities in the communities where we live. Local facilities for organized sports and exercise or the establishment of cultural centres, parks and other public recreation facilities are examples of such undertakings. I certainly regard the spread of public leisure facilities as a social benefit. My aim here, however, is to point out that these facilities exist within a certain discourse of leisure. They are established and maintained because interest groups and authorities in our societies strongly believe that a good life entails physical exercise and cultural stimuli. On the one hand, making such leisure activities available to the general population is a valuable service. On the other hand, the creation of structures that cause people to change their behaviour is an exercise of power. If we turn now to the history of the PRC, the link between power and leisure becomes even clearer.

The Maoist vision of a good life entailed selfless contributions to the collective, to serve the People and ultimately to be loyal to the Mao and the party state. These ideals were promoted through various propaganda campaigns, but also through the restructuring of Chinese society into a system of work units and farm collectives. Here the party state took active control over almost all aspects of everyday life. Political authorities dictated when and where a person should work, when and where to eat, when to wake and sleep and how to recreate and with whom. During the Mao years, leisure was thoroughly politicized, and if a person spent time on pet breeding or the collection of artefacts or other kinds of so-called 'petty bourgeois amusements', he or she would face severe criticism (Shaoguang Wang 1995: 155). The economic reforms introduced by Deng Xiaoping in 1979 entailed a gradual restructuring of the organization of work life. The reintroduction of private enterprises meant that an increasing number of Chinese came to lead their lives outside the structure of collective state units. The gradual withdrawal of the party state from the organization of people's everyday life, paired with an increased standard of living and a booming economy, has meant that the population in urbanized areas – from county towns to big cities – can choose the colour and flavour of their own life to a much larger extent than before. This significant change in the lives of the urban Chinese poses new questions concerning how the contemporary party state seeks to influence the leisure choices that ordinary people may now make. Therefore I examine the kinds of leisure activities that urban Chinese engage in, and the ways they talk about leisure. I also analyse what the current party propaganda says about leisure, and the role of the local branches of the party state in the facilitation of leisure activities. I want to use leisure as a case to demonstrate how the Communist party-state to a certain extent still seeks to dominate and control the everyday lives of the Chinese people. More important, however, studying Chinese leisure gives me the opportunity to highlight some of the popular countermeasures that arise in response to – or in spite of – official policies. The core question that I brought with me out in the field was 'to what extent may Chinese people govern their own lives in the face of the contemporary party-state?' During field research in Quanzhou the number of questions quickly outgrew the answers. It became necessary to ask whether government reports and articles about leisure in the state-controlled media really can reveal the intentions of the government and – following this question – can governments be said to have intentions at all? In Quanzhou I found clear discrepancies not only between the local government's vision for the development of local leisure places and the actual leisure activities that take place in the cityscape. I also found that what the authorities communicate in official reports and in the media is often quite different from the actions that government bureaus undertake. This is true both in terms of leisure facilitation, and in the local government's supervision and control of the leisure sphere. As a result I had to adopt my research strategy so that I could make comparisons between the practices of the relevant local authorities and those of the inhabitants they govern. I also needed to study the ways leisure is defined and descried in both official publications and everyday speech. Through alternating between the analysis of texts and interviews and observation and participation in a wide range of activities I have come to the conclusion that the local population has considerable agency and room to manoeuvre in the local leisure space. And, moreover, that the authorities' intentions and agendas are in practice much more diverse than they appear to be at the level of official discourse.

Lessons from Chinese studies of leisure

Chinese social scientists conducted the earliest research on Chinese leisure in the beginning of the 1980s, and the topic has since gained a certain popularity in the fields of economics and sociology. In the predominantly sociological Chinese literature on leisure I found two main tendencies that have had consequences for this study. First, several studies confirmed that the development of the Chinese commercial leisure market follows the rural-urban divide which characterizes the overall economic development in China. In rural areas and small towns the range of leisure activities is smaller and, moreover, the inhabitants have less money to spend (Ma Feifeng 2002: 14; Jun Liping and Li Jing 2002: 27. See also Davis 2000: 19 and Yunxiang Yan 2003: 37). These studies confirm the preliminary findings from my field research in 2003, namely that leisure activities were more common in an economically developed county town than in a rural township. As the links between economic development and the development of a leisure market on the one hand and people's income levels and their leisure spending on the other are already thoroughly established in Chinese scholarship (see for example Song Shuyang and Wu Xingwu 2002: 111; Jun Liping and Li Jing 2002: 27; Ma Feifeng 2002: 14; Wang Yalin 2003: 57; Zhang Taiyuan 2007: 107), this will not be a major topic of scrutiny here. Likewise, Chinese big city leisure, and consumption in particular, has already received a lot of attention from western and Chinese scholars alike (Ma Huidi 2004a; Ma Huidi and Zhang Jing'an 2004a. See also articles in Davis *et al*. 1995; Chen *et al*. 2001; and Latham *et al*. 2006b). Reading previous studies of leisure in China therefore made me confident that a detailed study of leisure in a medium-sized city is long overdue, and that the newly industrialized city of Quanzhou would be a good point of departure for such an analysis.

The second significant feature of the Chinese language materials consulted is the paradoxes in scholars' descriptions and analyses of leisure. Even when their data from surveys of leisure in big-city China give evidence of a vibrant leisure scene with a variety of activities, and despite the authors' positive characterizations of leisure as a phenomenon, articles on leisure written by Chinese scholars tend to take a moralizing stance and accuse the Chinese people of wasting their time on unproductive activities. As an example, in an article in the 2004 anthology *Zhongguo gongzhong xiuxian zhuangkuang diaocha* (Survey studies of the state of leisure life among the Chinese public),[1] Sun Xiaoli regards leisure as an opportunity for the liberation of mankind (Sun Xiaoli 2004: 77–80). The author furthermore lists the development of tourism, the spread of museums, and leisure businesses as positive changes in Chinese society. Sun then states that 'in order to establish a scientific, healthy and civilized lifestyle', the Chinese masses must at least be educated in 'modern concepts' such as scientific family planning, and a concept of consumption that does not encourage hedonism and the worship of money. They also need to adopt a concept of leisure where leisure is regarded as a resource 'that must be governed in a scientific, civilized and cherishing manner' (Sun Xiaoli 2004: 88). On the one hand, the author declares that leisure is a source of liberation for people in general. On the other hand, the Chinese population must be instructed so that this liberation is kept within the limits of the scientific and the civilized. Similar statements concerning the potential dangers of uncurbed leisure activities can be found in government-initiated propaganda campaigns, in publications from Quanzhou's local bureaucracy, and in the local press. More often than not, these sources communicate a view of leisure as a potential waste of time and resources, unless the population is guided towards 'healthy', educational activities. This official discourse of leisure, which permeates much of the written material analysed in this study, I term the 'PRC leisure ethic'.[2] This discourse distinguishes between so-called healthy (*jiankang*) and unhealthy (*bu jiankang*) or chaotic (*luan*) leisure activities. Leisure activities are described as healthy as long as they serve to bolster the legitimacy of the party-state. Conversely, unhealthy activities are discouraged, both directly, through legislative measures such as the rigid regulations for the management of Internet bars, and indirectly, through the characterization of certain activities or leisure places as chaotic or unhealthy. If we were to base our understanding of the Chinese leisure sphere on such documents alone, we would conclude that all leisure activities are supervised and dominated by the state and that little room is left for the initiatives and preferences of the individual. However, judging from the ways in which middle-class men and women in Quanzhou talk about leisure, and judging also from the leisure practices that have caught their interest, the official leisure ethic has little or no impact on the way people actually lead their everyday lives. This discrepancy between official discourse and local practices makes up the core of the present study.

When it comes to leisure, the people I observed and interviewed in Quanzhou were first and foremost interested in socializing and in experiencing something apart from their regular duties and responsibilities. Allusions to the utility of leisure as a resource or a distinction between healthy and unhealthy activities were rare among my interviewees. People did, however, frequently refer to the local ditty, 'you can only succeed if you exert yourself' (*ai pin cai hui ying*),[3] and were proud of the image of people in southern Fujian as industrious and able to endure hardship (*chi ku*). The tendency among the very same people to describe themselves as fun-loving (*ai wan*) makes for an attitude towards life where hard work and good fun are equally appreciated. The key data for this project stem from field research among Quanzhou's middle class.[4] To them, leisure meant going to a tea house or restaurant, reading, window-shopping, visiting a karaoke parlour or climbing the local mountaintop. Accordingly, these are some of the leisure practices we will return to in the chapters below.

The PRC leisure ethic

The discourse of leisure in terms of healthy and unhealthy activities I term the 'PRC leisure ethic', and I use this expression for two reasons. The first is that criticism of ordinary people's leisure practices is not a specifically Chinese phenomenon. As I argue in Chapter 3, the official leisure ethic, which finds its expression in the Chinese news media, propaganda campaigns and local policies for leisure management, bears a clear resemblance to the general sentiments of the Protestant work ethic and the popular culture critique in both Europe and the United States. As mentioned above, the right of individuals to spend their energies in the manner they themselves prefer has been contested in different societies and at different points in time. The discourse analysed in this study is therefore neither an essentially Chinese discourse nor a result of the introduction of Western sociological theories of work and leisure into Chinese society and scholarship. Nevertheless, as stated by Chris Rojek, 'leisure cannot be studied meaningfully in isolation from […] a historically specific system of power' (Rojek 1985: 7). The data from Quanzhou suggest that the official leisure ethic finds its justification in the changing political strategies of the Chinese party-state. This brings us to my second reason for naming this discourse the 'PRC leisure ethic'. The official discourse of leisure promotes an understanding of leisure as a resource that belongs to the greater collective, and one that should be put to use for the benefit of society. More specifically, the leisure ethic promotes activities that serve to increase the cultural competence (*suzhi*)[5] of the individual, and thereby indirectly the competence of the overall population. In this context, the concern for the individual and the quality of life that a rich leisure life can provide him or her is not considered a goal in itself. In this respect I find that the PRC leisure ethic is reminiscent of the Maoist ethic of the 1960s, as described by Richard Madsen (Madsen 1984: 107, 111, 129). I perceive a link between the propaganda calls for selfless contribution to the collective during high-Maoism, and the Party authorities' continuous concern for the supposedly uncivilized and unscientific ways in which ordinary Chinese live their lives. So, although the leisure ethic analysed in this study is a product of the social conditions of the reform era, its legacy runs back to the earlier decades of the People's Republic. I therefore consider the discourse as being situated in the historical and political context of the PRC.

Leisure in contemporary China studies

Leisure has yet to be counted among the central topics in Western scholarship on China. The fact that the leisure activities of the Chinese population have seldom been treated as a topic in its own right may be explained by the historical realities of civil war and social unrest that have characterized Chinese society throughout much of the twentieth century. Under such circumstances, there are matters of a more pressing concern to both social analysts and researchers than the question of the significance of leisure among the general citizenry.

During the course of the reform era, the policies of the Chinese Communist Party have in many aspects come to resemble the global mainstream market economy. In these circumstances the everyday life practices or ordinary Quanzhou people constitute a rich source of data for the analysis of interactions between government institutions and local inhabitants in urban China. In their analyses of everyday life as a social phenomenon, Henri Lefebvre, and later Michel de Certeau, have ascribed special importance to the mundane and trivial aspects that make up everyday life. The realm of everyday practices – of which leisure is but one aspect – is characterized as something hidden and evasive; it is the unnoticed, the inconspicuous, the unobtrusive, and that which repeats itself throughout the cycles of the week and the year (Highmore 2002: 145, 1, 128). According to de Certeau, it is these very qualities of inconspicuousness and invisibility that make everyday practices particularly important as an area for resistance toward the disciplining powers of bureaucracy and the agents of commercialization (de Certeau 1988: xiv).[6] Similarly, in his introduction to *Critiques of Everyday Life*, Michael Gardiner writes that the everyday 'has this resistant quality simply because its very presence is not always registered by the panoptic gaze of bureaucratic power' (Gardiner 2000: 16). The 'panoptic gaze' here refers to Foucault's idea of the *panopticon* of modern prison architecture as emblematic of the bureaucratized society where all individuals are subject to the controlling gaze of the authorities. It is tempting to analyse the Chinese party-state and its tools of governance in these terms. However, the diversity of the activities I observed during field work in Quanzhou confirms for me that in this case, what is true in western societies is also true in China: Even in the age of powerful bureaucrats, CCTV and internet censorship, the multitude of ordinary people's practices can never be successfully monitored by the authorities, nor completely subsumed by an official discourse. I agree with the theorists who regard everyday practices which go unnoticed by the authorities as areas from whence popular resistance can be launched. But, resistance is certainly not what leisure is all about. It is therefore imperative that we study in detail how everyday activities are utilized by the participants themselves as means of resistance and insubordination, as well as recreation. And it is vital that this research topic is explored also within the field of Chinese studies.

Anthropological and historical accounts that portray the lives of ordinary Chinese during the Mao era tell us that political authorities sought to dominate ordinary people's lives, even down to the organization of work, sleep, meals, and social activities (Madsen 1984: 138; Chan *et al.* 1992: 85, 97; Shaoguang Wang 1995: 152–6; Chan 1997: 96; Yunxiang Yan 2000: 224). Daily life was managed in much detail by local authorities through the system of work units (*danwei*) and the organization of labour in production units and brigades (Madsen 1984: 138; Chan *et al.*1992: 85). One of the few studies that explicitly analyses the party-state's attitudes toward leisure in this period is Shaoguang Wang's article from 1995 entitled 'The politics of private time: changing leisure patterns in urban China'. Wang writes that Party authorities sought to control people's leisure activities both before and after the Cultural Revolution. Starting from the early 1960s, people who engaged in hobbies such as fishing, gardening, and collecting stamps could either give them up or face criticism for 'wallowing in petty bourgeois amusements' (Shaoguang Wang 1995: 155). During the Cultural Revolution, Wang writes, there was in effect no demarcation between private time and public time and, moreover, the term leisure itself 'had become a dirty word' (Shaoguang Wang 1995: 156). In a subsequent footnote, however, Wang adds that for many Chinese, the climax of the Cultural Revolution in 1967–8 meant that 'for the first time in years [people] had plenty of free time and [...] no public authorities existed to impose officially sanctioned leisure patterns' (Shaoguang Wang 1995: 156, note 23). Shaoguang Wang's article focuses on the politicization of leisure under Mao and on the Party's gradual withdrawal from involvement in people's everyday lives under Deng. It is a pity, then, that the discrepancy between the official leisure discourse and examples of actual practices is relegated to a mere footnote. In Quanzhou, people gave similar descriptions of leisure life during the Mao era. A man in his late sixties offered the following description of leisure under high-Maoism: 'There was always space for people to make manoeuvres ... We were supposed to sing songs about Mao and such, but as soon as people knew nobody was listening or paying attention, up came the *erhu* and then the *nanyin* started.'[7] This indicates that popular leisure activities were not completely dormant during the Mao era. It is also an example of the opportunity for small acts of resistance, even in a society where private time is held to be nonexistent (Shaoguang Wang 1995: 155).

Several analyses of local conditions under Mao and Deng have proved important for the development of the present study. In *Chen Village under Mao and Deng*, Anita Chan *et al.* describe the effects of the political campaigns of the 1960s and 1970s on a sample of villages in Guangdong. Their analysis is mainly concerned with local power structures and the consequences of national politics on a rural community in the south of China. Little is said about the everyday life practices of the local villagers, apart from how the influx of urban youth, and the Maoist propaganda regime they represented, altered the rhythm of work and rest in the village (Chan *et al.* 1992: 97). A short footnote on page 67, however, tells us that

> [w]omen often did not eat with their husbands, but used dinner time as the chance to make the rounds of the neighborhood to socialize with other women. Whereas after dinner, the husbands could relax with male friends (unless there was a political meeting), the women had to work most evenings to finish the housework.

This short comment tells us not only about the unequal distribution of work and leisure in the 1960s, but the placement of this information in a footnote is also indicative of the marginal position of leisure in the analysis of social life at the time when the study was carried out.

Richard Madsen's monograph on morality and power in the same village community in Guangdong is another example of a study that informs us only indirectly of the leisure preferences of the local inhabitants. Madsen gives an account of the disappointment the sent-down urban youth felt when they got to know the real-life peasantry in this village community. The urban youth complained that the local men

> [...] liked to squat in several meeting places after dinner not to discuss revolutionary politics but to tell feudalistic stories from the *Water Margin* and the *Romance of the Three Kingdoms*.
> (Madsen 1984: 118)

It is no wonder that in these early Western studies of the consequences of Maoist policies, information about everyday life practices in local communities is eclipsed by descriptions of government structures and Party-initiated campaigns. On the one hand, the authors' aim was to describe in detail the results of the central government's policies and ideology at the levels of the brigade and the production team. On the other hand, the fact that field research inside the PRC was impossible at the time, and that data for these studies were gathered through interviews with émigrés in Hong Kong means that the researchers did not have the opportunity to observe the everyday practices that constituted village life during this period.

Gail E. Henderson and Myron S. Cohen, however, spent five months in a hospital *danwei* in Wuhan in 1979. Their book gives a more detailed account of how the management and spatial organization of the work unit influenced the social life and privacy of employees in general, as well as their own lives. Even so, the references to occasional outdoor movie screenings and annual celebrations organized by the work unit serve only as ornaments framing the main topic, which is the function of the *danwei* as a place of employment (Henderson and Cohen 1984: chapters 2 and 3 especially). The authors sum up recreational life in their work unit as follows: 'in general, evenings are uneventful' (Henderson and Cohen 1984: 15).

This description of the dullness of everyday life under collectivism brings us back to Lefebvre and de Certeau and their characterization of everyday life as the unnoticeable and the mundane. With this definition of the everyday in mind, we may ask whether everyday life in urban work units was as uneventful as Henderson and Cohen suggest, or were everyday joys and pleasures simply difficult for an outsider to detect or identify? The present study is not an historical enquiry and will therefore not provide a satisfactory answer to these questions. The questions that the reading of the above-mentioned monographs left me with did, however, encourage me to take special notice during my fieldwork of the types of leisure that are commonplace and seemingly uneventful, such as window-shopping and other forms of fun that people in Quanzhou enjoy on any given weeknight.

The image of leisure in the collective era as a dull affair is challenged by Yunxiang Yan's field-based study of the private lives of villagers in northeastern China from 1949 to 1999. Yan focuses on the changing power structures within the family, but also shows how the private sphere of the family home has been influenced by changes in the social life of the village as a whole. He argues that it was during the reform era that leisure and social life retreated into the home and became uneventful. His data indicate that the collective era, on the contrary, provided arenas for both participation and recreation, two important aspects of public life that disappeared from the village in the process of decollectivization (Yunxiang Yan 2003: 29–41). In rural Heilongjiang, the dismantling of the production brigade in the early 1980s meant an end to the funding and organization of public events and organized activity, from performances and volunteer work to team sports. Moreover, the collective headquarters in the village in question was demolished, and according to Yan, no public establishment has later replaced its function as a meeting place for the local men of the village. The former brigade-initiated activities, however compulsory in some instances, were a source of enjoyment among the villagers, writes Yan. According to one of his interviewees, the loss of arenas in which to socialize and places to meet has left the village streets 'dead' (Yunxiang Yan 2003: 29).

Yunxiang Yan writes that whereas the community he studied in the rural Northeast has lost much of its former public life, China's urban communities have experienced a different process, whereby 'commercialized arenas' have replaced the 'state-controlled public space' of the collective era (Yunxiang Yan 2003: 37). The development of new arenas of socialization, both in the leisure market and within the system of government-approved organizations, will be discussed in more detail below. Deborah S. Davis has argued that the urban consumer society in China has given new importance to horizontal ties such as family and kinship and to informal social relationships, and that these bonds in many ways 'challenge the vertical relationship between subject-citizens and state agents' (Davis 2000: 3). A similar point is made in Jing Wang's *Locating China*, where articles by, among others, Feng Chongyi contribute to an understanding of local popular culture as 'new forms of sociality' (Jing Wang 2005b: 18). These anthologies show that after the crumbling of the system of work units and household registration and the gradual development of a more flexible labour market, Chinese individuals face a range of new opportunities. As Link, Madsen and Pickowicz point out, however, the changes brought about by global trends in the Chinese economy and Chinese society introduce both new aspirations and new restrictions into the lives of ordinary Chinese. These in turn contribute towards increased social tension (Link *et al.* 2002). In *Popular China*, Link *et al.* warn Western analysts against interpreting Chinese popular culture as underground practices and forms of dissent (Link *et al.* 2002: 3–4). In the said volume, the authors demonstrate that popular practices in China often exist exactly where the unofficial meets the official realm of the party-state and its bureaucracy. It has been my aim to incorporate this perspective into my analysis of official discourse and leisure practices in contemporary Quanzhou.

Recurrent topics in recent English-language anthologies of sociological and anthropological analyses of urban China include the Chinese avant-garde art scene, the possible development of a civil society and analyses of the changing patterns of consumption. Moreover, the inclusion of perspectives from the field of human geography – the concepts of space and place in particular – have added new insights into the importance of the changing physical environment on both living conditions and everyday life practices in urban China.[8] Although the anthologies mentioned here contain several case studies of leisure practices and leisure consumption, little attention has been given in these studies to leisure as a phenomenon in itself.[9] The contribution of the project presented here is to use data from the context of China to the discussion of what leisure is, and furthermore, to shift the focus of attention from leisure as a form of consumption to leisure as a social arena in which the politicized leisure ethic is challenged by people's leisure practices. In this endeavour I am much inspired by Richard Madsen's analysis of discourses of morality in the 1960s and 1970s and Shaoguang Wang's analysis of how Chinese people's leisure was regulated under Mao and Deng (Madsen 1984; Shaoguang Wang 1995). Another study which directly addresses the question of popular leisure and the power of official discourses can be found in an article by Paul E. Festa (2006). Through the analysis of two government-commissioned papers on how contemporary *majiang* practises should be sanitized, standardized and transformed into healthy *majiang* (*jiankang majiang*), Festa demonstrates how popular culture is presented by Chinese scholars as a means for the moulding and cultivation of the Chinese populace. Although his analysis centres on the party-state's attempts at altering people's leisure practices by way of a normalizing discourse of healthy leisure,

Festa concludes that the discourse has limited effect on actual practices, and that the agents of the party-state fail to pursue the stated intentions with any consistency. These conclusions are, however, supported only with meagre reference to ethnographic data. While Festa's analysis focuses on the production of the official discourse of healthy leisure, I will explore in more detail the differences between this official discourse and actual leisure practices.

My analysis of discourse and practice also owes much to Sara L. Friedman's monograph about the Hui'an women (*Hui'an nü*) who inhabit one of Quanzhou's coastal districts. Friedman demonstrates how a very local discourse of propriety and gendered identity, combined with the national discourses of modernization, has consequences for the everyday life practices of young Hui'an women, from their choice of clothing to the leisure activities in which they engage. In her study, Friedman leaves no doubt of the influence of official discourses on the lives of ordinary men and women. At the same time, she describes the local state apparatus as 'riddled with internal contradictions' (Friedman 2006: 9). The consequence for Friedman's analysis is that she does not regard 'the state as a unified entity or agent that exists above society, dictating its every move' (Friedman 2006: 9). In this respect, Friedman's findings are similar to those presented below. The analysis of leisure discourse and leisure practices gives rise to questions of how power is exercised and the extent to which official propaganda can be used as an instrument of governance. Let us therefore turn to some of the theoretical challenges this project entails.

Discourse, language and reality

The scrutiny of an official discourse of leisure notwithstanding, this study is not conducted in the form of a discourse analysis. As a research methodology, discourse analysis involves a close reading of how social realities and power structures are constituted in a corpus of carefully chosen texts (Neumann 2002: 34, 51–2). Even if this is not primarily a textual study, I analyse the terms and expressions local authorities use to describe and evaluate leisure practices, and compare them to the expressions and practices of the local citizenry. It is therefore fruitful to consider my project as an enquiry into the relationship between discourse and practice.

Discourse analysis in the strictest sense not only implies specific research methods, but also relies on a set of theoretical stances, most notably the hypothesis that our social reality is constituted through and by language (Winther Jørgensen and Phillips 1999: 12–14; Larsen and Munkgård Pedersen 2002: 19–23).[10] I recognize the role played by language in the way we – both as individuals and as members of various social groups – make sense of the world, but the data from my fieldwork demonstrate that there is a difference between the world as it is represented in the official discourse of leisure, and leisure as it is spoken of and practiced by real people in physical places. As I will discuss in more detail in Chapter 6, when leisure consumers have first-hand experience of a leisure venue, for example a karaoke parlour, the assessment they themselves make eclipses the predominantly negative representations of karaoke that permeate the local media and reports from the Bureau of Culture. In this case, a purely textual analysis would unveil a moralizing leisure ethic in which karaoke is held in contempt, while the data from participant observation suggest otherwise. Karaoke may be considered an unhealthy form of leisure in official discourse, but people from all walks of life nevertheless enjoy meeting with family and friends in Quanzhou's karaoke parlours. This example shows that language and reality are not one and the same, and moreover, that it is productive to consider discourse and practice as equally significant aspects of reality. I therefore agree with Larsen and Munkgård Pedersen, who state that rather than analysing discursive practices in and by themselves, studies of social and material reality should pay more attention to the dissimilarities between discourse and practice (Larsen and Munkgård Pedersen 2002: 46, 61). This study of leisure practices thus provides an opportunity to test the power of official discourses over the everyday life practices of Chinese people, while at the same time demonstrating the agency on which Chinese individuals rely in their pursuit of leisure.

Space and place, power and resistance

Although I analyse the ways leisure is represented in speech and texts, I do not regard leisure as text, but as social practices that take place in physical environments. Henri Lefebvre's use of space – rather than language – as the central metaphor in the analysis of how power is exercised has therefore proved helpful, in particular in my analysis of public leisure places in Quanzhou (Lefebvre 1991). In Lefebvre's *The Production of Space*, 'place' refers to the physical sites where everyday life practices happen. 'Space', on the other hand, is the term reserved for the abstract space of plans and visions which authorities, represented by planners and technocrats, generate. According to Lefebvre, authorities seek to project their visions of an orderly space onto the physical places where people carry out their activities. The social production of space thus entails a form of social engineering on the part of the authorities. In this respect, Lefebvre's theory runs parallel to Foucault's analyses of how the physical environment of the prison has served as a technology for the authorities to discipline people's bodies, and for the promotion of a discourse of normality (McNay 1994: 93). In my analysis, I interpret the concept of healthy (*jiankang*) leisure as a representation of the idealized leisure space local authorities seek to promote. Conversely, I regard the local government's restrictions on so-called chaotic (*luan*) leisure practices as attempts to enforce the official definition of normal leisure behaviour. However, I also analyse the reception of this official discourse among the citizenry. My findings suggest that not only is the discourse of healthy and chaotic leisure of little consequence for the actual leisure practices that take place in Quanzhou, but also that the policies of the local government towards the leisure market are not pursued with any consistency by the relevant government agencies. From this, I conclude that the local population has more agency than Lefebvre's theory suggests and, moreover, that the authorities' intentions and agendas are in practice much more diverse than they appear to be at the level of official discourse.

Jing Wang has pointed out that 'Chinese statist regulation is sometimes merely rhetorical, at other times, consequential' (Jing Wang 2001a: 38). It is therefore vital that analyses of social spaces in contemporary China go beyond the level of official rhetoric, and examine the discrepancies between official policy statements and propaganda on the one hand, and the actual interaction between the state and individuals or groups of individuals on the other. My data from participant observation in organized leisure associations in Quanzhou show that officially approved leisure activities, however healthy, receive little or no support from local government. Added to the fact that the system established to secure the party-state's domination over popular organizations is enforced with remarkable flexibility, this indicates that the discourse of healthy leisure is – as Jing Wang states, – 'sometimes merely rhetorical'. The below analyses of the local government's management of Quanzhou's privately run leisure venues, and the cases of the local Internet cafés and karaoke parlours in particular, serve to demonstrate how the official discourse of leisure is also indeed consequential.

In his writing about power and knowledge, Foucault redefined power as a force that is neither unidirectional, nor purely negative (McNay 1994: 85). McNay has argued that the re-conceptualization Foucault made means that '[p]ower can no longer be analysed in terms of intentionality [...] or by focusing exclusively on legitimate and institutionalized centres of power, such as state apparatuses' (McNay 1994: 85). In his own analyses, however, Foucault nevertheless tended to overestimate the effectiveness of disciplinary forms of power and control. Peter Dews suggests that this is a result of Foucault's strong focus on official institutions, its governors and architects, combined with a tendency to neglect the 'voices and bodies of those being controlled' (Peter Dews in McNay 1994: 101). The same can be said of Lefebvre. Although Lefebvre wrote that authorities cannot always predict the consequences of their plans (Lefebvre 1991: 37), he nevertheless ascribed strong and unequivocal intentions to planners and technocrats. In my analysis of the leisure practices I observed and participated in while in Quanzhou, I have therefore supplemented Lefebvre's theory of space and place with the theoretical perspectives of Michel de Certeau and James C. Scott, who have analysed ordinary people's agency as forms of resistance (de Certeau 1988; Scott 1990).

The PRC leisure ethic promotes a leisure space where there is no room for unhealthy practices. The boundaries of the envisioned space are nevertheless constantly transgressed by the real-life practices of ordinary people. I consider these everyday transgressions as common people's strategies or 'ways of making do' (de Certeau 1988: 29–44) in relation to the relevant policies and regulations. The rules of the Quanzhou leisure space are re-written and modified by local people themselves through the leisure activities in which they engage. Moreover, in cases where controversy arises over the ways a leisure place is put to use, ordinary people may even resort to overt as well as covert acts of resistance, as demonstrated in the case study of leisure at Quanzhou's Qingyuan Mountain

Reserve in Chapter 8. As argued by McNay, it follows from Foucault's redefinition of power as a positive force that 'all power relations are potentially reversible and unstable', and that '[w]herever domination is imposed, resistance will inevitably arise' (McNay 1994: 101). In other words, there is always room for people to creatively interpret the official discourse, or opportunities to redefine the limits of the officially defined space. I argue that the existence of leisure associations that fail to be contained by official regulations, the continued popularity of the supposedly chaotic Internet cafés, and the local inhabitants' innumerable ways of undermining the local authorities' visions for the Qingyuan Mountain Reserve as a well-regulated leisure place reveal the limited efficacy of official discourses as a means of disciplining a population.

We cannot infer from the official discourse of leisure that the local government has one unambiguous agenda, and that this agenda is the disciplining of the Chinese population by way of official discourses such as the leisure ethic. On the contrary, if we look at the ways in which the local authorities govern the leisure market and the various types of associations in a city like Quanzhou, their policy implementation is just as paradoxical as the assessments made by Sun Xiaoli in the quote above. In practice, local leisure establishments are indeed an important part of the service sector promoted by local government. At the level of discourse, however, the authorities seek to curb tendencies towards overspending and increased materialism among the population. I argue that this contradiction is best understood as a continuation of the concern for the balancing of material and spiritual civilization. Ann Anagnost writes that in the implementation of Deng's reform policies, the co-development of the people's morality was regarded as necessary in order to prevent the expected negative effects of economic development and material comforts (Anagnost 1997: 84). The authorities feared that the introduction of economic reforms would cause urban elites to turn their back on socialist values and party doctrines.[11] The 1981–4 campaigns against 'spiritual pollution' can thus be seen as one attempt from the Chinese authorities at promoting frugality among Party members in general and the educated elite in particular (Friedman 2006: 231). I regard the PRC leisure ethic as a similar attempt by Chinese authorities to communicate a message of self-restraint and continued self-cultivation. This time, however, the message is directed towards the population in general. I argue that in effect the PRC leisure ethic serves to promote and endorse the leisure activities of the educated middle class, i.e. the kinds of cultural consumption that take place in the library, the museum, in night schools and in concert halls. By the same token, the leisure ethic voiced in Party propaganda, in scholarly writing and in the media characterizes the activities that take place in karaoke parlours, Internet cafés and shopping streets as wasteful and detrimental to the health of the population as a whole. This does not mean, however, that the agents of the party-state, be they local officials or publishers in the Party-dominated media, have the means to force ordinary people to choose self-study over karaoke. When people in Quanzhou did give priority to educational leisure activities, their reasons for doing so were far more complex than simple adherence to official discourse.

Scholars within the field of Chinese studies have recently argued that the Chinese party-state successfully utilizes the field of leisure consumption as a means to govern and pacify the populace (Jing Wang 2001a; 2001b; Tomba 2004: 3, Croll 2006: 30–1). In *China's New Consumers*, Elisabeth Croll states that the Chinese government has promoted private consumption in order to boost the legitimacy of the Party in the wake of the protests at Tiananmen in 1989, and in order to lessen people's opposition to the one-child policy (Croll 2006: 30–1). Croll writes that

> [t]he new policies encouraging spending and new forms of recreation confirmed one of my early contentions that the government deployed consumption either as an instrument of government or for compensatory popularity to soften the effects of unpopular policies [...]
> (2006: 30–1)

Another example can be found in an article by Luigi Tomba, where he writes that the development of an urban consumer society in China is 'as much the outcome of the social engineering project of the contemporary reformist state and its agencies as it has been a consequence of the opening up of the economy and society' (Tomba 2004: 3). Jing Wang is, however, the theorist who makes the strongest claims in this direction when she suggests that the Chinese authorities have substituted consumption for democratization in order to pacify the Chinese population (Wang 2001b: 73). The official discourse of leisure which I analyse in the following chapters has many characteristics in common with the campaigns and policies described by Jing Wang (2001a; 2001b). My data from participant observation in Quanzhou, as well as my analysis of how leisure regulations were implemented in the local context, show, in contrast, that the exact intentions of the authorities are difficult to identify. On the contrary, it seems that the intentions and agendas of local authorities may be as diverse as the practices of the people they govern.

When it comes to appreciation of the arts and the appropriate choice of leisure activities, the popular culture critique argues that ordinary people are easily led astray and must thus be guided by an informed elite. The Frankfurter school with its critique of the commoditization of culture provided the foundation for this line of argument, and for the dichotomized relationship between commerce and the arts. The relatively unimaginative character of the contemporary Chinese leisure market, with its karaoke parlours, snack franchises and muzak-ridden cafés, may serve to strengthen this impression of a growing commercialization and homogenization of the leisure sphere and a pacification of the population by way of consumption. This simplistic view of the leisure market overlooks the fact that what the consumer buys from a karaoke franchise is not simply a microphone and access to a standardized list of pop hits. What consumers pay for is just as much the opportunity to socialize with whomever they please in a comfortable environment and behind closed doors. As the following examples from the city of Quanzhou reveal, the activities that take place in commercial leisure places are not merely determined by commercial interests or the dominant discourses of the authorities; leisure activities are just as often initiated and presided over by the consumers themselves. This shows that in contemporary China, individuals may make room for their own preferred practices both in the places that are formally governed by market forces, and in the leisure space that is defined along the lines of the official PRC leisure ethic.

The organization of the book

Chapter 1 provides an introduction to the city of Quanzhou and its local leisure scene. I account for the methods I applied in my field research, and I give a short presentation of key contacts and interviewees in Quanzhou and describe how these men and women helped me find an entry point for field research in Quanzhou. Moreover, I give a short overview of the types of written materials I collected and analysed in this study, and I account for the strategies I used in order to identify prospective interviewees, as well as places and activities suited for participant observation. The problem of defining the Chinese middle class, and the questions that arise from my use of Mandarin as the primary language in a community of dialect speakers are also addressed in this chapter.

Studies of leisure generally lack a thorough discussion of what 'leisure' *is*. More often than not, leisure is defined as a special kind of time, i.e. 'the time that remains when paid work and other obligatory activities have been done' or the activities people engage in 'after hours' (Roberts 1999: 5, 3). When we look at everyday life practices in a local context, however, the point of departure must be how – in this case – Quanzhou's inhabitants define the hours spent chatting and drinking tea in the workplace, or the local hairdressers' practice of playing cards between customers. Is this considered 'work' or 'leisure', or both? In Chapter 2 I argue that leisure is best understood as a practice – goal-oriented or otherwise – in which the individual engages for the sake of pleasure or relaxation. I also look at leisure as a socio-cultural and historical phenomenon, and discuss the usage and meaning of the Chinese terms '*xiuxian*', '*xianxia*', and '*wan*' in academic writing and everyday speech.

Chapter 3 is devoted to an analysis of the PRC leisure ethic, its origins and significance in a local context. Here I map out the links between the PRC leisure ethic and the Protestant work ethic. The main focus is, however, on how the notion of leisure as a national resource, and the miscalculation of the amount of leisure available to the ordinary Chinese, cause scholars and government agencies to worry about the adverse consequences of idleness on the population as a whole. Based on my findings from Quanzhou, I argue that the underlying premises of the official discourse of leisure do not reflect the characteristics of Chinese people's leisure lives today.

Chapter 4 is concerned with specific examples of the discrepancy between the local government's visions and plans for a new museum district in Quanzhou and the kinds of leisure activities the new museums actually generate. I analyse some of the public leisure places in the Quanzhou cityscape using Henri

Lefebvre's theory of the social production of space. The chapter concludes that it takes more than visionary plans in order to alter the geographical distribution of leisure activities. The attraction of novelty notwithstanding, old, familiar leisure places will remain the most attractive for the general city population as long as new venues fail to be made accessible by way of public information and public transportation. This case study shows that despite the fact that going to museums is ranked among the healthy and educational activities promoted by the official leisure ethic, little is in fact done by local government to make leisure activities of this kind readily available to the local citizenry. This point is followed up in Chapter 5, where I make a comparative study of some of the so-called healthy leisure activities in Quanzhou, both those that are authorized by the local government and those organized unofficially by individuals or networks of friends and associates. The analysis shows that, in Quanzhou, the facilitation of leisure activities increasingly relies on agents in the commercial leisure market. The fact that the sheer cost makes many contemporary leisure activities inaccessible to low-income groups should therefore be of concern to the local authorities in their promotion of 'healthy' activities.

In the current situation, the official leisure discourse labels the activities the salaried middle class pursues, as healthy, while the leisure activities of the less privileged are more likely to be characterized as unwholesome. Chapter 6 is therefore dedicated to the analysis of some of the leisure places described as chaotic (*luan*) and unhealthy in propaganda materials and the local Party-dominated news media, namely Quanzhou's Internet cafés and karaoke parlours. While the latter are frequented by customers from different social strata, both the official discourse and local middle-class consumers link Internet cafés with urban 'others' – more specifically, young uneducated migrant workers. The chapter looks at the many ways in which parents and educators seek to dissuade young students from patronising local Internet cafés, for fear of the bad company they may keep there. The analysis shows that the influence of official discourse is strongest on middle-class individuals when it corresponds with their prejudice or uninformed opinions about the urban 'other'. When the local media warn against chaotic (*luan*) conditions in local karaoke venues, however, the middle-class customers seem to give more weight to their own experience than to moralizing admonitions in the local press.

Chapter 7 looks at the role of consumption as a form of leisure among Quanzhou's urban middle class. I analyse current consumer practices as a continuation of historical tendencies, rather than a radical break brought about by the reform policies of the last decades, and argue that the change in leisure consumption and consumption as leisure is a change of quantity more than quality. Based on the findings of the previous chapters and data concerning the practices of local consumers in Quanzhou, I question Jing Wang's claim that the Chinese party-state uses consumption as a ruling technology. I argue that this stance is based on a misjudgement of the Party authorities' power to govern the lives of Chinese individuals, and an underestimation of the agency of Chinese individuals as consumers. The spontaneous demonstration of popular agency is at the centre of Chapter 8, which is a case study of the various tactics Quanzhou's local inhabitants use to express their dissatisfaction with the way the local Qingyuan Mountain Reserve is managed by the local authorities. Here I rely on James C. Scott's theory of hidden transcripts and de Certeau's writing about ordinary people's ways of 'making do' in order to analyse Quanzhou people's attempts to reclaim their favourite leisure place within the larger perspective of popular acts of resistance.

1 Locating leisure in a medium-size Chinese city

If you were to visit Quanzhou, and if you were so lucky as to be accompanied by a local friend or business partner, you would inevitably be introduced to two of the most common forms of local leisure, namely a trip to the scenic Qingyuan Mountain and a relaxing break in a tea house. Your mountain excursion would most likely be taken by car, and on your way down from the peak you would

Figure 1.1 The skyline of contemporary Quanzhou.

stop at a small farm to enjoy a meal of free-range chicken and locally grown vegetables. You would then proceed to a tea house, possibly a renovated old mansion in a side street with a carefully constructed atmosphere of cultured recreation. Most likely, however, you would be invited to sample teas in a tea shop operated by a friend or relative of your local associate, who then would let you in on the secrets of the local speciality teas. While you were sipping tiny cups of local *Tie Guanyin* tea, arriving customers would sit down for a cup and a chat while waiting for colourful parcels of tea to be wrapped as gifts for their boss, their old teacher, or a potential business associate. You would soon realize that most customers were acquaintances or relatives of the shop owner, and before you were even let in on their plans, you would all go out to karaoke together. After an hour or so of singing, dice games and numerous toasts in brand-name liqueur, you would round off the evening with a foot massage.

This night out in town might leave you with the impression that leisure in Quanzhou is thoroughly privatized, commercialized and bland. That Chinese leisure is essentially an endless chain of dining, tea drinking, karaoke and massages is an opinion emblematic of the many foreign trade representatives I have met in China. The notion that leisure in Quanzhou – or indeed any medium-sized Chinese city – is bland is easily refuted, however, if you only take the time to observe what local residents are doing when they are not accompanying foreign or out-of-town visitors. Karaoke, cups of tea and a trip to the mountain might still be among the favoured activities, but the way leisure places are put to use vary considerably depending on when you go and who is accompanying you. This is equally true of the karaoke parlour and the public square, the scenic mountain slopes, and the local book café. These are all examples of leisure places that I will return to in the chapters below.

Once I became sensitive to the fact that local Quanzhou people put leisure venues and public places to use in widely different ways, I started looking at the cityscape from a new perspective. I began to pay attention to the areas that attracted townspeople and the places that were desolate, and I made note of the many instances when people made public sidewalks into private spaces or in other ways utilized areas of town in an unexpected manner. As a consequence of these observations, Lefebvre's theory of how space is socially produced became central to my analysis of leisure. And the very diversity of both leisure places and leisure practices is why I chose Quanzhou as my field site for this study. Being a city of close to one million people on the economically developed coast of Fujian Province, Quanzhou is home to a middle class for whom 'leisure' has come to mean anything from going to a tea house or restaurant, to reading, hiking, window-shopping or going to a karaoke parlour. However, leisure activities organized within the structures of the party-state are still part of the local leisure space. Accordingly, the practices of some of Quanzhou's cultural and leisure associations will also be analysed in the chapters below.

Quanzhou city past and present

Quanzhou is a dynamic city where skyscrapers and historical relics can be found within walking distance of each other, and where the local inhabitants take an equal pride in the history of Quanzhou as an ancient trading port and its current status as the flagship of economic development in Fujian Province. Quanzhou has more than 800,000 inhabitants, and is located by the Taiwan Strait in the Minnan area.[1] The city is situated at the foot of Qingyuan Mountain, and is administratively divided into the Fengze district to the east and the Licheng district to the west. Jinjiang River separates the city centre from its farthest suburbs to the west and south, and smaller rivers and channels run through the cityscape, sometimes along narrow back alleys, in other places lined by lush trees and flowers as a result of Quanzhou's 2003 bid for the Nations in Bloom awards.[2] Quanzhou is also the administrative centre of Quanzhou Municipality, which consists of four city districts (*qu*), three district-level towns (*shi*), five counties (*xian*), and a science and technology development zone (*kaifa qu*).[3] The municipal population numbers more than seven million people, among them 1.6 million labourers from all over China (Lin Fulong *et al. DNZB* 1 March, 2006: A4).[4] 98.2 per cent of the population is Han Chinese, and people from 48 other ethnic groups are also counted among the local inhabitants.[5] Some of Quanzhou's local surname groups, most notably the Ding and the Guo, can trace their lineages back to traders and merchants from the Middle East who became residents of Quanzhou during the Tang and Song Dynasties. These inhabitants are officially recognized as Arab descendants and count as members of the *Hui* ethnic group (Xiaojia Gu 2006). In addition, the Hui'an women who reside along the coast of Quanzhou's Luojiang district are well known for their traditional sartorial styles, strong same-sex networks and distinct marriage practices. They are not, however, officially recognized as an ethnic group (Friedman 2006).

Quanzhou's historical legacy

The Minnan area became part of the Chinese empire during the third century. Before that time, the area was inhabited by 'aboriginal tribal peoples' (Clark 1991: 3). In the late Han Dynasty, Han settlers from northern China gradually came to dominate the area, and traces of the amalgamation of northern customs and language with those of the coastal southerners can still be found in the Minnan dialect and in traditional performance arts. Today's Licheng district became the administrative centre of Quanzhou Prefecture in the mid-Tang period, and during the Tang and Song dynasties, Quanzhou developed into an important trading port. Here copper and iron and the famous locally-produced Dehua porcelain were exchanged for foreign goods. By the late Song period, Quanzhou was the 'biggest official commercial port in China' (Wang Mingming 1993: 29). Cultural relics in the Quanzhou area, from sacred Muslim tombs to Indian stone carvings and a Manichaean temple, bear witness to the variety of cultural and religious practices that converged here. Moreover, historians believe that Quanzhou is indeed the bustling port of Zaitun described by Ibn Batutta and later by Marco Polo (Xiaojia Gu 2006; Wang Mingming 1993: 29). As a consequence, Quanzhou is recognized by UNESCO as the starting point of the Maritime Silk Road (*Haishang sichouzhilu de qi dian*).

With the restrictions on trade imposed from the Ming Dynasty onward, Quanzhou lost its position as a commercial centre. The changes in the local economy had dire consequences for the inhabitants in the area. Since there was a shortage of arable land, people were forced to seek a livelihood elsewhere. During the late Ming Dynasty, the former trade routes were turned into smuggler routes (Wang Mingming 1993: 33). The continuation of these overseas connections facilitated large-scale migration from Quanzhou to Southeast Asia during this period. Some went in search of temporary employment, others settled abroad permanently. Later, in the wake of the clashes with Japan and European naval powers in the second half of the nineteenth century, the nearby city of Xiamen became one of the five most important treaty ports in China. This meant a further 'peripherization of Quanzhou' that lasted throughout the Republican period (Wang Mingming 1993: 35). It is only in recent years that Quanzhou has risen to new prominence.

Many of the Minnan Chinese communities in Southeast Asia have maintained strong ties to Quanzhou as their ancestral home, even during times when the political climate hindered their relatives in Quanzhou from making contact with residents of foreign countries. Since the opening up of China, the renewal of cultural bonds and kinship ties from the Quanzhou side has brought economic investments and industrialization to the region. Today, Quanzhou boasts of being the hometown (*qiaoxiang*) of 6.7 million overseas Chinese, and the ancestral home (*zuji*) to nine million Taiwanese, or 44.8 per cent of the population of the Republic of China (Quanzhou shi renmin zhengfu, 28 August 2008).

Whereas the city of Xiamen got an economic head start in the beginning of the reform period, Quanzhou's annual GDP now exceeds that of its old arch rival (190.1 billion *yuan*, compared to 116.8 billion in Xiamen).[6] The image of Quanzhou as a hometown of overseas Chinese and site for international trade and the legacy of openness to the outside world are now actively used by local authorities as a means to attract foreign investors and tourists to the area. As anthropologist Wang Mingming points out, the perceived existence of cultural pluralism and an 'open spirit' (*kaifang jingshen*) in ancient Quanzhou 'conforms with the new "open policy"' of the reform era (Wang Mingming 1993: 48). As an historical example of successful trade relations and international cooperation, Quanzhou supplies the contemporary party line with a certain historical legitimacy. Therefore, Quanzhou has come to occupy a special position in PRC historiography in the reform era, and is celebrated as one of Chinas' major historical cities.

Contemporary Quanzhou

The city of Quanzhou has seen considerable changes since the new economic policies and the process of industrialization embarked upon in the Xiamen-Zhangzhou-Quanzhou triangle 20 years ago. Much of the farmland on the outskirts of the city was appropriated for construction purposes in the early 1990s. The local government built several neighbourhoods of contemporary high-rises where flats were offered to state employees at subsidized prices. Local peasants were given monetary compensation for their loss of land, and many used the money to set up four- or five-storey buildings in the poorer areas of town. The former peasants now reside here with their families, and many of them make a meagre living from letting out rooms to out-of-town labourers or spaces for small shops at the street level. While much of the old town with its narrow lanes and two-storey buildings remains at the heart of the Licheng district, the Fengze district with its banking, finance, and hotel towers has, along with the newly developed neighbourhoods to the west and north of the old town centre, changed both the face of the city and the span of the city territory. The twin pagodas at Kaiyuan temple, which were once the most visible of Quanzhou's landmarks, have become overshadowed by a sparkling cityscape of glass and steel. Although the numerous *dasha* ('mansions') dominate the skyline, some of the most remarkable examples of Quanzhou's contemporary architecture can be found in streets in Beimen jie, Tumen jie and the newly restored parts of Xi jie, where shop fronts and residences show an amalgamation of the architectural characteristics of the fourteenth-century Qingjing mosque and the colonial style typical of the old commercial districts in both Xiamen and Quanzhou.

Although there are several factories within the city limits, Quanzhou's major industries are localized in the rapidly industrializing district-level cities of Jinjiang and Shishi, where workers from all over China are engaged in the production of shoes, sportswear and other consumer items for the national and international markets. Unlike in many other industrializing areas in China, the majority of Quanzhou's factories and enterprises are neither joint ventures nor township and village enterprises. More often than not they are privately owned companies established with assistance from relatives and contacts working or residing abroad. According to my interviewees, the amount of money in the Quanzhou economy acquired through overseas networks has reached 100 million *yuan*.

Quanzhou is a one and a half-hour bus ride from Xiamen International Airport and the local Jinjiang airport offers flights to all major national destinations. The mountainous Fujian terrain is poorly served with train lines, but the gradually expanding network of highways along the coast makes bus travel to China's big cities both relatively fast and affordable. Quanzhou's harbour is important for local industry, but despite the city's proximity to both the Jinjiang river and Quanzhou Bay, boat transportation and seaside activities are of little importance in the everyday lives of the citizenry. Although some of the main roads have been widened, the steady increase in the number of private cars, taxis, and motorbikes leaves Quanzhou's roads clogged. In an attempt to alleviate this problem, the local government stopped issuing license plates for motorbikes and electric scooters in 2007. Moreover, employers were asked to enforce flexible work hours and employees were encouraged spend their lunchtime siesta at work whenever possible, in order to prevent traffic jams during the morning, noon and evening rush hours. Transportation within the city limits remains slow and inconvenient and parking spaces are scarce. Luckily, most parts of the city are easily reached on foot or by bicycle. A network of highways was under construction between the city of Quanzhou and its important industrialized districts during my stay and the construction work left long stretches of road impassable at times. Moreover, only a short car ride out of Anxi county town, roughly one and a half hours from the Quanzhou city centre, the division between centre and periphery in the municipality becomes highly visible. Here, houses are of poor quality and dilapidated, industry is scarce, and transportation is made difficult by flooded dirt roads in poor repair. The production of the now famous *Anxi tie guanyin* tea has made a positive impact on the economy in this part of the municipality. When it comes to general industrial development, transport and education, however, the differences between the inland countryside and the coastal city districts of Quanzhou municipality mirror the rural-urban divide at national level.

The Minnan dialect (*Minnan hua*) is the language used among friends and family, in shops and markets, and among colleagues in informal settings. Mandarin proficiency is, however, a prerequisite for most jobs, and clear pronunciation is regarded as an asset for a prospective employee. Although many young people in Quanzhou are ashamed of their '*digua qiang*' (lit. 'sweet potato accent'), Quanzhou residents take pride in their dialect. Despite official projects to promote the use of *Minnan hua* in local broadcasts and the education sector,[7] the relative number of dialect speakers in the major cities of Xiamen and Quanzhou is decreasing.

Quanzhou culture, Quanzhou leisure

Tourists, both foreign and Chinese, will inevitably be introduced to what both official brochures and townspeople in general hold to be Quanzhou culture (*Quanzhou wenhua*). First, they will be offered cups of *Tie Guanyin*, which is local tea meticulously brewed, served in tiny cups of clay or Dehua porcelain. Then, the cultural heritage sites will be introduced, for example the Kaiyuan Temple with its twin pagodas, the Qingjing Mosque, and the statue of the daoist deity *Laojun* at Qingyuan Mountain, or possibly one of Quanzhou's five major museums. Finally, visitors will experience *nanyin*, a local song tradition that has become revitalized and gentrified by local culture bureaucracy initiatives. While tea culture is an important part of everyday life for people in the whole of Minnan, *nanyin* has lost much of its former role as the soundtrack of Quanzhou people's lives. According to local enthusiasts, *nanyin* should be the first sound a local baby hears, the music played at weddings and the sound accompanying the deceased to the grave site. This is no longer the case, initiatives by both the local culture bureaus and the education sector notwithstanding. *Nanyin* is performed at three open-air stages close to the Confucius temple (*Fuwenmiao*) every evening, but the audience is sparse and most locals admit that they take little interest in the genre. Popular music, in the sense of music appreciated by people in general, is the same in Quanzhou as in any other Chinese city. It is a mixture of Mandarin-language pop hits from mainland China and Taiwan, Cantonese pop from Hong Kong, and a few Korean songs. In addition, a genre of mostly sentimental songs in the Minnan dialect sung by performers from both sides of the strait are well-liked, and these songs are often on the menu along with the more mainstream pop music in Quanzhou's karaoke parlours.

As mentioned above, the commercial leisure market is dominated by karaoke, tea houses of different price ranges and quality, spa centres which are popular for their foot massages, and a variety of restaurants ranging from Brazilian barbeque and Philippine and Indonesian dining to regional cuisines from all over China. Together with book cafés, these are the most well-attended leisure establishments in Quanzhou. Other commercial leisure places include a number of gyms and yoga centres and a few Western-style bars. Quanzhou is also a university town. Although the campuses of Huaqiao University and the local teachers' college are situated outside the city centre, students and staff make frequent use of Quanzhou's leisure venues, particularly at weekends.

Several of Quanzhou's residential districts have their own activity centres, with leisure activities run by the neighbourhood administration or sometimes the users themselves. Neighbourhood leisure activities are mostly directed towards the elderly and the young in the form of art and music classes for school children and senior academies, dance halls and reading rooms for the elderly. For many residents in these age groups, the neighbourhood functions as the central leisure place in their everyday lives. The city also has two government-run cultural centres, the Youth Cultural Palace (*Qingshaonian wenhuagong*) and the Workers' Cultural Palace (*Gongren wenhuagong*). The former offers weekend classes for children, from ballet and drawing to computing and English. The Youth Culture Palace also houses the Communist Youth League (*Gongqingtuan*), the local branch of China Youth Volunteers (*Qingnian zhiyuanzhe xiehui*), and a spacious concert hall. The Workers' Cultural Palace advertises a range of computer classes, but none of my interviewees frequented the Cultural Palace, nor was it mentioned by anyone as a place of leisure. The open park grounds behind the Palace, however, are popular with both young and old. The grounds are used for morning exercises and there are outdoor pool tables and suitable seating for parties of card players. The area also serves as a fairground at festival times. Going to the movies is no longer as fashionable as was the case in the 1980s and 1990s (Shaoguang Wang 1995: 159). In Quanzhou, as in many Chinese cities, people find it more comfortable and also more affordable to watch movies at home or in Internet cafés. Quanzhou still has three cinemas, one of which serves as a stage for events organized by the local bureau of culture. The public parks around the city and close to the museum site west of the city centre are increasingly popular among the citizenry, but Qingyuan Mountain, with its pleasant mountain trails and small eating establishments, is by far the most popular area for outdoor activities in Quanzhou.

Middle-class leisure in Quanzhou

My analysis of leisure in Quanzhou focuses on how people utilize public and commercial places for leisure activities. As a consequence, I concentrated my field research on activities outside the home and individuals who have the economic ability to partake in a variety of leisure activities. These Quanzhou residents could afford to spend on activities and experiences beyond the routine expenses of food, shelter, health and education. They were women and men of all ages: young parents, families, elderly retirees, and youth without family commitments. They were employees in trade companies, teachers and employees in the local administration and culture sector – the media in particular. In short, they were part of the growing Chinese middle class.

To estimate the size and describe the composition of the middle class in a city like Quanzhou or in China as a whole raises problems in terms of categorization. Zhou Xiaohong has defined the contemporary Chinese middle class as consisting of those who own their own businesses or rural/township enterprises, small-business owners, individual entrepreneurs, officials, intellectuals associated with the Party and the state, Chinese administrators and key personnel in foreign enterprises, a vast number of administrators in enterprises and societal structures, those with higher education in law, business administration, etc., and those educated abroad in new and innovative trades and professions (lawyers, architects, accountants, planners, those within the movie and broadcasting industry, and so on) (Zhou Xiaohong: 2005: 5–6). And in Zhou's survey of the middle classes in Beijing, Shanghai, Nanjing, Guangzhou and Wuhan, a total of 11.8 per cent of the big-city population could be said to belong to the middle class on the basis of their vocations, income levels or patterns of consumption (Zhou Xiaohong: 2005: 5). My key informants and my interviewees for this project can be identified as officials and intellectuals associated with the Party and the state. Although their salaries were relatively modest, their connection to the state apparatus often provided them with economic privileges such as sponsored housing and the opportunity to have some of their restaurant bills and other expenditures covered by a work unit expense account. Fewsmith argues that if we want to estimate the impact of the Chinese middle class on contemporary Chinese society, we must pay attention to the significance of middle-class identity, rather than merely focusing on the exact size of the middle-class population. After all, as many as 59.6 per cent of the respondents in Zhou Xiaohong's survey identified themselves as belonging to the Chinese middle class (Zhou Xiaohong: 2005: 5). This tendency is also confirmed by Li Chunli's survey from 2001, where 46.8 per cent of interviewees in large- and medium-sized cities, as well as in the countryside, considered themselves middle class (Li Chunli in Fewsmith 2007: 3). According to Fewsmith, this tendency shows that 'a great number of people identify themselves with the tastes and aspirations of the middle class' (Fewsmith 2007: 7). Judging from their leisure practices, dress, accessories, cameras and computers, most of my informants in Quanzhou were at least aspiring middle-class citizens, in terms of consumption and income as well as vocation.

There is undeniably a bias in my material that stems from the fact that both my choice of research topic and my identity as an educated female foreigner made it easy for me to communicate with the educated middle class and people who had time and money to spend on leisure. However, six out of the nine months of my fieldwork, I lived in an apartment building in one of the city's poorer areas, and the contact I had with my neighbours there provided me with at least a rudimentary understanding of the everyday life conditions among the less privileged in Quanzhou. Furthermore, Chinese surveys show that Chinese men are much more likely to spend time and money on social activities outside the home (Wang Yalin 2003: 73). During my time in the field I socialized with men of different age groups and social status. I was allowed to join all-male parties for drinks as well as visits to dubious massage parlours, but there were certainly leisure activities to which I as a woman was not invited. Many of the women I interviewed in Quanzhou, both locals and women born and raised in other provinces, regarded the *Minnan* culture as particularly chauvinistic,[8] and held that women in Quanzhou were expected to socialize within the limits of the family home and spend time in the company of other women. My focus on leisure in public spaces means that this aspect of women's leisure – be it the leisure experiences of young wives or those of retired grandmothers responsible for cooking and looking after children or grandchildren – is poorly represented in my data. My female interviewees were mostly middle-class professionals, and more often than not they were unmarried, or their child was looked after by their mothers-in-law. Consequently, although there are many women among my interviewees for this project, their social status was less diverse than is the case with their male counterparts.

Gate openers and key informants in the field

Entering the field, both in the physical and the abstract sense, is very much a social process that starts during the planning of the research project and continues throughout the duration of fieldwork. In my case, I was fortunate to be part of a larger research project that assisted me in initiating my own work. I also had the advantage of having done field research in a different part of the Minnan area a couple of years earlier. So when I arrived in Xiamen in August 2005, I was met by colleagues and friends whose assistance remained essential throughout the following three periods of field research. After helping me decide on a suitable place to conduct my work, my main contact in Xiamen introduced me to people within her own professional network who were willing to assist me as door openers in the field. My use of the term 'door opener' rather than the more conventional 'gate keeper' (Burgess 1991: 47; Bailey 1996: 50) is a conscious choice. The term 'gate keeper' suggests that the individual in question is an obstacle, or a person who guards information that he or she is unwilling to share. The term 'door opener', however, conveys a more positive image of both the person in question and his or her function in the research process. In my experience, data is usually the outcome of dialogues and discussions between informants and myself; it is not something informants help me to 'find' or 'get'. This is why the development of trust and rapport with one or more key informants is vital to the facilitation of ethnographic field research. Some of the initial door openers in Quanzhou became just such key informants, contributing towards my project by sharing their life stories and opinions, by taking me along to social events and celebrations, and by introducing me to several other informants from their own personal networks.

Key informants are different from the average interviewee because of their role in facilitating the research by agreeing to introduce the researcher to relevant people and places. In my case, three of my key informants were experienced researchers themselves, and therefore took special interest in the project as peers. This allowed me the opportunity to discuss my questions and some of my preliminary conclusions with informants who were not only locals, but insiders in field-based research. At times, our differences in terms of academic tradition (and, for my part, the added challenge of discussing research methods in a foreign language) made it difficult for me to explain and defend my choice of research topic and methods. However, the objections and suggestions provided by these key informants forced me to explicate my topic and the goals of my research in a way that I believe has benefited the project greatly. The following key informants have been central for the execution of this project:

A   Male, from Quanzhou. Retired from central position in a local culture institution. Researcher. Broad professional network. Key informant in questions of local history, culture and administration.
B   Female, from neighbouring province. Director of a local cultural institution. Researcher. Broad professional network. Sociable and outgoing. Key informant in questions of leisure, culture, administration and family matters.
C   Female, from Quanzhou. Director of a local cultural institution. Researcher. Broad professional network. Key informant in questions of leisure, culture, administration and family matters.
D   Female, from Eastern Fujian. Graduated from university in Quanzhou. Employed in local trade company, later self-employed. Network among traders both local and international. Key informant in questions of leisure and youth culture.
E & F   Couple, both from Fujian. Employed in local administration and in telecommunications. Broad networks within administration and the culture sphere. Key informants in questions of organized leisure, local art forms and family matters.
G & H   Couple, he from Quanzhou, she from North China. Employed in finance and education. Broad networks in trade and economic life. Key informants in questions of local consumption and family matters.

Some of these were among the initial door openers, others took on the role of key informants after I had already spent some time in the field. Key informant D was one of several young people who approached me on their own initiative. The fieldwork literature cautions researchers against relying on so-called marginal informants and other individuals who seek your friendship, as sources in the field (see for example Agar 1980 in Johnson 1990: 55–6). However, unlike the stereotypical educated urban youth eager for language exchange, this young woman proved to be a resourceful contact whose assistance added much to the project.

Strategies for identifying interviewees

I used a dual strategy in the identification of interviewees for my research project. One was a form of 'judgement sampling' (Honigmann in Johnson 1990: 28), where I sought out individuals to interview on the basis of their positions in relevant organizations, institutions, or businesses. As part of my project design I had developed guides for semi-structured interviews, with questions about a given organization or business, general aspects of local leisure and cultural life, and the interviewee's own leisure activities. First, I interviewed my initial gate openers, who then pointed me in the direction of other prospective interviewees. This process helped me identify interviewees within different parts of the local leisure market, including museum directors, TV producers, library managers, performers of local traditional arts, and other employees in the local culture sector. Data from these interviews became decisive for my analysis of development in the local museum sector and the perception of 'healthy' and 'unhealthy' leisure spaces in Quanzhou. The personal and professional networks of these first interviewees determined much of my initial findings, and also my early focus on cultural institutions in Quanzhou. Therefore, in order to become acquainted with the perspectives of commercial agents and the Quanzhou inhabitants who were the actual users of local leisure facilities, I developed my own informal networks using a more data-driven or 'exploratory' strategy (Johnson 1990: 38). My research agenda developed in accordance with the topics I defined through the initial analysis of the first semi-structured interviews, the observations I made in the field as I went along, data from informal interviews, and a range of written materials I read while in the field. It was this heterogeneous collection of data that made possible the analysis of leisure practices in karaoke parlours, Internet cafés and book cafés, and on the slopes of Qingyuan Mountain. For this part of my research, I regarded every Quanzhou citizen as a well-qualified informant, in the sense that each individual's leisure practices, experiences and attitudes constituted potential data for my analysis. Even so, my search for interviewees and people and places to observe was far from random. I sought out people of different ages, gender and social status, in a variety of places and at different times of the day. For example, I would take evening rounds to each of the book cafés where I made a note of what kinds of customers were there at that point in time and what they were doing (reading, talking, ordering beverages, etc.). The next time I did this round, I would rotate the order of the book cafés so that I could observe each place at different hours. I would also make sure that I made observations during weekday mornings and weekends, and I used a similar strategy for my observations and interviews in different leisure places, from parks and squares to the library and Qingyuan Mountain. These rounds created many opportunities for informal interviews and I slowly got to know both staff and some of the occasional and returning customers. Although I did not follow a predefined interview guide on these occasions, I always had an agenda for my informal conversations, on which I relied in order to supply my semi-structured interviews with additional information and points of view.

Data generated through chance meetings, informal conversations, and other kinds of serendipitous circumstances make up a central part of my material for this study, both in terms of quantity and quality. To name a few examples, I met one of my key informants backstage at the local TV station, another key informant participated in a conference I was invited to attend, and the primus motor of the Professional English Club was introduced to me by a returning customer whom I befriended in one of the book cafés. The exploratory strategy rests on the researcher's readiness to improvise and be flexible. But to be open to and take advantage of the serendipities of fieldwork is an ideal that can often be difficult to achieve in practice. In my case, flexibility became especially important in the second period of fieldwork when I was struck with severe back pain, which affected both my mobility and spirit. One of my key informants then introduced me to a local acupuncture clinic, where a Dr Di not only offered excellent treatment but also took a keen interest in my project. He provided me with a choice of books and articles on local culture and politics, he invited some of his personal contacts in the local culture circles to visit me in the hospital, and he introduced me to several of his students and patients. All in all, the chance meeting with Dr Di actually made up for some of the time and opportunities I otherwise lost because of health issues.

The combined result of my judgement sampling and my exploratory approach to identifying interviewees is a heterogeneous collection of material that makes it difficult, but not altogether impossible, to make generalizations about leisure and leisure politics in Quanzhou. The predominance of the exploratory strategy is a deliberate choice in this study. I argue that the inclusion of a wide range of data from a variety of social contexts has resulted not only in a richer sample of data than would otherwise be the case, but also made it possible to address the more complex questions of how power is exercised and challenged in the context of everyday life practices.

Data from the field

The data presented here may be both heterogeneous and sundry, but in the process of assembling the various source materials – from interview data to propaganda posters – I have found patterns and consistencies that I hold to be of relevance for the understanding of leisure as a form of social practice. During my first round of fieldwork in Quanzhou, I was troubled by a nagging thought that my interviews were poorly executed and that the number of interviews was far too small. With the benefit of hindsight, I realize that these doubts stemmed from what Elin Sæther has identified as a positivist streak many field researchers struggle with. Even if we recognize that 'neither 12 nor 30 interviews make a representative selection', we still tend to think that a list of 30 interviews is better than a mere handful (Sæther 2006: 55). The amount of interviews and other data a researcher collects for his or her project is not insignificant.[9] However, in studies of everyday practices in particular, I have come to believe that it is important not to consider interviews to be more important than other forms of data. After all, not all information is mediated through speech or writing. Although many of the analyses in this study examine expressions and statements from interviews and texts, the conclusions are usually drawn from a combination of texts, interviews and participant observation.

Interviews, observation, participation

I find it useful to consider the relationship between the research interview and participant observation as a continuum rather than an opposition. The continuum stretches from passive participant observation via active participant observation to informal interviews, with semi-structured and structured interviews at the other end. As Bailey points out, the researcher can never be a completely objective observer. As long as the researcher is present in a situation, he or she is always to a certain degree involved in the actions that take place (Bailey 1996: 10). Fangen makes a similar point, stressing that field research always entails study within a society, as opposed to studying a society from the outside (Fangen 2004: 103). This means that, in field research, the artificially neutral observation of the laboratory kind is neither an ideal nor a possibility. In the field, observation means participation, because some form of social interaction always takes place between the researcher and the other people present in a given setting.

Therefore, at the one end of the continuum, I place what I call passive participant observation. When I made my repeated visits to different leisure places in order to record who was there at which hours engaging in which types of activities, I did not always participate actively in these activities. In many instances I observed people and practices from a distance, for example in Internet cafés, in public parks, on street corners, and at performances and events held throughout the city. However, being a foreigner in a medium-sized Chinese city, you can never pretend that your presence will go unnoticed, even in a public place. This does not mean that people in Quanzhou altered their behaviour significantly because I was present, but my presence in a street, a park or a square was noticed by many, and more often than not the word 'foreigner' (*laowai*) was uttered among the people I observed. To me, this demonstrates how even the most passive type of observation always involved at least some form of interaction between the people I was observing and myself as observer. I therefore regard observation as a form of social interaction akin to semi-structured and informal interviews.

The next item on the continuum I call active participant observation, which in this study refers to the cases where I participated in a given activity together with people in Quanzhou, while at the same time making observations of actions, speech and behaviour. As part of my field research, my informants took me along to karaoke evenings, on biking trips, on mountain hikes, to choir rehearsals, to churches and temples, to book cafés and to family dinners and celebrations. And although I sang, climbed, chatted and ate together with my informants, my experiences and observations, and my interpretations thereof, are necessarily informed by my identity as an outsider and as a researcher looking at everyday life in Quanzhou through academic lenses.

Next on the continuum I place the informal interviews I conducted with people of all walks of life while in the field. These interviews were neither scheduled nor structured by a set list of questions. Consequently, the power to steer the conversation was in these cases more evenly distributed between the interviewer and the interviewee(s). Some of the informal conversations I had in Quanzhou contributed more to my general understanding of local life than they contributed concrete data, or they generated opportunities for further interviews or participation in a given activity. Informal interviews usually started when someone, out of curiosity, asked me where I was from and what I was doing in Quanzhou. This gave me the chance to tell him or her a little about my research, and then to bring into the ensuing conversation topics of relevance to my study. I often used language problems as an excuse to ask informants to write down a Chinese character or an expression that caught my interest. In this way I could introduce pen and paper into the situation in a discreet manner. And, when I felt the need to make lengthy notes, I would excuse myself and take down notes in the rest room. The fact that not all the people I had informal conversations with could possibly know that they were in fact being interviewed raises the ethical question of informed consent, i.e. the interviewee's right to know that he or she is participating in a research project, and the right to refuse to answer questions. However, in the cases where informal conversations touched upon sensitive information, or when my gut feeling warned me that my conversation partner might not want his or her opinions quoted in print, I always gave a short description of my research project and asked for the person's consent.

At the other end of the continuum I place the semi-structured and the structured interview. Structured interviews, which I did not employ in this study, are characterized by a predefined list of questions that are the same for all those interviewed. Structured interviews are scheduled in advance, they usually take up a specific amount of time, and the interviewer must keep the interviewee from straying from the list of predefined questions (Bailey 1996: 72). In structured interviews the interviewer will also strive to influence the conversation as little as possible. The semi-structured interview, however, allows for more flexibility in terms of both form and content. Here, a prepared list of questions is combined with the flexibility and reciprocity characteristic of informal conversations. For each semi-structured interview I made an appointment to meet with a person for the purpose of interviewing him or her. I used a tailored version of the above-mentioned interview guide, and I asked the interviewee for consent and informed him or her of the right to decline to answer questions or to break off the interview. As an interviewer, I was participating, and was thus highly involved in the conversation. Even if the semi-structured interview allows the researcher to add follow-up questions and the interviewee to make digressions, the researcher remains in control of the conversation to a large extent.

The interviews usually took place in the interviewee's office or home. This meant that some interviewees were interrupted by colleagues or family members or by phone calls. In some instances, the people who entered in the middle of the interview sat down and contributed to the remaining questions. I took notice of how such interruptions and other environmental factors such as temperature, light, the time of day and so on influenced the conversation, the interviewees and myself. In some cases, these additional observations added much to my interpretation of the interview data.

In several instances I made follow-up interviews in order to check information that remained unclear and ask the interviewee to expand on questions that had come to my attention after the previous conversation. Some interviewees were interviewed both in more formal, semi-structured interviews and informally. In addition to the regular semi-structured interviews, I also conducted a series of 11 short interviews with customers in local book cafés, asking mainly about their reading habits. Unlike the other semi-structured interviews that lasted roughly one hour, these lasted no more than a quarter of an hour, and were not scheduled in advance.

I took notes in a combination of English and Chinese from all interviews, both semi-structured and informal. With as little delay as possible, I then wrote up the whole interview in detail, based on my notes and memory. Some of the information may, undoubtedly, have been lost or even distorted in this process. Despite being aware of this fact, I nevertheless chose to carry out my interviews without a recording device.[10] In the many informal settings in which I conducted my research, the introduction of a microphone and a mini-disc recorder would, in my opinion, have influenced the data collection in an equally negative way.

To help me identify patterns in my observation material and interview data, I made a table where I marked off the kinds of activities a given interviewee had expressed a liking for or an aversion to. I also noted whether s/he had ever participated in the activity in question, and whether or not I had actually observed his or her participation. This table made it easier to detect patterns concerning my interviewees' attitudes towards different forms of leisure, and the leisure consumption of which they had had first-hand experiences. This was especially useful in my analyses of leisure consumption and surfing in Internet cafés.

The relevance and outcome of each instance of participant observation and each interview I made in Quanzhou varied significantly. In some cases, an hour-long interview rendered little new information, but one random observation could open up a whole new range of questions to consider. This unpredictability is one of the factors that makes interviewing and participant observation both frustrating and fascinating as field methods.

Written sources

I located and read some of the key Chinese-language sources for this study while in Quanzhou – among others, Wang Yalin's survey study of urban leisure and an anthology edited by Ma Hui and Zhang Jing'an (Wang Yalin 2003; Ma Huidi and Zhang Jing'an 2004a. See also Ma Huidi 2004a; 2004b). I was also able to access the China Academic Journals database, first at Xiamen University Library and Huaqiao University, and later at the university library in Oslo, where I located numerous articles about different aspects of contemporary Chinese society. These have informed my analysis to a great extent. The latest versions of the local Quanzhou Gazetteer and Quanzhou Yearbook have also been important sources of information (Quanzhou shi difangzhi bianzuan weiyuanhui 2004a; Quanzhou shi difangzhi bianzuan weiyuanhui 2004b), along with a range of locally-published books about Minnan culture, folklore and performance arts. While in the field I also read and collected articles about cultural events, culture policies and consumption, as well as miscellaneous news from the local newspapers, *Dongnan Zaobao* and *Haixia Dushibao*.[11] Chinese news media are published in close cooperation with the authorities, and both TV stations and newspapers function to varying degrees as mouthpieces for the party-state. In Quanzhou, work units and offices of all kinds subscribed to *Fujian Ribao*, a paper published in the provincial capital, Fuzhou. This paper focuses on national and regional administration and politics, and was available from select newspaper vendors only. *Dongnan Zaobao* and *Haixia Dushibao*, in contrast, were readily available from small shops and newsstands, as well as ambulating breakfast carts. The two papers combine a non-controversial take on local politics with sensationalist coverage of crime and celebrities, and are widely read by the Quanzhou population. As these papers were significant sources of information for townspeople in general, I chose to follow local news through these channels. The collection of roughly three hundred articles, along with the online versions of these newspapers, has proved important for my understanding of the goings-on in Quanzhou, both while in the field and while developing my analysis. A selection of local paper articles from Fujian Ribao from the period 1978–80 has also provided relevant information about local consumption, media, culture and the arts in the early reform period. I also collected a variety of promotional brochures from local leisure establishments, real estate companies and other enterprises. These provide examples of how middle-class consumers are addressed by local businesses.

Miscellaneous sources

The Internet not only provided me with access to online written resources, it also proved an important means of communication with some of my informants. I had Internet access in my flat, and while writing up interviews and field notes I could also keep in touch with some of the young white-collar workers who used the Internet at work. Through online chat networks, we could make plans or discuss leisure activities and, moreover, I could ask questions about the working conditions of the interviewee in question. The chat sites make it possible to save a log from each conversation as a text file for future reference. I have remained in contact with some of these informants via the Internet since completing my last period of research in Quanzhou, and these occasional conversations make it possible for me to ask follow-up questions, and in addition maintain some form of relationship with those informants who also became my friends in the field.

The spread of cellular phones in China not only makes it easy to reach and make flexible appointments with key informants and prospective interviewees, but has also facilitated the development of new genres of popular culture. On special occasions such as Spring Festival, Mid-Autumn Festival and International Women's Day, people would exchange SMS-greetings in the form of short seasonal poems and ditties, often with a humorous content. I collected several of these messages and, together with regular SMS exchanges, these texts contributed to my understanding of how leisure-related terms, such as '*wan*' and 'FB', are used in the local context.

Some of my informants generously provided me with tapes and VCD recordings of local operas and puppet plays. In addition, I was given the opportunity to borrow recordings of a TV programme about the local tea culture from Quanzhou TV, and to participate in and observe their production of the 2005 Mid-Autumn game show, a game with questions from local history and culture. I also took numerous pictures and video clips in the field, some of which are included in these pages. A majority of the pictures document the many leisure activities I observed and took part in, while some show the city development which was – and still is – taking place in Quanzhou. I also used my camera to record posters, slogans and propaganda campaigns, among them the series of ten posters about 'Civilized Internet Use' (*Wangluo wenming*) and the moralist cartoon depicting how video games turned Little Huang into a criminal, discussed in more detail in Chapter 6.

Finally, I kept field notes, an average of two and a half single-spaced pages per day, throughout my nine months of field research. Here, I recorded the events of each day, new information and insights, questions and preliminary analyses, my plans, my failures, my joys and frustrations. The field notes can only provide partial renditions of actual events and conditions in Quanzhou at the time. This is equally true of the other source materials, be they texts written by others or pictures and film clips I recorded myself. Consequently, this study is not a true-to-life representation of leisure in Quanzhou. Rather, it is an analysis of certain aspects of the forms of leisure I have documented in the field.

Doing fieldwork in a foreign language

When I embarked on this research project, I had studied Chinese for several years. I had the skills needed to read scholarly articles and newspapers in Chinese, and I had already conducted three months of field research using Mandarin as my working language. I therefore felt quite confident carrying out interviews in Mandarin without an interpreter. However, the fact that I have relied on Mandarin when carrying out field research in a predominantly Minnan dialect-speaking area poses methodological problems. *Minnan hua* is a language only remotely connected to Mandarin, and unintelligible to native Chinese speakers outside southern Fujian and Taiwan. This means that Mandarin is a second language for many of Quanzhou's inhabitants, and some of the elderly and people who both work and reside in the rural districts speak little or no Mandarin at all. Witherspoon has stated that

> The greatest value of learning the language of another people does not come from interviewing informants without interpreters or from providing native terms in ethnographic writings; it comes from being able to understand what the natives say and how they say it when they are conversing with each other.
> (Witherspoon in Duranti 1997: 110, quoted in Borchgrewink 2003: 107)

If, as Witherspoon argues, the everyday speech that local people use between themselves is the most important source of information, my Mandarin proficiency was of little assistance in the Minnan region. Despite this insufficiency, I argue that it was possible for me to conduct meaningful field research in this area.

First of all, most people in Quanzhou speak Mandarin, although with a strong accent, and many among my interviewees were not originally from the Minnan area and knew little or no *Minnan hua* themselves. Non-native residents often complained to me that they at times felt excluded by their *Minnan*-speaking colleagues and friends, and it must be admitted that my presence as a Mandarin-speaking foreigner did not always prevent people from making conversation in their local dialect. My lack of proficiency in the local dialect has consequences for my choice of interviewees and the types of language-related data I could collect. Although the detailed description of the area-specific *Minnan* culture was not part of my research project, my dependence on Mandarin in the field had consequences for my understanding of those aspects of local leisure mediated through the choice of vocabulary. Admittedly, this problem could have been partly alleviated by appointing a native speaker as research assistant. I made the choice of not working with an assistant because I feared that his or her presence would only increase the distance between my informants and myself. During my last period of field research, however, I experienced benefits from being accompanied by one or two of my key informants during participant observation. As Borchgrewink argues, using an interpreter or assistant need not be an 'either/or' question (Borchgrewink 2003: 103). With the benefit of hindsight, I admit that working with an assistant on more occasions would have proved advantageous in this project.

Second, I found it useful to regard myself as still being a language learner. By this I mean that I made preparations that would help me understand as much as possible in conversations about my topics of interest. In preparation for fieldwork I assembled lists of vocabulary relevant to my planned study, from expressions like 'highbrow culture' (*yangchun baixue*) to the verb 'to gamble' (*dubo*). Although not all these terms turned up in the field, mastery of a broader vocabulary made me feel more confident during interviews – especially when meeting with cultured people. Moreover, while in the field I made notes of recurrent words and phrases I did not understand or did not know how to use. I then asked my key informants to help me understand the usage of the term(s) in question. Finally, during semi-structured interviews, I swallowed my pride and asked interviewees to repeat or rephrase their answers until I understood what they were saying. Most of the interviewees were patient, and although my repeated questions made me feel unprofessional at the time, the additional information I gained by asking again made it worthwhile.

Third, the ability to read Chinese characters made it possible to consult Chinese language sources which would otherwise have been inaccessible. Moreover, on several occasions I sensed that the fact that I had studied Mandarin and could keep a conversation going made interviewees who were my seniors in terms of both age and experience take my interview request more seriously than they might otherwise have done. The fact that ordinary people, once they overheard me speaking Mandarin on the phone or saw me carrying a local newspaper, initiated conversations with me in Mandarin, also suggests that in some cases meaningful field research can be accommodated without mastery of the local dialect.

A few words must be said about my use of academic English. My native language is Norwegian, and even though the relevant social science literature and many of the books and articles I have read about contemporary China are English-language publications, and although I have studied abroad in English-speaking countries, it is still a challenge for me to express myself in English. I chose to write my field notes in English in order to avoid translating Norwegian notes of Mandarin-based field experiences into the English of my final analysis. When taking notes during interviews, both formal and informal, I used the fastest method of note-taking, namely a mixture of Chinese characters, Norwegian and English. There is no denying that my rendering of Quanzhou people's dialect-ridden Mandarin into imprecise academic English may have consequences for the accuracy of my analysis.

2 What is leisure – in China and beyond?

What is leisure?

A study of leisure requires a discussion of what is meant by 'leisure', and similar terms such as 'spare time' and 'free time'. The way leisure is defined and measured has consequences for how we think about leisure and how leisure is regarded as a social phenomenon. And, as will be demonstrated in the following, definitions of leisure also influence the conclusions and policy recommendations scholars make on the basis of their research – in China and elsewhere.

In Chinese written sources the terms '*xiuxian*' and '*xianxia*' (leisure), and the more vernacular '*ziyou shijian*' (free time) are used interchangeably. In the case

Figure 2.1 Sunday leisure in West Lake Park.

of the English language, little or no differentiation is made between the terms 'free time' and 'leisure' in either everyday speech or academic writing. The word 'leisure' stems from Latin *licere*, which is also the root of the English term 'licence', meaning 'to permit or allow' (Seabrook 1988: 3; Rojek 1985: 17). The Oxford English Dictionary defines 'leisure' as 'freedom and opportunity to do something specified or implied' (Oxford University Press 2010). So, 'free time' and 'leisure' bring to mind elements of licence and freedom. However, contrary to what the root of these terms may suggest, sociologists and other scholars within the field of leisure studies argue that the element of freedom in leisure is illusory at best (Rojek 1985: 31). Some scholars stress that the distribution of work hours and spare time is governed by the structures of labour and capital, and, consequently, individuals are not 'free' to manage their own time (Thompson 1967; Roberts 1999: 2). Others hold that leisure choices are increasingly influenced by the logic of consumption and market forces (Seabrook 1988: 3; Gershuny 1992: 8; Jing Wang 2001b: 80), and that the term 'free time' should therefore be used with caution in analyses of leisure. Moreover, both the terms 'spare time' and 'free time' imply that leisure is basically a kind of *time*, and a time essentially different from work hours and activities in the work place. In order to shift attention away from the temporal aspect, the term 'leisure' (rather than spare or free time) will be the preferred term in this study.

Theoretical analyses of leisure can be divided into two rough categories based on their basic definitions of 'leisure': leisure as *time*, and leisure as *experience*.[1] Both approaches are problematic for several reasons, as will be discussed in detail below. On the basis of data from field research, I therefore argue that leisure is better understood as *practices* that take place in a variety of spaces and at different times throughout the day.

Leisure as 'spare' time

In Britain and the US, sociological studies of leisure have a history of more than five decades (van der Poel 2006: 97). Until recently, these studies have relied on quantitative surveys of the amounts of time respondents spend on work, household chores, hygiene and spare-time activities. The surveys measure the amounts of money people spend on leisure activities, record participation in different kinds of activities, or are detailed time budgets where each activity is measured by the minute. Data from quantitative studies of leisure are problematic for several reasons: first of all, interviewees have a tendency to underestimate the amount of money they spend on leisure. In addition, time budgets often fail to record activities that occur simultaneously (Roberts 1999: 17–18). For instance, if a person listens to an audio book while commuting, the time spent will be categorized as either 'commuting' or 'reading novels'. Similarly, a person who knits while watching TV will only report the minutes spent doing one of the two activities, not both. The final and most important problem in quantitative studies of leisure, however, is that the analyses rest on an oversimplified definition of leisure.

In quantitative studies of leisure, 'leisure' is generally understood as a kind of time ('spare' time) which is essentially different from time spent at work. Here, leisure is residual time, i.e. 'time which is not occupied by paid work, unpaid work or personal chores and obligations' (Haworth and Veal 2004: 1). Quantitative studies of leisure tend to overlook the fact that the division between work hours and 'after hours' is often less than clear. In Quanzhou, employees in private enterprises as well as in the local administration often spend their evenings accompanying prospective customers or visiting delegations to restaurants, tea houses and karaoke parlours. More often than not, business deals will be closed and commitments made in leisurely environments at a time of day long past 'office hours'. Looking at this phenomenon from the time perspective, these employees complete work-related tasks in their 'spare' time. The activities that take place, however, can be regarded in terms of both work (negotiating a deal or entertaining a delegation) and leisure (drinking, singing, enjoying gourmet food). This is one example of how the theoretical line drawn between work and leisure becomes rather blurred when actual practices are taken into consideration. It is interesting to note that using leisure places as a site for business transactions is nothing new in the Chinese context. According to Wang Di, Chengdu's tea houses served as a place for both business and pleasure during the 1930s and 1940s (Wang Di 2003: 93–4).

A contemporary example of the intermingling of work and leisure can be provided by Ms Zhang, a manager in a government unit in contemporary Quanzhou. She considered hosting dinners and taking visitors out for entertainment as work as long as these commitments kept her away from her family on weeknights. Like many managers at her level, she would often receive work-related phone calls at odd hours, and more often than not she went to work even during the two days of rest (*shuangxiu*), the weekend that has been guaranteed under Chinese labour law since 1995 (Ma Huidi and Zhang Jing'an 2004b: 5). Zhang felt burdened by the extra duties that fell to her as leader of a large unit. At the same time, she exercised considerable flexibility when it came to how she spent her time while in the office. She took care of personal errands and received social calls while on duty, as did all office personnel I met in Quanzhou. In Zhang's case, these freedoms were also extended to the junior employees in her unit, whom I often found reading papers and novels or playing computer games at their desks.

In the work units I visited repeatedly throughout my periods of field research in Quanzhou, the distinction between leisure and work was apparent to a lesser degree, however, than was the division between work-intense periods and periods with little or no activity. This shows that what Thompson describes as 'task oriented time' (Thompson 1967: 60–1) is not a phenomenon exclusive to peasant societies; contemporary bureaucracies are also influenced by 'seasonal' changes in the form of approaching deadlines for annual reports and auditing, or intensive planning leading up to big events. Drinking tea, chatting and surfing on the Internet, trading stocks and reading novels and magazines are just a few examples of the ways employees in Quanzhou spent some of their working hours during slow periods.

In *The Practice of Everyday Life*, Michel de Certeau analyses similar practices in France, where employees also use 'company hours' to complete tasks that are not work-related (de Certeau 1984: 25–6). De Certeau regards these practices in terms of popular resistance towards the domination employees experience in the work place. The examples I have given from Quanzhou do not represent acts of resistance. Rather, they are drawn from workplaces where the organization of work is flexible, a situation made possible by both the attitudes of the management and the nature of the tasks at hand (clerical work).[2] However, the examples from both France and China illustrate a type of work practice where work and leisure activities alternate throughout the day. On the basis of these examples, we can conclude that leisure is neither residual time nor simply the opposite of work. The understanding of the relationship between work and leisure as a dichotomy fails to account for the ways people actually combine or divide their time between work tasks and leisure activities.

Leisure as experience

While social scientists have analysed the temporal aspect of leisure, psychologists and philosophers have brought attention to leisure as experience. Joseph Pieper's anthology of lectures on leisure has inspired much of the philosophical writing on the significance of leisure for the well-being of the individual. Pieper draws a line from the ancient Greek philosophers' ideals of contemplation and intellectual reflection to leisure in modern times (Pieper 1952. See also Rojek 2006: 28). Or, rather, he uses recreation in ancient Greece as a vehicle for his critique of the hurried lifestyle in post-war Europe. Pieper's call for more time for reflection in everyday life has inspired the work of philosophically minded leisure scholars in China such as Ma Huidi and Yu Guangyuan, as well as western scholars in the field of development psychology, most notably Douglas Kleiber (1999: 4). Kleiber argues that spare time in itself is no guarantee of leisure. In order for there to be leisure, the individual must experience a sense of 'freedom *from* other demands' (work, school and the duties involved in everyday family life), as well as the 'freedom *to* act in particular ways' (Kleiber 1999: 4), more specifically the freedom to engage in the activities that the individual himself prefers. Kleiber thus defines leisure as 'the combination of free time and the expectation of preferred experience' (Kleiber 1999: 4). Seen from this perspective, 'leisure' is understood mainly in terms of an experience or sensation.

Leisure as experience is often associated with the concept of 'flow' (Stebbins 2004: 6), which is a positive experience of 'creative absorption' (Kleiber 1999: 2). In his research, Roger Manell describes flow as a mental state where people become so absorbed in an activity that they lose track of time and pay little or no attention to their immediate surroundings (Kleiber 1999: 2). Studies by Csikszentmihalyi and LeFevre indicate, however, that it is more common to experience flow during work than during leisure activities (Csikszentmihalyi and LeFevre 1989: 815, 821). This fact serves to highlight the similarities that do exist between work and leisure in terms of personal experience. Moreover, the frequent occurrence of flow during work further weakens the definition of leisure as the opposite of work.

When leisure is defined in opposition to work, it is not considered as a phenomenon in and of itself (Kleiber 1999: 1) but as the negation of work, i.e. 'nonwork'. This not only leaves us with an unsatisfactory definition of leisure, it also implies a simplified understanding of the meaning of work. Much has been written on the sociology of work, and a thorough assessment of the concept of work is beyond the scope of this study.[3] One more point must however be made of relevance to the relationship between work and leisure: the sociology of work often takes as its point of departure the theory of the Protestant work ethic, with its inbuilt perception of work as predominantly a duty to God and an aspect of the pain of mankind's worldly existence. Moreover, in these contexts, 'work' most typically refers to manual or industrialized forms of labour. As a consequence, much of what has been written about work takes the labours of work life for granted, and also ignores the fact that one person's leisure can be another person's job (Stebbins 2004: ix). As argued by Robert A. Stebbins, the common ground between leisure and work becomes evident when the amateur musician or dedicated collector turns his serious leisure practice into an occupation (Stebbins 2004). This, of course, does not mean that being a musician is not a 'real job', but rather that it is not the practice in itself – in this case the playing of an instrument – that is decisive when we characterize an activity as work or as leisure. The understanding of work as mere duty, opposed to the joys of leisure, fails to account for the fact that many trades and occupations offer stimulating tasks and development opportunities for the individual (Rojek 1985: 109), and that some employees do love their work.

Joy and satisfaction were the main motivators for the career choices made by independent booksellers I interviewed in Quanzhou. For Mr Xu, taking over the management of a bookshop merely meant an escalation of his own interest in reading and discussing literature, from leisure activity to full-time occupation. He now spends many of his 'off-hours' in the shop chatting with customers-cum-friends about literature and the quality of the teas they enjoy together in the book café. Wang, the manger of another small Quanzhou bookstore, even lives on the premises with his family, and treats the bookstore as an extension of his own living room. The family have their TV dinners in the shop area, where they socialize with friends and customers alike. When we talked about their way of life in the bookshop, Wang said: 'My friends tell me "your job is just leisure [*xiuxian*]!"'. He added that he himself regarded running a bookshop as a combination of work and leisure.

As pointed out in the Introduction, there is always a danger in ethnographic research that we as researchers pay more attention to what interviewees say than the material and social conditions that surrounds them. Although Wang, like the other bookstore managers I interviewed, talked about the book trade with pride, and although he clearly enjoyed his current occupation, I cannot say for certain whether turning his love of books and reading into an occupation was a conscious choice or simply a matter of securing a livelihood for his family.

Nevertheless, given that the experience of flow can occur in both work and leisure, and the sensation the individual experiences when enjoying work assignments and leisure activities is 'qualitatively speaking the same' (Stebbins 2004: xi), the distinction between work and leisure cannot be explained with reference to experience only. As the data from Quanzhou work life demonstrate, a definition of leisure must account for actual leisure practices in the environments in which they take place. In other words, the study of leisure must account for the various ways in which individuals engage in leisure activities at home, in public spaces and in the workplace.

Leisure as practice

My aim in this project is to analyse the actual leisure activities in which people in Quanzhou engage, and in the following I refer to the numerous practices that individuals pursue for the sake of pleasure or relaxation as 'leisure practices'. Leisure practices include both goal-oriented activities such as exercise, learning a language or playing an instrument; activities that involve excitement and pleasure such as various games or getting a foot massage; and activities that have no specific purpose, such as hanging out, having fun, or even doing 'nothing'. Acknowledging that individuals are not free to make unimpeded decisions concerning the ways in which they spend their time, I use the term 'pursue', rather than 'choose' in my definition of leisure practices. A thorough discussion of the exercise of choice – or presumed exercise of choice – in relation to leisure activities cannot, however, be facilitated within the limits of this study. The main focus here is on the actual activities that individuals pursue as a result of some sort of personal motivation, be this recreation, diversion, socializing, or other. Activities that are undertaken in a person's 'spare' time but forced upon the individual by authorities – be they parents or agents of the party-state – cannot be regarded as leisure practices, but rather as the fulfilment of duties. One example of such a 'leisure duty' is the stereotypical case in which Chinese parents force their only child to take piano lessons and spend afternoons and weekends practicing against the child's own will. Another example of 'leisure duty' is the many instances in recent Chinese history when local Communist Party branches have initiated '(in)voluntary work' activities (*yiwu gongzuo*)[4] through the system of work units. Party representatives in the work units would dispatch employees to an appointed place to contribute in a given manner, in celebration of Elderly People's Day, Spring Festival and other public holidays. This practice was widespread even up to the 1990s (Rolandsen 2010: 139). Yet another example of leisure as duty is when economic disparity forces people to take on an extra job in their 'spare' time. Although activities that generate income are counted as a form of leisure in certain Chinese surveys, such undertakings can hardly be characterized as leisure activities (Wang Yalin *et al.* 2004: 108).[5]

These examples bring us back to Kleiber's claim that leisure involves 'freedom *from* other demands' and the 'freedom *to* act in particular ways' (1999: 4) and to the lexical denotation of 'leisure' as 'freedom and opportunity to do something specified or implied' (Oxford University Press 2010). Both these definitions refer to leisure as something people do, and as acts in which people engage, i.e. practices. The problematic term here is, again, 'freedom'. As pointed out by Rojek *et al.*, 'individual choice is *situated* and freedom *conditioned* by social, cultural, political and economic variables' (Rojek *et al.* 2006: 11). Ordinary people's leisure 'choices' may be impinged on by the social organization of work in the given society, by the structures of the market economy or by social constraints such as gender, age or race.[6] However, the argument that individuals are not free is questioned by theories of agency that show that even in cases of strict social control, people as individuals and collectives do exercise freedom to a certain extent (Scott 1990: Ch. 4). The question of governmental control and popular agency becomes especially important in a study of leisure practices in the PRC. Until a mere two and a half decades ago, leisure practices were checked by the Communist party-state down to the level of the individual. This was made possible not only through direct surveillance in work units and brigades (Henderson and Cohen 1984: 27, 46; Lü and Perry 1997: 3), but also by way of self-censorship that individuals took up in fear of the consequences of being 'criticized for "cutting themselves off from the masses" and "lacking collectivist spirit"' (Shaoguang Wang 1995: 153–4, footnote 19).[7] As demonstrated by the example, recounted in the Introduction, of the elderly man who confessed to playing local folk music at a time when the culture of the 'old society' was banned, people will always find spaces where they can exercise a certain amount of freedom. Analysing the leisure practices that do take place in present-day Quanzhou brings to light both the restraints and the liberties that characterize the field of leisure in China today.

Leisure in historical and socio-cultural contexts

The ways we think about leisure (as time, as experience, or as practice) are closely linked to coexisting social and cultural values, such as our work ethic and notions of freedom. To what extent do historical context and socio-cultural values determine the manifestations of leisure in a given society? Or, in other words, is the leisure of yesterday the same as leisure today? Furthermore, is leisure in China essentially different from leisure in a Western context, that is, leisure as a product of the specific historical context of European industrialization? Answers to these questions depend not only on how we define leisure in itself, but also on how we analyse the history of leisure.

Leisure and history

The history of leisure as a social phenomenon is much debated, within both the disciplines of leisure studies and social history. In leisure studies, 'leisure' is analysed as a sociological phenomenon subject to the changing structures in society. As an academic discipline, leisure studies has its roots in historical and sociological enquiries into the changing working relations brought about by the industrial revolution. More often than not, leisure is held to be an essentially modern phenomenon. As an example, Kenneth Roberts writes that

> [...] the leisure in our lives is a product of the modern organization of work, our market economies, civil liberties that we enjoy, and the weakening of the family, community and religious controls that prescribed and enforced common ways of life in earlier times.
>
> (Roberts 1999: 1)

Roberts links leisure to the social organization of modern society and sets 'our lives' apart from 'life in earlier times'. A similar stance can be found in historian E.P. Thompson's writing on how the gradual change in work organization made leisure a new part of the everyday lives of the English working classes (Thompson 1967). Thompson – and to a certain extent Roberts – regard leisure as a product of the industrial revolution. It is a matter of dispute among historians whether or not leisure as a social phenomenon was in fact caused by the industrial revolution. Some historians argue that there is no essential difference between leisure in pre-modern and modern times, and that the pastimes of the ancient Romans and the festivals in medieval times may be regarded as leisure in the modern sense (Balsdon 1969: 130–68; Marfany 1997: 158, 179). Peter Burke, on the other hand, describes an historical process where leisure gradually becomes a 'routinized' and 'separate domain' in people's lives (Burke 1995:149). Burke perceives a link between the relations of production in society and the emergence of leisure. He does not, however, support Thompson's and Roberts' stance that leisure is a product of industrial production and thus intrinsically bound to modern societies.

On the basis of the definition of leisure as a type of practice in which individuals engage for the sake of pleasure or personal fulfilment, it is possible to argue that there is no essential difference between leisure practices today and in the past. The fact that historical records and accounts – from both China and elsewhere – inform us almost exclusively of the lives and conditions of the elites means that we know very little about the everyday activities of commoners in the past. In *Streetlife Chengdu*, Wang Di has attempted to circumvent this theoretical challenge by searching between the lines, so to speak, for materials about ordinary people's lives in a variety of written sources (Wang Di 2003: 93–5, 167). Comparing Wang's material to that of my own research, I find that there are several similarities between the function of the tea houses in Chengdu at the turn of the twentieth century and the function Quanzhou's local tea houses have as places of leisure today. At both points in time, tea houses have been considered public places and have been frequented by people from all walks of life. In historical Chengdu, some tea houses were luxurious and expensive and therefore available only to the wealthy and well-connected.[8] This is also the case in today's Quanzhou, where local back-alley tea shops serve as tea houses for the less affluent, while going to brand-name tea houses, karaoke parlours and the like is only a possibility for the salaried middle class. My point here is to show that going to the tea house has been a widespread leisure activity in China, both in pre-modern times and after China embarked on a process of modernization and industrialization. And, moreover, that from the point of view of the individual and his or her actions and experiences, there is no essential difference between going to a tea house in Chengdu in the early twentieth century and going to a tea house in China today. Even if the development of a middle class of consumers in recent decades means that participation in the elite version of Chinese tea culture has become attainable for a proportionately larger number of people, it is only the spread of high-class tea drinking (the quantity) rather than tea drinking as a leisure practice (the quality) that has changed. Therefore, following Burke's view of leisure as a phenomenon that gains increased importance throughout history, this study regards the difference between leisure in the past and leisure in the present not as a change in essence (from elite 'culture' to common 'leisure'), but as a gradual increase in the access to and availability of leisure activities among the populace seen as a whole.

Leisure and culture

Assuming that leisure is in essence the same phenomenon across time, how do we understand leisure as a cultural phenomenon? Kenneth Roberts has analysed leisure as a social product, i.e. a result of the material conditions in the society in question. Based on this underlying premise, Roberts writes that

> [w]hat leisure is can vary from group to group within a country depending on each group's circumstances, but the variations between societies, certainly between types of civilizations, are even more profound.
>
> (Roberts 1999: 2)

Sepp Linhart makes a similar argument in his study of leisure values and leisure activities in 1980s Japan. According to Linhart,

> [t]he long working hours of white-collar workers, in ministries and the main offices of big companies alike, are often the result of what in Western eyes is a non-efficient, leisurely way of doing work, in which much time is devoted to maintaining good human relations. Leisure at night in the company of colleagues is certainly not work. Some take part only because of social pressure, but for many it is surely enjoyment and pleasure, and similar arguments can be made for playing golf with company members on Sundays.
>
> (Linhart 1988: 306)

Linhart suggests that the important cultural value of maintaining social relations lies at the root of the merging of work and leisure in Japan, and that this practice is alien to 'Western eyes'. The way Ms Zhang must spend evenings entertaining associates and visitors to her Quanzhou work unit is reminiscent of the Japanese practices described by Linhart. It is tempting, then, to explain the amalgamation of work and leisure activities by way of specifically East Asian cultural values. However, if we look at one of the other characteristics of the organization of work and leisure in Ms Zhang's work unit, namely the employees' tendency to read novels and play computer games in the office and Ms Zhang's own flexible juggling of personal errands and work-related tasks throughout a regular day, these practices have parallels in offices and work units in other parts of the world as well.

Monica Heintz, for example, describes similar practices in her analysis of the work ethic in post-socialist Romania. Based on her field research from 1999 to 2000, she argues that the period under communism lead to the prevalence of '"free rider" behaviour' in Romanian society. She describes this behaviour as a 'lack of involvement and responsibility for the enterprise and communal goods' (Heintz 2002: 107). Heintz analyses a situation where employees have recently lost their former privileges of state-sponsored social security, and where low wages and benefits have kept workers from performing well in their jobs. She illustrates the situation with a popular joke in the Romanian workforce: 'They pretend they are paying us, and we pretend we are working' (Heintz 2002: 111). The historical context of collectivization can explain the scope of both free-riding and also the outsourcing of knowledge and skills as a form of 'moonlighting' (Heintz 2002: 108; Tomba 2004: 21) among state employees in Eastern Europe as well as in China. Davis and Sensenbrenner write that 'for urban residents in the Mao years, the workplace was the locus of production, consumption, identity, and often even residence' (Davis and Sensenbrenner 2000: 77). More often than not, these government units and state enterprises were overstaffed, and workers became accustomed to spending time in the work place without specific tasks to complete. In an historical study of rural development in China, Philip C.C. Huang describes the result of this work organization in regard to time use and efficiency in a rural context:

> Under the collective, leisure was a negative incentive. For team and brigade cadres, idleness looked bad to their superiors. For individual team members, no work meant no labor points. But in the absence of alternative employment, there was no incentive to finish a task quickly. So long as someone put in his hours and the work got done, that was good enough. Given surplus labor, the collective system led to the phenomenon of what the peasants in Huayangqiao call 'loitering work' (*langdang gong*). It was better to do the job slowly, stand around, loiter about, and so on, than to take time off.
> (Philip C.C. Huang 1990: 219)

The propensity among Chinese and Romanian workers to loiter or take care of personal business while in the office cannot be explained by reference to socialist collectivization alone. I argue that their free-riding and moonlighting is also akin to some of the examples given by de Certeau in his writing on French employees' resistance to workplace management (de Certeau 1984: 25–6). There is essentially no difference between the leisurely break the Chinese clerk takes to play a game of chess on the computer and that of the French secretary who writes love letters at the office desk on 'company time'.

The examples from such diverse societies as China, France, Romania and Japan suggest that the merger of work tasks and leisure activities inside and outside the work place is a product of neither East Asian culture nor socialist collectivism; similar practices of intermingled work and leisure coexist as an aspect of everyday life around the globe. This serves to strengthen the conclusion that the relationship between work and leisure is far more complex than is conveyed by the prevalent understanding of work as the opposite of leisure. If we look at the different types of leisure activities in which people engage throughout the world, it is evident that leisure takes different forms in different cultures and among different peoples. As an example, cricket is an activity typical of Commonwealth nations, while East Asians take a special interest in karaoke. While forms of leisure may vary, leisure as a social phenomenon does not.

Leisure in China

The above discussion of leisure has accounted for the origin of the term 'leisure' and different understandings of what the term refers to in social science. The aim of this study is to broaden the understanding of leisure as a social phenomenon by way of data from contemporary China. This necessitates a discussion of how concepts of leisure are expressed in Mandarin Chinese, and how, when and by whom specific terms are used. First, however, I will give a short summary of the findings provided by surveys of leisure activities in China conducted by Chinese scholars.

Chinese scholars' studies of leisure are, not unlike many Western language studies, characterized by large-scale surveys of time distribution. These surveys show that a majority of the Chinese spend their spare time with family and friends at home (Shaoguang Wang 1995: 165; Wang Yalin 2003: 55); moreover, that Chinese in general spend most of their spare time in front of the TV (Shaoguang Wang 1995: 159; Luo Jiaming et al. 2004: 160–1; Wang Qiting et al. 2004: 147–8; Wang Yihong 2005: 129; Chang Qinyi et al. 2007: 124). Ken Roberts' study of leisure in Britain claims that the amount of time people spend watching TV depends on whether or not they have access to and the opportunity to engage in other activities (Roberts 2002: 168). This may also explain why watching TV is such a widespread leisure activity in China; the choice of leisure activities in most communities, and in rural areas especially, is rather limited (Ma Feifeng 2002: 14; Wang Yalin 2003: 57; Zhang Taiyuan 2007: 107).[9] Shaoguang Wang has argued, however, that the fact that people in China spend so much time in front of the TV is largely a result of the cost involved in commercial leisure activities. Most Chinese watch TV simply because 'their resources cannot stretch beyond the requirements of basic everyday necessities and easily accessible pastimes' (Shaoguang Wang 1995: 167).

Chinese surveys show that both occupation and income level are decisive for the kinds of leisure activities in which the Chinese engage.[10] Managers in national enterprises, as well as in private and foreign companies, enjoy more diverse leisure activities than do people at lower income levels (Wang Yalin 2003: 88–97). Age and family situation are also significant for the type of leisure individuals enjoy: youth under the age of 25 spend more time socializing outside the home than do young parents and the elderly, and the youngest have the most varied leisure lives (Wang Yalin 2003: 83–4). My observations of leisure in Quanzhou follow these overall trends: people do spend much of their spare time at home, and participation in costly leisure activities is enjoyed primarily by those who have the required combination of spare time and money.

As for the social distribution of spare time, recent surveys show that self-employed workers (*geti laodongzhe*) have the lowest amount of spare time of all groups of employees. They often work during weekends and spend little time on entertainment or exercise. Interestingly, Wang Yalin's survey data from Shanghai, Tianjin and Harbin show that the employees who have the most spare time on their hands are those working in Party and government administration: they may work long hours on regular work days, but they hardly do any housework and have more time off during weekends and national holidays than any other group (Wang Yalin 2003: Ch. 5). It is somewhat ironic, then, that in their analyses, Chinese leisure scholars tend to express concern for the way ordinary workers, youth and the unemployed 'waste' their time. The fact that cadres have more spare time and spend more money on recreation than do other groups of employees is often ignored. This is an example of how the aforementioned PRC leisure ethic passes judgment on the popular culture enjoyed by those with low cultural capital, while the leisure consumption of the Chinese bureaucratic and economic elite is regarded as unproblematic.

Leisure in Mandarin

Since the time of Malinowski, anthropologists have stressed the importance of indigenous categories and local terms for the understanding of the social and cultural practices of 'others' (Beals *et al.* 1977: 528; Borchgrevink 2003: 96, 98). The value of local terms and concepts for anthropological analysis has lead researchers to study languages relevant to their geographical field. In his writing about field research in China, Stig Thøgersen points out that Western researchers are often well-versed in the official terminology, which they know from government reports, books and other media, as well as from Chinese scholarship, but pay too little attention to how people use different terms to describe social phenomena in different situations. In order to collect data that reflects to a larger extent the realities of Chinese people and the ways in which they relate to the party-state, Thøgersen advises that the researcher pay attention to the usage of 'language codes' (Thøgersen 2006: 110–26).[11] He identifies two main codes in contemporary China: 'Ganbunese', 'the official language of the state apparatus and its cadres (*ganbu*)'; and 'Baixingnese', named after 'ordinary people' (*laobaixing*) (Thøgersen 2006: 112). Thøgersen demonstrates how a switching of codes from Ganbunese to Baixingnese can be applied by a writer or speaker as a device to signal a distance between himself and the 'mental universe of Ganbunese, and implicitly from the party-state' (Thøgersen 2006: 112). These language codes described by Thøgersen are not characteristic of a given social stratum in a society. Rather, they are language devices individuals use in order to express, in indirect terms, their relation to or distance from the official discourse of the party-state.

As part of the preparations for my first field trip to Fujian in 2003, I read sociological articles in Chinese in order to familiarize myself with both the state of the field and the terms used in discussions of leisure in China. The terms I planned to use in my interview guides, such as '*xianxia*' (leisure) and '*ziyou shijian*' (free time) turned out to be of no use to me in my field study of leisure among rural teenagers. The middle school students I interviewed at the time did not recognize the term '*xiuxian*' at all, and when asked to describe which activities they engaged in during their 'free time', the most prevalent answer was 'I don't have any free time' (*Meiyou shenme ziyou shijian*). In order to get the young students to talk about their basketball playing or love of dancing, I had to switch to Baixingnese and simply ask 'what do you usually do after classes?' (*Xia ke yihou ni pingshi zuo shenme?*), or 'where do you go to have fun?' (*Ni qu nali wan?*). As a consequence, I have made the way people talk and write about their leisure practices a key element in my analysis of leisure in contemporary Quanzhou. While 'leisure' in Ganbunese is often expressed in terms of problems and vices, Baixingnese speakers talk about relaxation, pleasure and having fun.

Xiuxian *and* xianxia

The Chinese scholars Yu Guangyuan and Ma Huidi have written extensively on the meaning of leisure in Chinese culture and on the significance of leisure in contemporary societies. In their writing, they distinguish between leisure as a temporal resource (*xianxia*) and leisure as a spiritual good in the lives of all people (*xiuxian*). Chinese scholars in general use the terms *xiuxian* and *xianxia*, and also *ziyou shijian*, interchangeably (See for example Zhou Xiaohong 2005; Tian Cuiqin and Qi Xin 2005; Sun Xiaoli 2004; Wang Qiting, Li Xin and Shi Lei: 2004; Wang Yalin 2003). Of these terms, *xiuxian* is by far the most frequently applied, often in combination with the derogatory term *xiaoqian*, meaning to while away time or divert oneself (Luo Jiaming *et al.* 2004: 160; Wang Qiting, Li Xin and Shi Lei 2004: 144).

Concerning the roots of the term '*xiuxian*', Yu Yuanguang writes that the character *xian* (闲) refers to matters of little importance, as in the distinction between *zhengshi*, which is a person's proper duty and business, and *xianshi*, which translates as an unimportant matter, or other people's business (Yu Guangyuan and Ma Huidi 2006: 86). *Xian* is the first syllable in a variety of compound words, and as Yu points out, most of these words are to be found in derogatory descriptions of actions or people, such as *xianche* (chit-chatting), *xianhua* (gossiping), *xie xianwen* (to write irrelevant words within a text); *xianguang* (to stroll about), *xianshua* (to enjoy oneself at leisure), or *xianwan* (to play around while at leisure). *Xian* is also used in longer expressions such as *chi xian fan* (to lead an idle life, be a loafer), *guan xianshi* (meddle in other people's business), *xianchou* (to worry for no reason), and *sheng xian qi* (get angry for no reason) (Yu Guangyuan and Ma Huidi 2006: 86).

Although the term *xian* is often used to convey a derogatory meaning, leisure as a concept is described in both negative and positive terms in the key texts of the Chinese cultural tradition. Ma Huidi finds that in classical texts such as *The Analects* and the *Book of Changes*, *xian* has a range of positive references, among them 'morality, moral standards, restrictions and restraint' (*daode, fadu, xianzhi, yueshu*), and also in the form *xianjing*, which refers to being 'gentle and refined', or *anning*, which means 'calm, tranquil and free from worry' (Yu Guangyuan and Ma Huidi 2006: 90). The Chinese character for the syllable *xiu* (休) which as a verb means to cease, rest or recuperate, shows a 'person stopping to rest under a tree' (Wenlin Institute 2002). According to Ma Huidi, the character signifies the harmonious relation between man and nature, which to Ma is one of the ideal states of leisure (Ma Huidi and Zhang Jing'an 2004a: 5; Ma Huidi 2004a: 15). The tranquillity depicted in the character *xiu* and the negative connotations of idleness and meddling associated with *xian* are indicative of the ambiguous usage of the term *xiuxian* in contemporary Mandarin.

Xiuxian is an expression used in formal speech and written language. In academic writing, *xiuxian* is the term authors use when they write about what leisure ought to be, while Chinese people's actual leisure practices are mostly described in negative terms as 'idleness and pleasure-seeking' (*chi he wan le*) (Yu Guangyuan and Ma Huidi 2006: 86) or 'having fun' (*wan*) (Zhang Jian 2004: 212). As for commercial texts, the term *xiuxian* frequently appears in newspaper articles (Huang Zuyang 2006: A6, *DNZB* 23 February), in advertisements promoting leisure wear (*xiuxian fuzhuang*) and other kinds of leisure goods (*xiuxian jingpin*), and in bright neon characters flashing outside leisure centres (*xiuxian zhongxin*). In her introduction to the book series *Chinese Scholars' Leisure Research*, Ma notes that during the course of the last decade, *xiuxian* has become one of the most frequently used terms among the Chinese, and that the characters '休闲' can be seen everywhere (Ma Huidi 2004a: 3). Ma is right in pointing out that these characters are ubiquitous in the Chinese cityscapes in the form of neon signs and advertisements. But in everyday speech, or – to be more specific – in the Baixingnese language code, the term is hardly ever used in reference to leisure activities. *Xiuxian* is, however, used for example in the description of how a person dresses (*chuande hen xiuxian*; [he or she] dresses in a leisurely manner) or in reference to a place that has a relaxed atmosphere (*bijiao xiuxian de shudian*; bookstores that are rather relaxed). In Quanzhou you will not be invited to a 'leisure centre' (*xiuxian zhongxin*) to enjoy a foot massage; you will be invited to '*qu xijiao*' (lit. get a foot wash) at a '*zuyu dian*' (a foot-bath shop), or you will simply be invited to go out and have fun (*qu wan*). The few times I heard the term *xiuxian* spoken in Quanzhou was during semi-structured interviews, where the interviewees tended to use a more formal vocabulary closer to the written style. I also noticed cases where the interviewee would switch to Baixingnese when we talked about leisure in a more informal setting, such as over a meal or when going shopping together. My material from Quanzhou shows that the most common term used with reference to leisure in oral expressions[12] is not *xiuxian*, but the simple expression *qu wan*.

Wan, *or having fun*

In the everyday Baixingnese language code, the term used with reference to leisure practices is '*wan*'. In Baixingnese, *wan* is a term with positive connotations. It can refer to a range of leisure practices from activities in the home – such as watching TV, chatting on the Internet (*wan QQ*[13]), socializing with friends and relatives, eating out, going for a hike or window-shopping (*qu guangjie*), to name but a few examples. In Quanzhou, people invited me to 'come and have fun' in their homes (*Qing lai women jia wan*) and even in their offices (*Qing lai women bangongshi wan*).

The term '*wan*' is not exclusive to Baixingnese. *Wan* is also used in Ganbunese, but always in the context of social criticism. In Quanzhou I met university teachers who criticized students for spending too much time having fun (*wan*) rather than paying attention to their studies. I also interviewed officials in the culture sector who criticized the general public for expecting museums to be entertaining (*haowan*) rather than educational. This shows that it is not the term '*wan*' in itself that refers to leisure in a positive or negative way; the connotation depends on the context in which the term is used. When educators and scholars talk of 'leisure' (*xiuxian*), they refer to a specific range of activities such as reading, going to a museum, or taking physical exercise, i.e. healthy and commendable leisure activities. '*Wan*' is reserved for the activities Yu Guangyuan listed as negative connotations of the term *xian*: being idle, strolling about, enjoying oneself, or playing around while at leisure (Yu Guangyuan and Ma Huidi 2006: 86). In Ganbunese, '*wan*' refers to the leisure practices that authorities find to be objectionable, but that common people love and engage in every day.

It is not only authorities who criticize certain leisure practices by way of a careful choice of words. Among young Chinese white-collar workers, the term 'FB' (pronounced as in English) is sometimes used with special reference to spending money on food, alcohol and karaoke, which is a common leisure practice among the middle classes. An IT-worker in her mid-twenties explained to me that the word 'FB' has its origin in Internet slang and is a shortened form of the term *fubai*, which here means 'corrupt'. FB is used as a description of having fun (*wan*), but also points to the many ways that Chinese leaders – in her words – 'eat up the people's funds at big banquets and in hotels'. Asking a friend, 'have you "FB'd" lately?' (*Zuijin you mei you qu FB?*) is synonymous with asking – in a humorous manner – whether he or she has been out consuming excessively, in the manner of corrupt cadres. This sarcastic reference to the infamous spending among Chinese officials is another example of the ways terms can be actively utilized in the Baixingnese language code to express criticism of Chinese authorities. This example shows the importance of interviewees' choice of words as a source of information in the study of leisure as a social phenomenon.

The different ways in which the inhabitants of Quanzhou talk about leisure practices are significant because the choices of words indicate the status of and preference for certain leisure practices in this society at this point in time. During field research in Quanzhou, I found that some people even described their own leisure practices as 'nothing'. For example, when I asked a young driver about leisure activities in Quanzhou, the man held that people in this town do 'nothing'. He then went on to describe this 'nothing' as 'watching TV, taking a meal together, going window-shopping, etc.' (*kan dianshi, qu chi fan, guang-guangjie, dengdeng*). The activities he accounted for were examples of the popular culture which is accessible to most people in Quanzhou. In the words of this young man, these leisure practices are best described as 'nothing'. The authoritative Ganbunese language code devaluates the leisure practices of common people by insisting that the various kinds of *wan* are negative for society. The following chapter is devoted to the detailed analysis of the PRC leisure ethic, which informs the derogatory evaluation of leisure practices in contemporary China.

3 The utility of leisure and the dangers of idleness

As demonstrated in the previous chapter, the ways an interviewee talks about leisure tell us something about the person's attitude towards certain leisure activities or towards leisure in general. In the same chapter, I also presented some examples of the scepticism expressed by Chinese leisure scholars concerning the types of activities in which ordinary people engage; in other words, a criticism of contemporary Chinese popular culture. Since the beginning of industrialization, political, clerical and scholarly authorities have fronted a similar critique of mass culture in Western Europe and the US. Popular pastimes ranging from drinking and spectator sports to pop music and computer games have at different times been regarded as harmful to society (van der Poel 2006: 98; Donnelly: 1988: 70; Gans 1974: 19). In Europe, the perception of popular culture as a negative influence on the general population has its roots in the moralist discourse Max Weber called the Protestant work ethic, and in the wave of elitist denunciation of commercial mass culture in the mid-twentieth century, fronted by the philosophers of the Frankfurter school in particular. In recent years, new forms of leisure such as computer gaming and net surfing have come under attack (Johnson 2005). A similar scepticism towards mass culture is present in the contemporary Chinese government's regulation of leisure activities, in the official propagation of healthy leisure, as well as in Chinese scholarship on leisure. I argue that, in the Chinese context, this scepticism takes the form of a leisure ethic that serves to strengthen the legitimacy of the party-state by promoting adherence to the goals of stability and economic growth. The leisure ethic thus implicitly serves to sustain the leadership of the Chinese Communist Party. Within this discourse, leisure is regarded mainly as a resource that should be exploited for the sake of the national collective. In this chapter, I analyse the underlying premises of the discourse that I call the PRC leisure ethic, and the ways in which Chinese studies of leisure serve to reinforce the metaphor of leisure as a national resource, which is characteristic of this discourse.

The Protestant work ethic and popular culture critique

Throughout history, attitudes towards leisure have been closely related to the prevalent moral stance in the given society. At the time of the industrial revolution, England was strongly influenced by Puritan ethics in general, and in particular by what was later called the Protestant work ethic. The Protestant work ethic is based on Calvin's theory of predestination, which states that only by working diligently, making oneself useful to the community and amassing wealth – albeit not for the sake of profit – can one prove that one believes oneself to be among those chosen few predestined for salvation (Stebbins 2004: 24). The Puritans preached that 'the end is near', and as a consequence, spending time in idleness or engaging in leisure activities came to be regarded as sinful. During the same period, the practice of translating man-hours into wages established the idea that time is money. Thompson writes that the Protestant work ethic thus imbued man with a 'moral time piece' (Thompson 1967: 87). Together with the principle that industriousness is superior to the pursuit of pleasure, this logic lies at the heart of the capitalist value system, as pointed out by Weber (Rojek 1985: 68).

In eighteenth- and nineteenth-century Europe, popular culture in general and ordinary people's leisure activities in particular were regarded with scepticism by both social commentators and authorities (Thompson 1967: 86). It was generally held that ordinary people were unable to govern their own leisure time and, moreover, that poverty was caused by idleness (Thompson 1967: 75, 86); employers attempted to discipline workers, whom they characterized as people spending their spare time in 'debauchery rather than physical and mental recovery' (Roberts 1999: 27. See also Bauman 1998: 9–10). Bauman stresses that the focus of industrialized society was the conquest of nature and the progress of mankind. Thus, any resistance towards the discipline of an industrial society was considered an irrational and ignorant 'resistance to progress' (Bauman 1998: 6). Philosophers, politicians and men of the cloth argued that the labouring classes needed guidance in order to make the right choices concerning how to spend their time, and in both Europe and, later, the United States, moralist campaigns were held to 'teach people to wish for a better life' (Bauman 1998: 6).

From the latter part of the twentieth century onward, historians, sociologists, and scholars within the developing field of cultural studies have raised the claim that everyday life, popular culture and leisure activities are social phenomena worthy of scholarly attention. While some theorists continued to lament the fact that the ascetic Protestant work ethic was on the wane (Goldstein and Eichorn 1961: 557), others came to envision the development of a 'leisure society' where all people, regardless of social status, worked fewer hours and spent their leisure time and wages pursuing leisure activities (Gershuny 1992: 4, 22).[1] Although 'leisure' has gradually come to be imbued with a positive value, this does not mean that the twentieth century saw a straightforward progression from one historical stage of mentality (critique of leisure) to another (defence and promotion of leisure); the same time period also witnessed a new critique of popular culture, this time based on sentiments other than Puritan ethics.

In his writing on popular culture critique in the US, Herbert Gans identifies two main points of view: a conservative stance, heralded by such writers as T.S. Eliot and Jose Ortega y Gasset, that expresses a resentment towards the increasing social, economic and cultural power of the masses (Gans 1974: 54), and the socialist stance, voiced by the Neo-Marxist Frankfurter school among others. The latter makes the argument that the culture industry transforms culture into a commodity, and that this process 'functions to induce uncritical mass obedience to the existing power order in society' (Rojek 1985: 114). Not only were the socialist critics fearful of the culture industry, they were disappointed in the masses and their failure to support the socialist advocacy of high culture (Gans 1974: 54; Bauman 2001: 10). Both of the above-mentioned stances express scepticism towards the ability of ordinary people to make their own life choices, be it the choice of what to buy, which music to listen to, or for whom to vote.[2] Aspects of this critique of popular culture can still be heard in present-day discussions of the potential dangers of contemporary leisure activities such as watching TV, playing computer games or surfing the Internet. In his book *Everything Bad Is Good for You: How today's popular culture is actually making us smarter* from 2005, Steven Johnson argues against the prevalent distinction between the wholesome genres of high culture, such as the novel, and the 'junk-food culture' of the commercial leisure market. Johnson claims that concern over violent contents and swearing makes parents and educators overlook that a computer game or a chapter of a contemporary TV series actively engages its audience (Johnson 2005), and is as complex and stimulating for the viewer as novels from the literary canon are for the reader.

Johnson's defence of popular culture addresses the attitudes towards ordinary people's leisure preferences in the US. Contemporary popular culture critique and its counter-critique are not, however, particular to Europe and the US. Asef Bayat has analysed the restrictions of popular culture expressions such as dancing, drinking, and all kinds of 'fun' in Islamist states, and he sees these restrictions as a form of social control. Bayat stresses that what he calls the rhetoric of 'anti-fun', or 'anti-fun-damentalism', is not a question of religion or culture, but rather a means used by authorities to exercise power over ordinary people. After all, Bayat writes, restrictions on popular culture can be found in a variety of social contexts,. from the policies of secular Bolsheviks to the writings of Iranian religious leaders (Bayat 2007: 434, 443). Shaoguang Wang strengthens this argument, stating that

> [...] by cultivating and imposing a particular ideal of acceptable leisure activity, the modern state, capitalist and Communist alike, aims to draw all social groups into 'rational recreation' to curb the potential dangers of free time.
>
> (1995: 150)

The readiness of authorities – be they governments or cultural elites – to criticise the cultural preferences and leisure practices of ordinary people, is clearly a widespread phenomenon. The irony is that leisure critics seem invariably to promote what the critics themselves regard as an ideal way of life (Gans 1974: 52), i.e. their own value systems or moral sentiments. Moralism and distrust of the abilities of ordinary people to make their own leisure choices has characterized approaches to leisure in the Western cultural sphere. These attitudes are also present in the official discourse of leisure in the PRC.

The characteristics of the PRC leisure ethic

In the reform era, the Chinese Communist Party has sought a balance in the development of 'material civilization' (*wuzhi wenming*) and 'spiritual civilization' (*jingshen wenming*). Party ideologues have feared that a growth in material wealth would lead to 'brutalization of life and social disorder' (Anagnost 1997: 84). It has therefore been imperative for the Chinese authorities that material development be checked by a matching degree of 'ethico-moral development' (Anagnost 1997: 84). I argue that the official leisure discourse with its promotion of so-called healthy and educational leisure complements the party-state's efforts to generate a spiritual civilization among the Chinese population. Ann Anagnost writes that in, the post-Mao era, the discourse of class has been replaced by the discourse of *wenming* (civility/civilization/civil behaviour) and an increased focus on people's 'quality' (*suzhi*) (Anagnost 1997: 74). Rather than evaluating the individual on the grounds of his or her class background as was the case under high-Maoism, Chinese individuals are now distinguished by their level of cultural competence. According to Anagnost, the authorities' concern with levels of quality 'constructs the necessity for a national pedagogy' to assist the improvement of the Chinese population (Anagnost 1997: 78). Through this civilising process, writes Anagnost, 'the party seeks the completion of its own identity as the authority necessary for a polity not yet ready for self-representation' (Anagnost 1997: 78). I regard the PRC leisure ethic as part of this 'national pedagogy' of the party-state; it is one element in a larger official discourse that seeks to shape the life choices and aspirations of the general population. This discourse, which I call the PRC leisure ethic, can be summed up as follows:

> *It is the duty of the individual to make use of his or her leisure in a way that increases his or her cultural competence. The self-development of individuals is beneficial because it secures an increasingly skilled workforce. This work force will contribute towards China's continued growth and development, on which the legitimacy of the current regime rests.*

The leisure ethic is based on a central 'metaphorical concept' (Lakoff and Johnson 1980: 4–5), namely that leisure is a resource, and the imperative message is that this resource must not go to waste, but be exploited for the benefit of the greater collective. Even though the actual allocation of spare time and the responsibility of making the 'right' choice of leisure activities is placed at the level of the individual, the utilitarian logic of the leisure ethic still applies; the good life is presented as making oneself useful to the collective, which in this case means the Chinese party-state.

It is tempting to trace some of the values promoted in Chinese scholarly articles on leisure back to Confucian ethics. Contemporary sociologists' preoccupation with the duties of the individual towards the collective is in some ways reminiscent of the Confucian stance that to be truly human is to be faithful to one's duties in society (Madsen 1984: 13). In his article on Japanese leisure values, Sepp Linhart regards the idea that 'work is good and play is bad' as being part of the Confucian values of the past (Linhart 1988: 305), and in a recent article about women's leisure in Taiwan, Lucetta Tsai claims that it is the Confucian norm of frugality and filial piety, rather than economic dependence, that restricts women's access to leisure in Taiwanese society (Tsai 2006). A thorough discussion of the relevance of Confucian values for present-day ethics – or indeed present-day leisure practices – is, however, beyond the scope of this study. My point here is simply to show that the critique of leisure, or the Puritan preference for work over leisure which is inherent in what I call the PRC leisure ethic, need not stem from a Chinese adaptation of a Western discourse of work ethics or from Western popular culture critique. Even if the conclusions that Chinese leisure scholars draw are similar to those made by leisure critics in the West – be they conservatives or neo-Marxists – the underlying arguments are not the same. Whereas Western conservatives have feared the influence of the masses and the neo-Marxists criticise the commoditization of culture under capitalism, the PRC leisure ethic is shaped by other factors. As will be discussed in more detail in the next section, the PRC leisure ethic is shaped by market fundamentalism and economism, and a concern for China's competitiveness in relation to other nations. Moreover, as argued in the introduction, the PRC leisure ethic also bears resemblance to the Maoist ethics of the 1960s. Shaoguang Wang illustrates the politicization of leisure during the Mao era with examples drawn from newspaper headlines from 1964 which read 'Value Your Spare Time' and 'You Must Behave Yourself Even in [*sic*.] After-Hours' (Shaoguang Wang 1995: 155, quoting from *Zhongguo Qingnian*, May 1964).[3] Wang writes that '[t]hose who failed to participate in officially organized leisure activities risked being criticised for "cutting themselves off from the masses" and "lacking collectivist spirit"' (Shaoguang Wang 1995:153, quoting articles in *Zhongguo Qingnian*, June and September 1956). A parallel can be drawn between the 1960s' 'Maoist ethics' and the contemporary focus on leisure as a resource that should serve the national collective. This rhetoric is also present in the recent socialist values campaign, 'Eight Honors and Eight Disgraces' or 'Eight Dos and Don'ts' (*Ba rong ba chi*), fronted by Hu Jintao. In this campaign, slogans four and eight read as follows:

> To labor industriously is honor; to love leisure and hate labor is disgrace.
> Arduous struggle is honor, arrogant excess and wanton leisure are disgrace.
>
> (*Yi xinqin laodong wei rong, yi haoyiwulao wei chi.*
> *Yi jiankufendou wei rong, yi jiaosheyinyi wei chi.*)
>
> (Teslik 2007)

These slogans serve to demonstrate how moral principles are promoted in present-day China. In doing so, both the Party and Chinese leisure scholars rely on a moralist rhetoric reminiscent of Northern European Puritanism. As I will demonstrate in the following chapters, this sentiment is echoed in the PRC leisure legislation, official propaganda and the state-sponsored media. The danger of treating a diverse field of study in a reductionist manner not withstanding, let us proceed to an analysis of the leisure ethic as it is communicated in Chinese academic writing on leisure.

The PRC leisure ethic in academic writing

In China, social scientists are state employees who write within an academic tradition where research articles are expected to produce policy recommendations. Judging from the articles I analyse here, this places the scholars in an uncomfortable position. More often than not, Chinese survey studies of leisure draw conclusions that support the PRC leisure ethic even when the theoretical framework and the data point in a different direction. It is therefore necessary to ask whether these scholarly studies consciously serve to reinforce the official discourse of leisure, or whether scholars are merely paying lip service to the same discourse. A more thorough examination of the origins of the PRC leisure ethic and the way it informs Chinese research on leisure is therefore necessary.

In the beginning of the 1980s, sociologists such as Wang Yalin, Yu Guangyuan and Ma Huidi conducted pioneering studies of leisure in China. During the last two decades, Chinese sociologists, economists and educationalists have continued to describe and analyse the new lifestyles and the changes in people's quality of life that have taken place during the reform era, predominantly among China's urban population. This research relies heavily on methodology developed within the European and US sociology of leisure, giving priority to time budget studies and quantitative surveys of people's everyday activities. The leisure of different social groups (based on gender, age, employment status), the development of leisure industries, and juvenile delinquency are recurrent topics within this field (Wang Yalin 2003: 2).

In terms of theory, Chinese scholars discuss leisure as a source of personal development (Sun Xiaoli 2004: 78, 81; Wang Yalin 2003: 51). Yu Guangyuan, for example, writes that the increased amount of spare time in Chinese society 'facilitates numerous forms of personal development', and Zhang Jian states that leisure offers students an opportunity to experience a different kind of self than the self they experience during classes (Yu Guangyuan 2004: 1; Zhang Jian 2004: 208). Despite this theoretical point of departure, and even if most articles refer to Karl Marx's definition of 'free time' (*ziyou shijian*) as time a person may 'freely allocate' (*keyi ziyou zhipei de shijian*) and spend on 'rest and recreation' (*yule xiuxi*) (Wang Qiting *et al.* 2004: 144), scholars within the field of Chinese leisure studies are reluctant to admit individuals the right to spend their time in whichever way they please.

In their recommendations, several leisure scholars call upon the Party and government departments to provide the Chinese population with a form of leisure education that can guide people in their choice of leisure activities. Wang Zhongwu recommends that the government should provide national consumer education in order to alleviate the dangers new consumer products and new forms of leisure consumption pose to people's mental and physical health. This education should instruct people to adjust their excessive and wasteful consumer habits, and tutor the people in national consumer policies and moral consumer norms so that they can become lawful, rational, conforming and standard consumers (Wang Zhongwu 2005: 125). Moreover, in a recent study of leisure among workers who had recently arrived in the city of Ningbo from nearby rural areas, the authors are critical of the quality of their interviewees' reading materials, the number of hours they spend in front of the TV, and their propensity to play *majiang*. The authors' advice to the authorities is that new urban residents should be 'timely, correctly, and passionately guided (*yindao*) towards healthy aesthetic standards' and taught to 'make cultural consumption choices that lead actively upwards' (Chang Qinyi *et al.* 2007: 123). Similarly, Ma Huidi and Zhang Jing'an argue that leisure education is needed in order for people to achieve 'leisure qualifications' (*xiuxian zige*) (Ma Huidi and Zhang Jing'an 2004b: 4). Meng Lei, on the other hand, advises that if only people of low culture and low income would emulate the cultural tastes of the middle classes, their professional ethics and 'elevation of human quality', then good work ethics, healthy lifestyles and a stable social order would ensue. (Meng Lei 2007: 26). Meng's reasoning brings further evidence to Anagnost's claim that the Chinese discourse of social class has been replaced by a discourse of civility and civilization.

The dichotomy of healthy (*jiankang*) versus unhealthy (*bu jiankang*) leisure, and the belief that ordinary people need guidance (*yindao*) in order to make the right choice of leisure activities are, I argue, characteristic of the field of leisure studies in China.[4] The concern for the quality of Chinese people's leisure activities is evident from the numerous calls in scholarly writing for people to take up 'civilized' (*wenming*), 'healthy' (*jiankang*), 'rational' (*heli*) and 'scientific' (*kexue*) forms of leisure (Zhang Jian 2004: 210; Sun Xiaoli 2004: 81. The usage of these terms in China is discussed in some detail in Shaoguang Wang 1995). A discussion of what actually constitutes healthy, scientific, 'rational' or civilized leisure is, however, seldom included in these writings.

Børge Bakken stresses that Chinese authorities continue to regard social stability as one of the preconditions for the execution of reform policies (Bakken 2000: 6), and I interpret the warnings against unhealthy leisure in official discourse – and in scholarly writing – as a sign of the Chinese authorities' fear that idleness among the populace will lead to public disorder and chaos. Some leisure scholars hint at the grave consequences of letting people while away their time. The fear of the consequences of idleness is most clearly present in writings within the sub-field of leisure education (*xiuxian jiaoyu*), where educators and sociologists discuss how to teach healthy leisure habits to young students (see for example Li Guangnian 1995; Tai Rongli 1995; Rong An 1995; and Zhang Zujun 1997). Zhang Jian, for example, claims that if Chinese youth spend their time as they please, this may lead to trouble and wrongdoing, which is harmful to society (Zhang Jian 2004: 213–15). As examples of 'unhealthy' activities, Zhang Jian lists karaoke, playing billiards or video games and watching VCDs/DVDs (Zhang Jian 2004: 220). These are all popular culture activities enjoyed by the general urban public in China. Zhang Jian argues that unless young students are provided with healthy organized leisure activities, they will spend their weekends sleeping in and having so much fun (*da wan*) that they will be neither rested nor prepared for their studies on Monday (Zhang Jian 2004: 212). This rationale echoes the worries voiced among early British industrialists who held that the alternation of days of work and days of rest led to the so-called 'worship of Saint Monday', where workers were exhausted on Mondays after the joys of their Sunday evening off (Thompson 1967: 75). The above examples reveal a tendency whereby, on the one hand, scholars celebrate the development of a more diverse leisure scene in urban China, while on the other, the very same leisure practices are held to be detrimental to the development of the population.

This contradiction is present in the writings of Ma Huidi in particular. She defines leisure activities as something one 'engages in out of one's free will when one has fulfilled one's work obligations, obligations in the home, and towards society' (Ma Huidi 2004a: 3). At the same time, Ma stresses that leisure is a social resource (*shehui ziyuan*) (Ma Huidi and Zhang Jing'an 2004b), and that the ability among the general population to make use of this resource is decisive for the successful development of the Chinese nation. As she herself puts it: in the twenty-first century, 'the people's quality and cultural accomplishment is the foundation of the nation's core competitive power' (Ma Huidi 2004 2004a: 4). I find that this contradiction between leisure as an intrinsic value in the life of the individual and leisure as a resource that should benefit the national collective runs through much of Chinese writing about leisure. Furthermore, I ascribe this contradiction to two characteristics the majority of the articles I have consulted have in common: first, a miscalculation of the amount of leisure available to ordinary Chinese people, and second, the central metaphor of leisure as a national resource.

Contradictions in methodology

With few exceptions, Chinese sociologists' analyses of leisure and their subsequent policy recommendations are based on surveys of how urban residents distribute their time between work and leisure. These quantitative analyses do not take into consideration the complexity of the relation between work and leisure, but regard them as exhaustive entities.[5] As pointed out in Chapter 2, the perceived dichotomy of work versus leisure fails to render the intermingling of work and leisure activities in the workplace and in public spaces. This is a methodological challenge shared by those who pursue quantitative studies of leisure both in China and elsewhere. More problematic, however, is the fact that rather than basing their conclusions on the empirical data collected, leisure scholars in China tend to base their generalizations and recommendations on leisure as it is rendered in the national legislation pertaining to the amount of work hours per day and the number of holidays per year. According to PRC legislation, employees within the state sector are entitled to take time off for the Spring Festival, Labour Day and National Day holidays, also known as the 'three golden weeks' (*san ge huangjinzhou*). If one adds the two days of rest at the weekend, this should amount to an average of 114 resting days per year.[6] These numbers express the guidelines that Chinese authorities have laid down for the regulation of work hours in China; they are normative, not descriptive. Nevertheless, even in studies where the data analysis clearly demonstrates that the amount of spare time enjoyed by different groups of employees varies significantly, the authors make their judgements and recommendations with reference to the normative work-time legislation, and state that every worker in China is entitled to 114 days of rest.[7] My data from field research in Quanzhou shows that not only are state employees often called in to work during the 'golden weeks', but a significant number of employees, although predominantly in the private sector, still work at least half a day on Saturdays. This indicates that the basic amount of people's spare time is overestimated in Chinese writing on leisure.

Conclusions concerning the spare time available to pupils and students are based on similar generalizations. As an example, Ma Huidi and Zhang Jing'an write that students in high school and at university enjoy 140 to 160 days of holidays each year (Ma Huidi and Zhang Jing'an 2004b: 5), but they do not discuss the fact that students from the level of junior high and upward are given excessive amounts of homework during both the 'golden weeks' and regular weekends, which makes their 'spare' time less than leisurely (Zhang Jian 2004: 214; Rolandsen 2004: 50–8). As for spare time among the peasantry, Ma and Zhang claim – without reference to empirical data – that because of the process of mechanization in agricultural production, peasants may 'rest for approximately half of the year' (*quannian yue you bannian xiu*) (Ma Huidi and Zhang Jing'an 2004b: 5). This 'fact' is left uncommented on, even though an article in the same anthology states that 'work for wages makes up a proportionately large amount of the annual income among peasants' (Sun Xiaoli 2004: 75), which in turn suggests that many peasants do find ways to occupy themselves, including outside of the agricultural busy seasons.

Furthermore, most articles on Chinese leisure postulate that the modernization of societies leads to a general increase in leisure time, and it is argued that China is about to enter the 'era of the leisure economy' (*xiuxian jingji shidai*) (Wang Yalin 2003: 4), and that China is gradually becoming a 'leisure society' (*xiuxian shehui*) (Wang Yihong 2005: 123). If a leisure society is defined by the size of its leisure-related economy, the growth in the Chinese service sector (35 per cent of the GDP in 2004, compared to 20 per cent in the 1980s) may serve to confirm this claim (Sun Xiaoli 2004: 78). The hypothesis that industrialization and modernization have led to an increase in the amount of spare time available has, however, been refuted in Western leisure theory (Seabrook 1988: 10; Chick

2006: 48; van der Poel 2006: 101). In the 1950s and 60s, after the introduction of the eight-hour work day, sociologists and economists expected that the average work week would be even further reduced, and that the overall amount of leisure and leisure consumption would increase accordingly, as data from the US suggested. In this situation, social scientists argued that 'people had to be prepared and educated in order to be able to spend this free time in a responsible and edifying way' (van der Poel 2006: 99). Contrary to the scientists' predictions, however, work hours in the US increased, the anticipated 'leisure society' failed to manifest itself, and the hypothesis that industrialization leads to increased leisure was discredited (van der Poel 2006: 101). The hypothesis is nevertheless sustained in Chinese studies of leisure.

Jonathan Gershuny has argued that, objectively, work hours are decreasing in Western societies, and that the experiences people in modern, industrialized societies have of a 'time famine' and the belief that everyday life is running faster are merely subjective perceptions (Gershuny 1992: 22). These subjective impressions are nevertheless important for our understanding of what everyday life looks like from the point of view of the urban middle class in a city like Quanzhou. Judging from interviews and conversations with Quanzhou's middle-class professionals, the problem they face is not an increasing amount of spare time, but rather a feeling that 'everything goes faster', and the experience of being pressed for time in their attempts to fit work, family life and recreation into their schedules.[8] These may be mere subjective perceptions of the general pace of life. Even so, these notions do at least challenge the assumption that the amount of spare time among the Chinese is increasing, and that this, as Chinese leisure scholars argue, poses a social problem.

Summing up, Chinese scholars' analyses of leisure in China tend to be clouded by an overly simple concept of leisure and a focus on normative legislation rather than the realities of actual leisure practices. This constitutes an underlying premise that guides the conclusions and recommendations provided in Chinese writing on leisure; namely, that people have too much idle time on their hands, and that this time resource ought to be put to use for the benefit of the country. The metaphor of leisure as a resource is significant because it places the PRC leisure ethic firmly within the larger discourse of the cultural competence – or 'quality' (*suzhi*) – of the Chinese population as a factor in the development of the Chinese nation.

Leisure as a resource

Desmond McNeill has argued that terms and concepts borrowed from economic theory influence not only the way we talk about social phenomena, but also the way we think about society. Terms like 'human resources' or indeed 'human capital' possess a certain explanatory power, but once we as researchers or social analysts apply these 'economistic' terms, we are in danger of 'viewing the individual person as [a] potentially productive asset rather than as a human being' (McNeill unpublished manuscript: 8). The PRC leisure ethic, as it is communicated in Chinese scholars' writing about leisure, is characterized by a view of the individual as a means to increase national economic production. The leisure ethic requires that the individual give priority to national interests over his or her own desire for enjoyment and relaxation. From this reasoning, it follows that spending one's (spare) time inefficiently is a sin against the state and the common national goal of wealth and prosperity. 'Sinners' are not threatened with any concrete sanctions. But, by rhetorically linking 'idleness' (*xiaoqian*, also *xiuxian*) and 'having fun' (*wan*) to a lack of cultural competence (*suzhi*) in a person, or even with delinquent behaviour, the academic texts signal that such conduct ought to be socially censured.

In Chinese leisure research, the metaphor of leisure as a resource occurs in both normative statements and in admonitory remarks. One such normative statement is Ma Huidi's claim that leisure is a social resource, while Sun Xiaoli's statement that a scientific concept of leisure means to regard leisure time as a kind of wealth, a wealth 'that must be governed in a scientific, and civilized' manner is an example of an admonitory remark (Ma Huidi and Zhang Jian 2004b:4; Sun Xiaoli 2004: 82). Sun furthermore writes that to arrange one's leisure in a proper manner 'symbolizes the distinction and level of the lifestyle of the modern man' (Sun Xiaoli 2004: 82). It is clear from the context that engaging in leisure activities in a proper manner means to make oneself useful to society. More importantly, however, the people whose work hours and leisure is up for discussion – and indeed the preferences these people may have concerning their leisure – are completely excluded from these assessments of the significance of leisure in Chinese society.

In their analyses, Chinese leisure scholars tend to take leisure activities out of the realm of everyday practices and place them within an economistic framework. This is what Wang Yalin does when he states that Chinese society 'possesses far more leisure time resources (*xiuxian shijian ziyuan*) than the amount of work-time resources the society applies toward creating material and spiritual wealth' (Wang Yalin 2003: 43). I see in these articles a mirror image of the drive for economic growth that has come to shape the party-state's policies in all sectors in China.[9] Victor Lippit characterizes this relentless drive for economic growth within Chinese politics as 'market fundamentalism', defined as 'a belief in the market system as always desirable, and the inability to grasp the pervasiveness of market failures' (Lippit 2005: 445). This fundamentalism is also emblematic of economic policymaking in Western societies, but in these environments the role of the market is often contested by political parties as well as popular groups and associations within the civil society. Importantly, in China, intellectual social reformers like He Xuefeng seek to promote an alternative path for China's development.[10] Moreover, as I discuss in Chapter 7, members of local cultured middle class in Quanzhou are critical of what they perceive as increasing materialism in their local environment. Nevertheless, contemporary Chinese society has very few arenas where ordinary people's views can be brought to the government's attention and cause significant change.

Leisure and the fate of the nation

The PRC leisure ethic is utilitarian in the sense that the overall aim is the good of the population as a whole, and that the actions of the individual should contribute to this end. The Protestant work ethic is also a utilitarian ethical code; leisure is regarded as a means to an end, i.e. increased productivity in this world and salvation in the next. Whereas the Protestant work ethic used a religious discourse of sin and salvation to ensure workers' commitment to wage labour, the PRC leisure ethic invokes the early modern discourse of the necessity of a strengthened Chinese nation in a world of competing states (Ma Huidi 2004a: 6; Li Yisun 2007: 2). According to Ma and Zhang, '[t]he future does not belong merely to educated people, it belongs even more to those who have learnt how to utilize their leisure in a clever way' (Ma Huidi and Zhang Jing'an 2004b: 2). The proper utilization of leisure is regarded as decisive for China's future. For this reason, scholars argue that the Chinese population must be taught how to 'spend' leisure resources with care. Wang Zhongwu writes that Chinese people's tendency to stress entertainment and pastimes (*yule xiaoqian*) rather than intellectual development (*zhili fazhan*) has consequences for the human capital of the family, and also for the 'construction of spiritual civilization in our society' (Wang Zhongwu 2005: 125). Here, leisure is regarded as part of the family wealth and, indirectly, the national pool of human capital. Again, the leisure of the individual is reduced to a mere resource that ought to be exploited for the benefit of the national collective. The concern for the cultural competence of the Chinese population is also evident in Sun Xiaoli's proposal that more technology theme parks and science museums should be built in China. Sun argues that to make such institutions available 'would increase the economic sustainability of the nation' (Sun Xiaoli 2004: 79). A similar point is made in a study of consumption in Henan Province, where Ma Feifeng states that the lack of diversity in the local leisure market 'affects the improvement of the residents' cultural quality' (Ma Feifeng 2002: 14). This brings us back to Ann Anagnost's discussion of the discourse of civility in post-Mao China. Anagnost describes the civility discourse as 'a discourse of "lack", referring to the failure of the Chinese people to embody international standards of modernity, civility, and discipline' (Anagnost 1997: 76). Anagnost shows that the concept of the people's low quality serves as a 'master trope for explaining the "historic failures of the nation"' (Anagnost in Festa 2006: 22). In Chinese leisure studies, the question of how leisure is used and governed as a national resource ultimately becomes a question of China's role in the international arena. This is most clearly expressed by Li Yisun, who stresses that the development of a cultural economy has come to be the measure of national strength, and he warns that unless China takes measures to stem the flow of global commercial culture into China, the nation will inevitably fall into a trap of 'self-colonization' (Li Yisun 2007: 2–3). Chinese leisure scholars' solution to this challenge is that the general population take up healthy, educational and preferably native Chinese forms of leisure (Festa 2006).

This leaves us with a view of leisure not as a source of personal development, nor as a good that the individual can allocate freely, but as a resource in the form of the cultural and human capital that sustains China's competitiveness on the global scene. With its call for Chinese individuals to spend their time so as to increase their cultural competence, the PRC leisure ethic can be seen as a normalizing discourse that works in unison with the overarching discourse of China as a nation that 'lacks' competence and is therefore perceived as lagging behind.

Lip-service or subservience?

These examples, drawn from scholarly studies of leisure, demonstrate two general tendencies within said field of study: namely, the overestimation of the amount of leisure that Chinese people enjoy and a strong concern for how ordinary people make use of leisure as a resource. The relationship between these academic texts and the official discourse of leisure is complex. As I have already pointed out, the metaphor of leisure as a national resource runs counter to scholars' theoretical point of departure, which is invariably that leisure is a positive factor in the lives of Chinese individuals. And, more often than not, the leisure practices described in the analyses differ significantly from the leisure activities proscribed in the closing sections. The noteworthy discrepancy between the data and the policy recommendations made in Chinese studies of leisure leads one to ask whether the recommendations are to be taken at face value, or whether the authors as state employees in the People's Republic are simply paying lip-service to the dominant leisure discourse heralded by the authorities of the party-state.[11]

Iver B. Neumann writes that in order to analyse newspaper articles from the Soviet Union in the 1980s, knowledge of the genre is of great significance. According to Neumann, articles from this period were typically divided into an introductory section that repeated the dominant representation of the world, i.e. the party line, and then a second section, where ideas and information which had yet to be curbed by the demands of the Party discourse could be presented. These two parts were usually separated by the simple term 'however' (*odnako*) (Neumann 2002: 51). If we look at articles in the field of Chinese leisure studies as a genre, and the sociological articles in particular, the dogmatic stances and judgemental attitudes towards popular leisure can be found in the concluding remarks and in the policy recommendations. In the main sections, where data is presented and commented upon, the evaluation of leisure is almost neutral. There is no convention similar to the Russian 'however' that can signal a shift from a possibly feigned adherence to the party line and to the real matter in hand. Moreover, although Chinese researchers are employed by the government, I find it difficult to believe that the presence of censorship and self-censorship in Chinese academia can be deciphered in such a straightforward manner. As a consequence, I do not interpret the moralist sentiments and negative assessments of popular leisure practices in these scholarly articles as examples of how Chinese intellectuals pay lip-service to the official party line. Rather, I see it as an evaluation of ordinary people's leisure from the perspective of an educated elite. When Chinese leisure scholars speak warmly of libraries and museums and warn against the dangers of gambling and excessive drinking, they promote their own norms and ideas about the good life, much in the same way the various schools of popular culture criticism in the Western tradition have done. As argued by Herbert Gans, the mass culture critique in the European context 'is largely a statement of aesthetic dissatisfaction with popular culture content, justified by an incorrect estimate of negative effects and based on a false conception of the uses and functions of popular culture' (Gans 1974: 51–2). I therefore see no reason to regard Chinese scholars' writings on leisure as conscious attempts at suppressing popular practices. It is nevertheless a fact that the focus on leisure as a resource in these articles and the overestimation of the amount of poorly utilized leisure hours in Chinese society serve to reinforce the PRC leisure ethic. And, as I will demonstrate in Chapter 6, this leisure discourse informs the national leisure legislation and the enforcement of this legislation at the local level.

The above examples from Chinese leisure studies and the comparison with similar historical and current discourses in Europe and the US show that attitudes toward leisure and evaluations of various leisure practices are shaped by the dominant discourses in the society in question, be it the Protestant work ethic or the concern for China's level of civilization. Moreover, the examples from Chinese scholarship show that the ways researchers define and measure leisure has consequences for the assessments and recommendations they make on the basis of their findings. In the case studied here, the normative assessments of leisure in Chinese scholarship have more in common with the ideals of the PRC leisure ethic than with the actual leisure practices that can be observed in contemporary Chinese cities.

The PRC leisure ethic is, I argue, an aspect of the more overarching official discourse of civility on which Chinese authorities rely in order to curb the negative consequences of market reform. I regard this discourse not as a coercive tool in the hands of authorities but as a normalizing discourse that communicates to the population which kinds of behaviour are permissible and which are not (McNay 1994: 94–5). I consider the leisure ethic to be part of the 'moral regulation' authorities use in order to 'educate its citizens to ideological norms of civility' (Rojek 1995 in Festa 2006: 9–10). In Anagnost's words, it is part of the 'disciplinary impulses [that] operate at the level of political signification' (Anagnost 1997: 77). As stated in the Introduction, it is problematic to infer that Chinese authorities, be they local government officials or Party ideologues at the national level, consciously intend to govern the population by way of normalizing discourses. In her study of propaganda campaigns directed towards women in Hui'an, Sara L. Friedman concludes that the local state apparatus works in contradictory ways. Similarly, Festa's study of the sanitation and standardization of the game of *majiang* shows that the party-state communicates mixed messages when it comes to leisure consumption (Friedman 2006: 9; Festa 2006: 28). Both studies indicate that it is problematic, even, to suggest that the discourses authorities use and propagate are decisive for the actual policies and the ways in which they are carried out. With this challenge in mind, the following chapter analyses the ways in which a selection of public leisure places in Quanzhou is presented by the local authorities, and the discrepancy between official visions of leisure and 'image politics' on the one hand, and the leisure activities that actually take place in the cityscape on the other.

4 Leisure in the Quanzhou cityscape

In Quanzhou, the local city administration provides physical places designated for leisure activities, such as museums, parks and public squares. But the leisure space envisioned by local administrators does not necessarily correspond to the map of leisure places that the city population live by. Lefebvre describes this phenomenon as a discrepancy between the 'conceptualized' space 'produced' by authorities and space as it is 'lived' by inhabitants (Lefebvre 1991: 38–9). Inspired by Lefebvre's theories of the social production of space, this chapter discusses how designated places for leisure are produced, and how and why some attempts at creating places for leisure fail to generate activity and attract people.

Figure 4.1 Elderly people enjoying a game of *majiang* at *Tongfo si*.

Envisioning a leisure area

Two monumental buildings stand out in the western part of Quanzhou: the Quanzhou Museum (*Quanzhou bowuguan*) and the Mintaiyuan Museum (*Mintaiyuan bowuguan*). The museums are situated near each other in a geomantically auspicious environment at the foot of the Qingyuan Mountains and facing the West Lake Park. The museums were completed in 2005 and 2006, and are therefore new additions to this district. Until just a few years back, this area was farmland, and what is now the West Lake was a water reserve used for flood regulation. The stretch of land between the museum area and the mountains still has large village settlements. Neighbouring farmers till their land and dump their garbage right next to Mintaiyuan Museum Square. One of the museum curators, Mr Song, described with enthusiasm the local authorities' plans for a connected tourist area (*lüyou qu*) or even a leisure area (*xiuxian qu*) between the lake and the mountain. The official information booklet from the Quanzhou Museum already presents the museum area as 'an ideal spot for [...] tourism and leisure, a base for patriotic education and a place for [the] life-long education of citizens (*guomin*)' (Quanzhou bowuguan 2005). The booklet describes the area as a place for the 'citizens', but the citizens referred to are not Quanzhou's city population (*shimin*), but rather citizens of the Chinese nation (*guomin*). This indicates that, for local planners, the museums may be more important as showcases for visitors than as accessible leisure places for the people who live in Quanzhou.

The plan for a recreation area connecting the museums with West Lake Park is already partly realized. Each museum now has a vast public square that stretches towards the park. Moreover, a visitors' centre is currently being built at the foot of the mountain to cater to tourists who come to experience the scenic Qingyuan Mountain. There is a steady stream of visitors to the mountains, and West Lake Park is also popular with the local residents. The two museums, however, have so far only partly succeeded in becoming the leisure area portrayed in the information booklet. One of the curators explained it this way: 'Going to a museum is not part of the leisure culture that local residents enjoy.' Based on observations and interviews, however, I argue that there are two main reasons why the local townspeople are absent from the museums.

First, there is the question of accessibility. The opening up of the western district of Quanzhou is an ongoing project. Townspeople still speak of West Lake Park and the museum area as being 'far out of town'. As one of the museum employees put it: 'This place is too remote, there is nothing here, and behind us there is only countryside.' The cost of a taxi ride to the museums is more than twice the regular fare,[1] and the only bus line connecting the museums to the town centre was added in late 2006 and runs both infrequently and irregularly. Many townspeople have yet to visit either of the two new museums.

The second reason is admission policies. The Quanzhou Museum is open to all paying visitors, but the cost is ten *yuan*, which regular townspeople hold to be a steep price for a one-time admission. In 2005, the Quanzhou Museum hosted a dinosaur exhibition for children in the hope that this would attract more visitors.

Because of extensive production costs, the ticket price for the exhibition ended up being as much as thirty *yuan*, which would make a trip to the museum a considerable expense for a Quanzhou family. This may explain why the exhibition failed to attract the number of visitors expected by the museum administration. The Mintaiyuan Museum is free of charge, but this does not make the collection more accessible. Visits must be booked in advance, preferably by a representative from the relevant work unit (*danwei*) or a travel agency. When I asked the local China Travel Agency for information about the museum, they were not able to provide me with information about opening hours or how to get there. As of 2007, neither of the Quanzhou museums had employees responsible for information directed towards the public or the local service sector. As a result, information about the museum collections and the occasional events organized by the museums fails to reach the general populace.

Why build museums, and for whom?

With a municipal population of some seven million and more than half a million residents in Quanzhou city proper, the museums have a potential audience. But as a consequence of deficient transportation, lack of information, and general inaccessibility, the main body of visitors to the museums now consists of pupils on excursions, delegations of officials, and a few organized tourist groups who all arrive in chartered minibuses or limousines. The text in the Quanzhou Museum information booklet echoes the official leisure ethic and its promotion of educational leisure. But the fact that the rhetoric of useful and goal-oriented leisure is used by the local administration does not mean that local people's leisure is at the heart of their concern. In this case it seems that the discourse of healthy leisure is merely utilized by local authorities as an alibi for the construction of a showy building complex.

Discussing the development of the museum area in an interview with a senior member of staff in the local culture sector, the interviewee claimed that the Quanzhou Museum was a mere 'image project' (*xingxiang gongcheng*) conceived by the local mayor's office in order to show off the wealth of the municipality. He compared the museum to other prestigious projects such as the building of big bridges or super highways. 'This museum was not initiated because the Mayor loves art and culture,' he said. 'If that were the case, the Mayor would have supplied the best developers, made sure that the entire infrastructure was planned in accordance with the needs of the museum, and head-hunted the most professional people to be in charge, luring them to Quanzhou with the promise of a big house, a car, a maid ... This was not the case.'

A similar comment was made by a curator in one of the older museums in the city centre, who criticized the local government for repeatedly utilizing the museum in its marketing of Quanzhou to tourists and investors. To her, these were just 'fine words' (*haohua*). In practice, the funding from the local bureau of finance covers little more than wages for the museum employees, and it is increasingly difficult for the museums to acquire funding for the development of new exhibitions. 'Nowadays, people expect to be entertained in a museum. They don't come out of an interest for history – it is not enough,' the curator explained and added: 'The displays need to be eye-catching; there must be some activities, pictures, maps. The displays that we have at present are simply not good enough.'

While the local government has provided museums as public places for leisure, museum curators in Quanzhou said that they lack the funding, experience and administrative skills needed to develop the kind of leisure centres that they themselves want their institutions to become. During my last visit to the Quanzhou Museum in the spring of 2007, the two-year-old museum was visibly worn. The paint in the entrance hall was blemished and cracked, and the stage in the conference hall had a fracture running along its length. In Quanzhou, there is clearly a discrepancy between the museum district as conceived by the local administration and the everyday reality of running the museums and attracting an audience.

In an article about urban development and culture policies in China, Carolyn Cartier presents a similar case from Shenzhen. Here, local authorities have invested in concert halls and other culture venues without paying much attention to whether or not these places are put to real use. Cartier holds that in contemporary China, 'the state's cultural economy has relied on the built environment as a basis for the definition of cultural development' (Cartier 2005: 67). She writes that in the case of Shenzhen, urban planners have taken for granted that '"culture" inherently exists in the space of a building' (Cartier 2005: 67). Thus, the existence of a culture centre has been understood as proof of the existence of 'culture'. My examples from Quanzhou support Cartier's theory that, in some cases, places for culture and leisure are built in order to prove the local administration's level of cultural competence, or in Bourdieu's terminology, their possession of cultural capital (Bourdieu 1986: 133). The aforementioned senior member of staff put it this way: '[T]he Mayor wanted a museum just like a rich man wants to show off his wealth by adorning himself with an expensive watch.' Quanzhou municipality can take pride in a number of museum buildings, both old and new. But as the lack of visitors to the museums indicates, the existence of designated buildings does not automatically facilitate leisure practices.

Space as a social product

In *The Production of Space*, Henri Lefebvre presents his theory of space as a social product. Lefebvre holds that space is neither 'empty' nor a passive receptacle, but a product of social agents – more specifically, a product of the undertakings of social engineers (Lefebvre 1991: 15, 87, 89, 190). Through their planning and administration, authorities (such as scientists, planners and technocrats) make abstractions of space. According to Lefebvre, this 'conceptualized' space conceived by the authorities is 'the dominant space in any society' (Lefebvre 1991: 38–9). Foucault regarded discursive formations as sets of rules which to a certain extent govern what we can talk about and how (Larsen and Munkgård Pedersen 2002: 18); Lefebvre ascribes a similar function to the conceptualized spaces produced by technocrats and planners. Thus, 'space' in Lefebvre's writing can be understood in terms of a dominant discourse that governs the ways ordinary people (users, inhabitants) may act and live out their lives in a given society. Lefebvre describes the production of social space in terms of a 'spatial economy', which

> [...] valorizes certain relationships between people in particular places (shops, cafés, cinemas etc.), and thus gives rise to connotative discourses concerning these places; these in turn generate 'consensuses' or conventions according to which, for example, such and such a place is supposed to be trouble-free, a quiet area where people go peacefully to have a good time, and so forth.
>
> (Lefebvre 1991: 56)

In Lefebvre's 'spatial economy', people's actions seem to be fully governed by the dominant discourses, consensuses and conventions conceived by the authorities. Lefebvre stresses, however, that 'even technocratic planners and programmers [...] cannot produce a space with a perfectly clear understanding of cause and effect, motive and implication' (Lefebvre 1991: 37). This means that even within Lefebvre's seemingly structuralist analysis of society, the domination of the authorities is far from total: there is room for people to act against or outside the consensuses and conventions of socially produced space. The museum district in Quanzhou is a case in point. At present, the realities of the Quanzhou museum area are far removed from the 'conceptualized space' presented in the information material. Local planners and administrators may have envisioned a museum area that would generate educational leisure activities, or, alternatively, an ensemble of impressive buildings that would prove the cultural capital of the municipality. However, it is important to note that the actions of the people of Quanzhou are not governed by the consensuses or conventions of this conceptualized leisure space. In her reading of Lefebvre, Mayfair Yang points out that the spatial practices of ordinary people and the authorities' representations of space are different aspects of the same space, and that resistance takes place not outside the space of power, but constitutes an alternative 'order of power' within the shared space (Mayfair Yang 2004: 725–6). In Quanzhou we see that the museums have thus far failed to generate the type of visitors' interest that the planners envisioned. At the same time, local townspeople have appropriated the public square in front of the Mintaiyuan Museum as their new favourite leisure spot, and thereby contributed in their own way to the production of the local leisure space. The following section analyses why townspeople have taken up leisure practices in this particular square.

The characteristics of a leisure place

The public square in front of the Mintaiyuan Museum has colourful ornaments and musical water fountains. During the day, women from the nearby village areas take young children there to play, and on Sundays and public holidays the square swarms with people flying kites, enjoying the musical fountains, and purchasing snacks from the many vendors whose carts line the periphery of the square. The neighbouring Quanzhou Museum faces its own public square, which stretches all the way to the northern entrance of West Lake Park. This ground is paved with local stone and adorned with stone carvings and flower displays, as

Figure 4.2 'Leisure square. No parking!'

well as a sign that reads 'Leisure square. No parking!' (*Xiuxian guangchang, jinzhi tingche*). Now and again a motorbike or a cart will cross the square, as does the occasional transport of visitors to the museum, but I never observed a single person at leisure in this 'leisure square'.

Both squares have the same transportation challenges as the museum area in general: the distance to the town centre is significant and buses are few. Also, both squares were completed in 2006 and should thus enjoy the same novelty status. What makes the Mintaiyuan Square a place where leisure practices bloom, while the leisure square' in front of the Quanzhou Museum functions primarily as a thoroughfare?

The decoration of Mintaiyuan Square is eye-catching. There is an impressive water mirror flanked by 48 imaginatively designed pillars covered in colourful porcelain mosaics. At the weekends and on national holidays, visitors can take pleasure in a fountain display that moves in time to classical music streaming from loudspeakers around the square. The square is spacious enough for kite-flying, which is enjoyed by young and old, especially at weekends. You can also see people squatting by the fountain and the row of pillars, talking or simply watching the lively scene (*kan renao*). Mintaiyuan Square has become a place where people go to socialize, relax and have fun (*wan*).

The 'leisure square' in front of the Quanzhou Museum does not share in this atmosphere at all. The grey stone square pales in comparison to its multi-coloured neighbour. Moreover, half of the square is closed off behind the museum's monumental gate, which also houses a ticket booth and security personnel. The gates and the thoroughfare make the square less welcoming than the spatially inviting Mintaiyuan Square.

While the distance from the town centre makes both squares equally inconvenient as leisure places for local townspeople, Mintaiyuan Square has attractions that Quanzhou Museum Square lacks. This shows that, although a place may be relatively inaccessible, the attraction of opportunities for relaxation, socializing and *renao* is enough to catch people's interest. Thus far, the attractions inside the museums fail to conjure the kind of resonance among local people that the lively Mintaiyuan Museum Square does.

An example similar to the case of the museum squares can be observed in the Quanzhou city centre. Fengze Square is an open circular area with a stunning marble sculpture at its centre. The circular staircase at the base of the statue is a popular meeting place, and also provides welcome rest for tired shoppers entering and leaving the mall that lines the square. In May 2006, Maritime Silk Road Square was opened across the road from Fengze Square. This new square is situated in a narrow ravine between a twenty-storey hotel and an equally tall apartment complex. Five monumental statues illustrating the hallmarks of Quanzhou's culture and history fill up the narrow space and make the square seem overcrowded. At its opening in the spring of 2006, a local paper welcomed this square as a 'splendid destination for the sightseeing and leisure of townspeople and tourists alike' ('"Haisi" diaosu...' *DNZB* 10 April 2006). I never observed anyone lingering in the square or admiring the artwork. The square is built as a

76 *Leisure in the Quanzhou cityscape*

Figure 4.3 Kite-flying on a Sunday afternoon at Mintaiyuan Museum Square.

lid over the city sewers, and because of the considerable weight of stone statues (Chen Xiangmu 2006), the material chosen for these sculptures is concrete covered in gilded paint. Several people expressed their disappointment at how cheap the statues look. Some also hinted that the square was a project initiated by one of the vice mayors with the sole purpose of promoting Quanzhou's brand name status as the 'starting point of the historical Maritime Silk Road' (*Haishang sichouzhilu de qi dian*). Others held that the square and the statues are part of the adjacent hotel's recent redecoration project. Regardless of whether the square was conceived by local politicians to promote the city's image or by a hotel investor in search of new customers, the fact remains that Maritime Silk Road Square fails to attract sightseers and townspeople in search of leisure. The two squares are conveniently situated in the new part of the city centre; they are accessible and open to everyone. But while Fengze Square facilitates both relaxation and opportunities for people to chat and watch the *renao*, Maritime Silk Road now functions mainly as a much needed parking space for hotel guests.

Convenience and attraction

Looking at a variety of leisure places in Quanzhou, it becomes clear that in order for there to be a successful leisure place, what is needed is a balanced combination of convenience (location, accessibility, cost, benefit) and attractions (novelty, relaxation, entertainment, *renao*, an opportunity to socialize), as the following examples further demonstrate.

Leisure can be practiced in the most unlikely places. Every morning around nine o'clock, a group of middle-aged men gather to play cards on the steps of a local branch of the China Construction Bank. These men are day labourers and motorbike taxi drivers. At nine, the rush hour is over and business is slowing

Figure 4.4 Young workers watching the *renao* at Fengze Square.

Figure 4.5 Playing cards on the steps outside China Construction Bank.

down. This gives these men a chance to snatch a moment of leisure while waiting for customers and prospective employers to approach them. The reason the men gather in this particular spot is that the number of residents and businesses in the area increases the likelihood of getting a job offer. At the same time, they obviously prefer spending their time in the company of peers, playing cards and chatting, rather than sitting on their bikes waiting to be approached. Whether or not this practice is best described as leisure depends on how we define work and leisure. I argue that although these drivers are compelled to wait at the crossroads, their card-playing is to a certain extent comparable to the practices of office clerks who drink tea with friends, read novels or play computer games in the workplace, as discussed in Chapter 2. The steps in front of the bank prove to be a convenient leisure place for these men, as it is close to job opportunities and provides relaxation and the opportunity to socialize – and in addition, the chance to win a few *yuan* in the game.

Most neighbourhoods (*xiaoqu*) in Quanzhou have a small designated area with simple exercise equipment where residents can work out. Before office hours, this is a place for the exercising early birds, but in the late morning and after lunch housewives and grandmothers flock there with their children and grandchildren. The work-out machines are a novelty in Quanzhou and are quite popular among the increasingly health-conscious populace. The exercise grounds function the way the urban planners intended, as places for exercise. Inadvertently, however, these areas also function as a place for small talk and play.

Next to the exercise area in Park Drive *xiaoqu* there is a small kiosk where the residents can buy their newspapers and magazines. This kiosk is also a leisure place where people stop for gossip and friendly chats with neighbours and the saleswoman. The kiosk is open from half past eight in the morning until eleven at night. Not surprisingly, the kiosk and the area surrounding it is the site for both work and leisure for the saleswoman. In the morning hours, she spends time with other women in the exercise area and walks over to the kiosk whenever a customer approaches. In the evenings, a group of friends gathers inside the small booth to play cards with her. These are often the same group of people, but passers-by also frequently lean over the counter to follow the card game and shout out their advice on how to play a good hand. In Park Drive *xiaoqu*, the kiosk and its exercise area are convenient leisure places for the residents. They provide accessible no-cost entertainment and an opportunity to socialize close to home.

The level of expense involved is significant for the kinds of leisure activities people in Quanzhou are able to pursue. Xiao Li, who sells tea leaves out of a small shop in one of the poorer quarters in Quanzhou, mentioned several times that she would like to take her daughter and sister for a day trip to the Qingyuan Mountain. She reckoned that the tickets alone would set her back 80 *yuan*, and so she has yet to take the trip. For Xiao Li and her family, going to Qingyuan Mountain or to Quanzhou Museum would mean a considerable expense in itself. The day trip would also mean the loss of one day's income for the tea shop, which she runs by herself. For the white-collar middle class the cost of a ticket to Qingyuan Mountain or even a half-year pass is of little significance. Nevertheless, as will be discussed in more detail in Chapter 8, even people with good incomes often prefer to access the mountain via 'secret' paths in order to avoid the ticket booths. Similarly, in Quanzhou, people tend to choose karaoke spots where they have a VIP card or can otherwise get a discount, even if the choice of this spot means that they will need to take a taxi to get there. The choice is motivated not so much by thrift as by the enjoyment and status involved in making a bargain. To flaunt a VIP card with a considerable discount is appreciated by one's peers, and the practice of borrowing membership cards and pin codes from colleagues, friends and relatives is widespread. This means that the karaoke spots that offer a discount programme that leaves the customer with a sense of a good bargain are especially attractive among prospective customers.

The utility of a social network (*guanxi*) in this context is considerable, and not only in order to enjoy leisure activities at a bargain price. Some leisure events can be accessed only by way of *guanxi*. This is especially true of the shows and performances organized by the local bureau of culture during the Maritime Silk Road Culture Festival or in celebration of the Chinese New Year and other major festivals. Tickets for these shows, featuring acclaimed local opera troupes, traditional marionette art and popular singers and actors, are not for sale. Tickets are free of charge and are distributed through the system of government work units and via personal connections. Shows of this kind receive much attention and acclaim in the local press, but the fact that this entertainment is a government-sponsored benefit for a circle of well-connected people is never mentioned. This example serves to show how access to leisure entertainment in Quanzhou relies not only on personal income but also on a network of social connections.

The leisure place in Quanzhou that attracts most people is the area along and east of Zhongshan Road, together with Confucius Temple Square (*Fuwenmiao guangchang*) and the grounds surrounding the Workers' Culture Palace (*Gongren wenhuagong*) and the Tongfo Temple (*Tongfo si*). This is where people of all ages go to enjoy window-shopping, cafés and book cafés, listen to live traditional music, or simply watch the *renao*. For years the temple square was occupied by a vegetable market, but in 2000 the local government invested 120 million *yuan* in its restoration (Huang Shuikan 2005: 91–2). The area now doubles as a centre for the local tourism industry and a public leisure place enjoyed by both locals and visitors. In the early mornings, people from the surrounding neighbourhoods meet at the square or by the small lake next to the Culture Palace to practice *taijiquan*, play badminton and do other kinds of exercise. In the late mornings, the lush trees by the Culture Palace give shade to card players, and on some days, a small choir that consists of elderly and retired people can be found beneath the trees. Along the lakeside and inside the courtyard of the nearby Tongfo Temple, the elderly meet to play *majiang*, drink tea, worship and gossip in the mornings and early afternoons. This is also the place to get a shoeshine, and a range of spectacles and false teeth are also on offer from the vendors there.

Towards the evening, younger people fill the streets, often in groups, in search of affordable fashion items and novelty snacks. In Confucius Temple Square, two outdoor stages present performances of the local *nanyin* song tradition. The audiences are offered seats and a cup of tea free of charge. The *nanyin* performances are most popular among the elderly, but as the performers are mostly young women in their twenties, they also attract an audience of younger friends and acquaintances. Families come to the area during the weekends when the temple square is a veritable fairground, offering bumper cars, a tiny shooting gallery and other activities for children. During annual holidays and festivals, the area around Confucius Temple Square and the Workers' Culture Palace is a spectacle of outdoor amateur performances, traditional riddle-guessing and food stalls offering delicacies from all over China. This is also where the townspeople go to watch the displays of colourful paper lanterns during the Lantern Festival, which the locals boast of as being the most *renao* festival in this part of Fujian. Access to these grounds as well as the *nanyin* performances are free of charge and open to everyone, and the cost involved in the funfair rides for the children is insignificant. Bus lines from all over town stop at or nearby the square and the Culture Palace, which is often where people agree to meet when they plan to go out together.

While the local administration plans for a new leisure area west of the contemporary city centre, the leisure map by which Quanzhou townspeople navigate still centres on the historical layout of the city centre. Nevertheless, a closer look at Quanzhou's changing urban space shows that the expansion of the city limits and new residence patterns influence the ways townspeople think about and move around in the cityscape.

Changing practices in a changing cityscape

Until the beginning of the twentieth century, Quanzhou retained its design as a fortified town with seven gates and a town centre oriented by an axis running from south to north. In 1921 the local bureau of public works was established, and the task of mapping and surveying began in order to facilitate improved transportation and sewage systems.[2] The city walls were gradually torn down, and the final blow came in 1939 when town walls all over Fujian were demolished in order to make the towns less visible to Japanese bombers. During the 1920s, broadened concrete roads were introduced. Among these was the new central axis of the town, which since the Anti-Japanese war has been known as Zhongshan Road. The site for early car traffic, the town's first cinema and the local Red Guard headquarters, this road has been the centre of activities in Quanzhou from the Republican era and throughout the Mao era.

Throughout the years, the Confucius temple complex on Zhongshan Road has been the site of several cultural institutions and has thereby retained its central position in the cityscape. In the period from 1958 to 1982 it was the home of the Quanzhou Library (Quanzhou shi tushuguan 1991: 1), the Young People's Culture Palace (*Qingshaonian wenhuagong*) was situated there from 1981 to 1998, and until 1985 it also housed the Quanzhou Museum. While the Quanzhou Museum has been relocated to the new museum area in the western periphery of Quanzhou, the library and the Young Peoples' Culture Palace have been moved east, to the new city district of Fengze. The activities of the Youth League and the Young Volunteers' Association as well as the many weekend classes for children now take place in a designated building across from Fengze Square. Fengze district (*qu*) was established in 1997, and I was told that when the Young Peoples' Culture Palace was moved to Fengze in 1998, people were frustrated because, at that time, Fengze was held to be 'far out of town'. With its popular mall and inviting public plaza, Fengze Square has now become a new nodal point in Quanzhou, often referred to as the 'new city centre' (*xin chengshi zhongxin*). This is mainly due to the many residential neighbourhoods built in this new district since the beginning of the 1990s.

People who live in the new Fengze neighbourhoods have a variety of shops and restaurants from which to choose, and transportation to and from the central leisure area around Zhongshan Road is convenient and cheap. In practice, Fengze is no longer 'far out of town'. With its shopping malls, culture institutions, and accessible transport, the Fengze district has become part of the larger inner-city centre which is now steadily gravitating from the central Zhongshan Road towards Fengze in the east. This shows how the new residence patterns combined with transportation and commercial activity influence townspeople's perceptions of centre and periphery in their hometown. New neighbourhoods have also been built in the vicinity of the West Lake Park, but people who live in the western part of town complain about the lack of transportation and shopping opportunities in the area. Thus far, both the museum district and the neighbourhoods in the western part of Quanzhou are far removed from the city centre, and a sense of a 'new' centre has yet to be realized in this part of town.

It is not only the distribution of residences and shopping areas that is shifting in Quanzhou. Qingyuan Mountain is another leisure place which has gained a new position on the Quanzhou leisure map. Old Xie, a man in his seventies who grew up in the southern part of town, told me that when he was in primary school their class would go on an excursion to Qingyuan Mountain once a year. 'Our school was down by the river near South Gate, and I remember that I thought back then that to walk to the mountain was *very* far. And it was three or four kilometres,' he said, and added that '[...] hiking on Qingyuan Mountain was not part of everyday life until 20 years ago.' The reminiscences of this elderly man tell us that his subjective perception of the distance between the city centre and the mountain area has changed. Moreover, his small anecdote indicates how Quanzhou people's leisure habits have also changed: going to the mountain really has become part of everyday life. Whereas Xie as a young pupil had to walk the distance, Quanzhou inhabitants can now take one of several bus lines, hire a taxi, or even drive their own cars up to the mountain. In effect, the mountain has moved closer to the city. And, as a consequence, the mountain has become a major site for townspeople in search of recreation and exercise.

The gravitation of Quanzhou city centre towards the east is not only a result of the need to provide new housing for a growing city population, but also part of long-term plans for a greater urban Quanzhou that stretches along the eastern coastline of the municipality. The municipal administration itself is expected to move from its present location close to Zhongshan Road to the easternmost part of Fengze district. Two new institutions of higher learning are already in place in the eastern suburbs, and several villa (*bieshu*) areas are under construction. The local authorities also plan to relocate Quanzhou Library to this future municipal government complex. The director of the library was critical of these plans. He compared the situation to that of the new museums, saying that the area by West Lake 'would also be a good spot for the library, but on the other hand, it is far out of town. A museum is not somewhere you go every day, and so the spot is okay for their use, but for a library ... the ideal place is in the middle of town.' While the urban planners in the local government conceive of a new administrative centre which is geographically closer to the industrialized areas in the municipality, the library director feared that relocation would mean moving the library away from where people live. His vision for the new Quanzhou library is a network of smaller branches that would be easily accessible to the town population in general. His assessment of the easternmost city suburbs was that 'only few people actually live in that district, [and] we should think carefully about whom the library is to serve'.

Some affluent families have moved out to these suburbs already, but as public transportation is scarce at best, they rely on private cars to get to and fro. Many of the villa settlements are veritable ghost towns, where empty houses have been left to decay pending the construction of shopping facilities, restaurants and office complexes. At present, a second generation of investors buy deserted, mouldy villas from disappointed owners, and it is doubtful whether public works and commercial activity will reach the area in time for the second owners' villa dreams to be realized. For now, all development hinges on the moving of the municipal government. As for the future of Quanzhou Library, the library director stated that this is all up to the mayor. According to him, the library itself, and even the Bureau of Culture, has little or no influence over its relocation: 'When the leadership says "here", then that's where it will be' (*lingdao shuo 'nali', jiu nali*).

The analysis of some of the public leisure places in Quanzhou indicates that there is a limit to the authority of city planners when it comes to shaping people's everyday life practices in the changing cityscape. To use Lefebvre's terms, the notions of centre and periphery in Quanzhou depend not solely on how space is 'conceived' and 'produced' by local authorities (Lefebvre 1991: 26, 40). The 'lived' practices of the townspeople who are the users of transportation networks, leisure places and residential areas are also an important factor in the production of the local leisure space. Moreover, if the building of the new museum area in Quanzhou is indeed the result of a mayor's desire to make a display of the material and cultural capital of the city, then the discourse of leisure for the 'life-long education of citizens' in the museum brochure cannot be taken as proof that the local administration governs in observance of the official leisure ethic. If the museum area was conceived as an 'image project', the data from Quanzhou serves as an illustration of how local government units pay lip-service to a leisure discourse that is not, in fact, the principle governing their actions and policies.

A closer examination of the above examples shows that there exist two divergent narratives concerning how the Quanzhou leisure space is governed. If we consider the local people's practices described above as one narrative of the local leisure space, this narrative tells us that Quanzhou townspeople utilize urban leisure places as they themselves see fit. People use the museum area as a place for socializing and kite-flying rather than visiting the museums' collections; and despite the planned repositioning of the city centre, the area close to Zhongshan Road remains the centre of Quanzhou inhabitants' leisure and social life. However, both the library director and the senior member of staff who accused the mayor of initiating a mere 'image project' cast the local mayor in the role of an autocratic ruler who can rearrange the cityscape at his own discretion. This second narrative is one of despotic rule. How do we explain the coexistence of these conflicting images of local authorities' command over the leisure space?

This question brings us back to Jing Wang, who characterizes the regulatory practices of the Chinese authorities as being sometimes 'merely rhetorical, at other times, consequential' (Jing Wang 2001a: 38). In their regulation of the field of leisure, Chinese authorities make use of both rhetorical devices and direct intervention. As I will argue in the following chapters, when seeking to guide the population towards the kinds of healthy leisure that serve to bolster the discourse of civility (*wenming*), the authorities rely mainly on propagation through the media and through slogans and poster campaigns. However, when dealing with leisure activities that, according to the official leisure ethic, are detrimental to the development of the Chinese population, local authorities do exercise consequential regulatory power.

Detailed study of the instances when the leisure ethic unquestionably informs the authorities' supervision of the field of leisure increases our understanding of the impact of official discourses on the lives of ordinary people. The following chapters therefore analyse a range of popular leisure practices, both healthy and chaotic, and the different strategies the authorities adapt in order to regulate them.

5 'Healthy leisure' in transition

In January 2007, Quanzhou's Bureau of Education, in cooperation with one of the local newspapers, suggested the following leisure activities to ensure a 'healthy, safe, and happy' (*jiankang, anquan, you yiyi*) New Year holiday for middle school students: reading novels; and writing essays about one's education plans or the ongoing construction of a Harmonious Quanzhou ('Hanjia...' *HXDSB*, 31 January 2007, B3). In the spring of the same year, a row of colourful posters outside the Quanzhou Library encouraged passers-by to 'Surf the Internet in a healthy manner and keep net addiction at a distance' (*jiankang shangwang yuanli wangyin*). These are examples of how local state-run institutions communicate the logics of the leisure ethic to the Quanzhou public. Both texts

Figure 5.1 Young and old reading and relaxing in one of Quanzhou's book cafés.

seek to promote so-called healthy (*jiankang*) leisure practices, and do so by making allusions to the dangers of the conversely unhealthy practices (the threat of an unsafe holiday, or net addiction). In this regard, these texts echo Chinese leisure scholars' scepticism towards popular culture, and towards leisure practices in which ordinary people engage without proper guidance, as discussed in Chapter 3. At the level of discourse, the impression is that the provision of healthy leisure is a public concern. In practice, however, little is done by Quanzhou authorities to facilitate healthy activities for the local townspeople. People in Quanzhou do practice leisure activities that are healthy according to the leisure ethic, such as reading, self-study, outdoor sports, or participation in social associations. But, importantly, they mostly do so without any significant support or funding from the government.

This chapter centres on two distinct parts of the Quanzhou leisure sphere, each in its own way exemplifying the conditions that shape so-called healthy leisure activities at a local level. The first example discusses how and why privately run bookshops have taken over the function of public libraries. In Quanzhou, book cafés (*shuba*, lit. 'book bar') are now the chief facilitators of reading as an educational or a purely recreational leisure activity. The second part analyses the relationships between the local government and organized leisure groups, both the 'popular' organizations (*minjian shetuan*)[1] which are directly linked to the Party apparatus, and those groups or associations that exist outside the Party realm. These cases serve to demonstrate that the organization of healthy leisure activities in Quanzhou relies increasingly on the infrastructure of the commercial leisure market and the informal networks and resources of committed individuals. This means that while the leisure ethic may dominate the official PRC discourse on leisure, local authorities do very little in the way of actively steering the populace in the direction of a 'healthy' leisure life.

The decline of the library and the rise of the book café

> The library is the knowledge treasury of mankind; books make up the ladder of historical progress. Would you like to climb this ladder to the highest peak of scientific knowledge?

This is how Quanzhou Library presented itself to readers in a 1991 brochure. The quote equates reading with the promise of progress, which is the central aim of the PRC leisure ethic. The act of reading is here regarded as having a clear purpose, namely the steady upward progress of the Chinese populace in the 'scientific' manner upheld by the Chinese party-state. Chinese leisure scholars express a similar concern for the development of the Chinese populace, and persistently promote reading and self-study as 'healthy' (*jiankang*) pursuits along with such activities as sports, appreciation of the arts, travel and going to museums (Zhang Jian 2004: 210; Sun Xiaoli 2004: 78–9; Ma Huidi 2004a: Ch. 5 especially). In these contexts, the public library is regarded as the designated place for reading and for the acquisition of reading materials, a perspective which explains why Ma Huidi so strongly laments the fact that in the period from 1996 to 2001, the number of library loans and library card holders in China's major cities was declining. These data have lead Ma to the conclusion that the Chinese public – and young people especially – are losing their interest in books and reading (Ma Huidi 2004a: 156; Yu Guangyuan and Ma Huidi 2006: 88). However, it is also the case that Chinese readers flock to privately run bookshops in search of reading materials and a comfortable place to read. By shifting the perspective from the library to the readers and reading as a leisure practice, the following analysis shows that it is in fact the role of the library as a public institution that is diminishing, not people's interest in reading.

Were have all the readers gone?

Quanzhou Library is located on a central street in the newest part of the city centre. Overlooking a park and situated within easy walking distance of bus stops, a movie theatre and popular shopping streets, I expected the library to be considered a familiar landmark among local inhabitants. To my surprise, few of the people I met during my period of fieldwork in Quanzhou knew where the library was. Those who knew of the main library were seldom aware of the newly erected district branch in the liveliest part of the old town centre. Quanzhou Library has a local history collection, a reading room with old and new editions of a range of newspapers and magazines, and a general collection of fiction and reference material – all in all a collection of 800,000 volumes. In addition, the library runs an Internet café with web access for library card holders. The building is ventilated through open windows and hatches, which leaves the books mouldy in summertime and the staff and readers frozen during winter. When I visited the library for the first time in 2005, parts of the collection were stored in piles on the sixth floor of the building, while the more popular titles were made available on shelves that were moved closer and closer to each other to make space for new acquisitions. Local government units have approved of plans to build a new library (Quanzhou shi gongcheng zixun gongsi: 2002), but the project has thus far not been given priority by the local government.

In interviews, one of the librarians stated that Quanzhou Library's current funding was far from sufficient. The director of the library claimed that the funding from the local treasury 'followed the positive development in the Chinese economy in general', and that even if books have become more expensive than before, the economic situation of the library had not changed. Mr Hu, a retired cadre from the Bureau of Culture, who had himself been involved in re-establishing Quanzhou Library after the Cultural Revolution, claimed that the economic situation for the library had worsened over the years. According to him, local libraries now struggle to find money to pay for electricity, not to mention new books. 'The library was supposed to "serve the people",' said Hu, referring to the old Communist Party slogan. He then added a comment typical of a disillusioned old cadre: 'The people who work there are satisfied with doing as little as possible – they will get their pay anyway, no matter how few people actually use the facilities.' The number of visitors to Quanzhou Library decreased from more than 20,000 each month in 1991 (Quanzhou shi tushuguan 1991: 2) to a mere 5,000–6,000 in 2006. The library director described their institution as a 'place for culture and leisure' (*wenhua xiuxian changsuo*), but apart from the ten to 15 elderly men who were returning visitors to the newspaper reading room, I encountered very few people in the library. Whenever I passed through the general collection, the place seemed deserted and remarkably silent.

The data from the Quanzhou libraries suggest the same tendency as recorded by Ma, namely that the Chinese government's investment in public library facilities is insufficient, and fewer people use the libraries (Ma Huidi 2004a: Ch. 5). Even if fewer people use public libraries, this does not necessarily mean that the actual number of readers is decreasing. While libraries experience a drop in the number of loans and visitors, privately run bookshops have become important leisure places for the reading public in China. Foreign visitors to Chinese bookshops are often surprised not only by the number of customers, but also by the way customers squat leisurely between the bookshelves to read and even make notes from the reading materials on display (Meyer: 2005). In later years, larger bookshops in China have introduced chairs and tables to facilitate these reading habits. These book cafés also offer reasonably priced snacks and drinks which add significantly to the booksellers' earnings. Although book cafés in China are usually run by the same management as the bookstore in question, the layout of the café areas resemble those found in larger bookstore chains in Europe and the US: a defined space with a number of small tables and a counter where the customers can order refreshments. In the US, the first book café opened in Washington in 1976 (Livingston 1981 in Miller 1999: 399), and the in-store café has now become an indispensable part of the 'bookstore "experience"' as it is marketed by both superstores and independent booksellers in North America (Miller 1999: 397, 399). When asked about sources of inspiration, none of the bookstore managers in Quanzhou referred to the book café as an international trend. Famous bookstores in Beijing and Shanghai were mentioned by one manager, but the main inspiration in the Quanzhou book market was a pioneer bookstore manager who opened a book café in the nearby town of Dehua and later brought his business idea to the city of Quanzhou.

In 2007, three of Quanzhou's privately run bookshops had sizeable book cafés, the smallest of which had 15 tables. The largest makes up roughly one-third of the 2,000 m^2 Book City ('Citonghua tushu cheng' 2007: 60), and has a well-equipped snack bar, three tables placed in view of an artificial brook, and a small elevated area with a white grand piano on display. 'Up till 1999, people seldom went to the bookshop to read,' says Mr Gong, the current manager. 'After book cafés were introduced, people have come to think of them as similar to their own living rooms or studies.' At weekends, couples with children are a frequent sight in Quanzhou book cafés, but during weeknights, chairs and tables are occupied by high school and college students who enjoy the opportunity to read extracurricular materials for free. Young employees of overseas trading companies often use the book cafés after-hours in order to work on their language proficiency or increase their understanding of business management. People meet in the book cafés to talk business, to date, or to meet with friends over a cup of tea.

Data concerning reading and book sales in big-city China point in different directions. Time-allocation surveys show that the amount of time Beijingers in general spend studying or reading papers and books is decreasing significantly (Wang Qiting *et al.* 2004: 146).[2] These data echo the decline in library loans. But in contrast, the amount of money Beijing households spent on books rose during the period 1992–8 (Zhang Taiyuan 2007: 105). Moreover, in a 1998 survey involving respondents from big cities such as Shanghai, Shenzhen, Tianjin, and Wuhan, reading ranked as one of the most popular leisure activities, second only to watching TV (Shaoguang Wang *et al.* 2006: 318). According to the *New York Times*, sales figures from book retail have recently earned China the title of 'the world's fastest-growing book market' (Meyer: 2005), and the Chinese publication industry has seen an annual growth rate of 8–10 per cent since the mid-1990s ('Just how big...' *Beijing Review* 3 March 2005). Juxtaposed, the data show that Chinese consumers buy more reading materials than ever before while at the same time the number of minutes they spend reading each day is decreasing. The field research for this study cannot satisfactorily explain the evident contradiction between the decreasing time spent on reading and the increase in book sales. The increasing amount of online reading material and the role of net surfing as a possible substitution for more traditional leisure reading add to the complexity of this phenomenon. Here it is sufficient to point out that it is doubtful whether quantitative survey studies with their clear-cut categories of 'shopping', 'reading' and 'social interaction' (for examples, see Wang Yihong 2005: 52–3; Wang Qiting *et al.* 2004: 146) can account for the mixture of consumption, reading and socializing that takes place in Chinese bookshops today. Consider the following extracts from interviews with readers in the Book City book café:

'Going to the bookshop is my leisure of choice,' says Ms Chen, a PhD in her late thirties. She often takes her daughter book-shopping on the weekends, or rather, they go out to 'read in the bookshops' (*qu shudian kan shu*). By this, she means that they will 'stay there the whole afternoon, read for a while, buy some books, have some snacks in the book café, and then read some more'. The example of Ms Chen serves as an illustration of the many cases where there is no clear distinction between shopping and reading as a leisure activity. The role of the book café as a place to combine reading with relaxation and socialization is also evident in the example of Ms Dai, a returning customer in several of the Quanzhou book cafés. Ms Dai works in a local enterprise and visits book cafés two or three times a month, usually when she is escorting her child to an afternoon art class. When her work requires it, she will read books relevant to her profession and take notes for later use in articles and reports at work. When given the opportunity, she chooses new publications and also more relaxing titles. Most times she reads in the book café, but she also confided that she 'sometimes return[s] home with a whole stack of purchases from the bookstore'. She often comes to Book City alone, but also told me that 'when my friends and I have not seen each other for a while we may say "What about meeting in the book café?" and then we'll sit there and have good talk...'. The day I interviewed her, Ms Dai was accompanied by Mr Jiang, an old classmate of hers who is an employee in the local district administration. To him, going to book cafés was 'both a hobby and a habit'. He added that 'when there's little to do at work, or whenever I have time, I come here to the book café to read or have a little chat'.

These examples show that people go to bookshops in order to read, but also that spending time in a book café can be a leisure activity in itself, much like going to a café or a tea house. In addition, visiting a bookshop can be the conclusion to a round of window-shopping, as in the case of Ms Fang. She has the habit of ending her frequent stints of window-shopping with a visit to one of her two favourite book cafés. Some times she also goes to the book café to study. Working with foreign trade, it is important for her to sustain and improve her language skills, and so she reads English or French as least once a week. To Ms Fang, the abundance of self-study materials – and the opportunity to enjoy refreshments and music while reading – makes the in-store book café an ideal environment for studying. Moreover, for young adults like Ms Fang, the book café also offers a more comfortable place to spend time after work or during lunch hours than do the tiny flats or dorm rooms provided by companies and work units. The use of the book café as an alternative to spending time at home among young people was evident on weeknights and afternoons, when Quanzhou's book cafés were filled with middle school and college students bent over textbooks in pairs or small groups. One of the bookstore managers held that the book café attracts students because they have too many distractions at home (TV, computer etc.). In his mind, the book café environment offered them a more appropriate space for learning. From my observations and interviews, I conclude, however, that what brought young students to the book café was basically the opportunity to do homework together with classmates in an environment where they were not under the supervision of parents or teachers.

The bookshop as library cum *leisure place*

Looking at how readers spend time in these bookshops, one is tempted to ask whether these businesses primarily function as book sellers, coffee shops, or even libraries. At the opening of the 2,000 m² Quanzhou Book City in 2002, the store promoted itself as 'the first and largest private library in the whole country'.[3] Quanzhou Book City now offers different kinds of loan programs. On a regular borrower's card you can borrow a book at the cost of 0.3 *yuan* per day; to borrow a book for a year costs 106 *yuan*. Each customer can only borrow one volume at a time, and as of April 2006, an average of 5,000 volumes were on loan from this bookshop at any given time. The local city library operates on similar terms. Here, readers pay a deposit of either 50 or 100 *yuan* which entitles them to borrow two books for 21 days or four books for 30 days respectively. Even if the library's deposit is refundable, 'the bookshops always come out on top,' as one of the library employees stated. 'They have new books, and they can provide soft drinks and air conditioning. The library has neither.'

I asked book café customers whether or not they also used the local libraries. The answers below indicate how the increasing number of bookshops and the services that they provide have altered people's reading practices:

> Mr Jiang assessed the loan services in this way: 'The library is poorly managed, and by that I mean that the environment is not relaxing and you must pay a deposit for loans. In the bookshop you pay for the actual loans.' As a consequence, Jiang preferred the bookshops' loan services to that of the library. For the most part he borrowed books for his child, and at times he would also bring his child to the bookshop so that they could browse the shelves together.

> 'New books arrive too late in the library,' says Ms Dai. 'Some years ago, there were very few bookshops. At that time I did use the library. Now I only go there for information about things that happened in the 1980s or 1990s.'

> 'I live nearby, so I often come here [to Book City], sometimes as often as five times a week,' says Ms Dong, a young woman in her twenties who works in the food industry. She has been to both of the local libraries, but does not visit them often. She also does not buy books anymore, 'because now there are so many book cafés'.

> Ms Li, a college student who frequently goes to book cafés to read Japanese and to meet with friends, states that she never goes to the library, because 'the books are old, and they don't have the kind of books I like to read'.

> Comparing the library to her favourite bookshop, a local MA student told me that she would 'never go to the library to have a good time *(qu wan)*', only to look up material for her thesis.

The library is clearly losing its position as 'knowledge treasury', as well as its intended function as a place of culture and leisure. At the same time, reading as a leisure practice has gradually moved from the public libraries to the privately run commercial bookshops.

As discussed in the previous chapter, the physical environment is a significant part of the attraction when people choose to use a leisure place. Concerning the environment of Quanzhou Library, the director said that the fact that their building is deteriorating is only part of the problem; he also perceived a change in readers' expectations in terms of convenience and comfort. He explained that when the library was built in the late 1980s, 'demands were different. Now readers prefer an environment where they can relax, a place that is convenient and comfortable.' I asked him to explain what he meant by a 'comfortable environment', and he promptly listed the city's popular book cafés. The following quotes from book café customers confirm that a visit to a book café is not only about reading, but also about the chance to linger in pleasant surroundings:

> 'Book cafés have a certain elegance...,' says a doctor in his forties, currently reading a book on management. The nurse sitting across from him at the book café table had brought a medical manual, a notebook and pencils. 'I love to listen to music while I read,' she says, sipping her iced tea.

> 'I like the environment in the book café, and people who read are often cultured people (*suzhi gao*),[4] so I like to make friends here' says Mr Li, a young sales representative who comes to the book café five to six times each month to read and take notes for future reference. He also uses the local libraries frequently. According to Li, the most significant difference between the library and the bookshop is the interior.

The comfortable environment is an intrinsic part of the book cafés' attraction. But, as was concluded in the previous chapter, the success or failure of a leisure place rests on the right combination of both attraction and convenience or accessibility. Quanzhou's three book cafés and the two libraries are situated in the city centre and also in close proximity to each other. Moreover, neither the book cafés nor the libraries make use of advertisements or publicity campaigns to promote their services. The data from Quanzhou shows that the bookshops and libraries are equally accessible to the population, with one important exception: their opening hours.

The libraries in Quanzhou followed the rhythm of government offices in general: they were open from eight in the morning and closed for three hours at lunchtime. Afternoon hours were from two–thirty till five–thirty.[5] The libraries were open during weekends, but even so the limited opening hours on weekdays meant that the libraries were often closed during the period of the day when people generally have the most time for leisure activities. Quanzhou bookshops opened at ten in the morning and closed at ten-thirty at night. Their peak hours were from five in the afternoon onward, but lunchtime usually also brought a surge of customers. The extended opening hours made the bookshops more accessible as leisure places than the public libraries. This, together with the notion among readers that the libraries fail to provide new or interesting reading material, contributes towards the declining importance of the library in the leisure lives of Quanzhou readers. One of the local bookshop managers put it like this: 'The public libraries have not been able to keep up with the developments that have changed the way people live. Now, bookshops are the public libraries.'

'Charging the batteries'

The previous chapter concluded that lack of public information and facilitation made official places of leisure – such as museums and public squares – unattractive to the general public for practical reasons. The local libraries in Quanzhou seem to be facing the same challenge. The examples from the Book City book café confirm that even if fewer people make use of the space officially designated for reading, i.e. the library, this does not mean that people do not read. In their eagerness to bring attention to the fate of public libraries, leisure study scholars like Ma Huidi tend to overlook the novel-reading practices that take place in establishments outside the realm of official institutions. As a result, conclusions about the Chinese readership are made without taking into account the fact that bookshops and book cafés are increasingly popular in China. The official PRC leisure ethic is thus fuelled by the fear that the cultural competence (*suzhi*) of the Chinese people is inferior or failing. The anxiety caused by the notion that Chinese people do not read is linked to the overall concern for the intellectual capacity of the national workforce. In the official leisure discourse, reading is regarded as an educational activity that can serve to augment the cultural competence of the populace. However, as the above vignettes of bookshop customers indicate, some readers do use the book café as a site for self-study and educational reading, or 'charging the batteries', as it is sometimes called. Does this mean that the official leisure ethic, with its praise of reading as a healthy activity, finds resonance among the middle classes in Quanzhou? In order to answer this question, an analysis of the Chinese concept of 'charging the batteries' is needed.

A bookseller in his thirties gave me the following description of local inhabitants' willingness to invest in education: 'The economy in Quanzhou is quite developed, and people in this city have money on their hands. They are willing to spend on their child's education, and the young are eager to "charge their batteries" (*chongdian*)'. In this quote, the expression '*chongdian*' refers to a person's engagement in some form of education. In Quanzhou I also heard people use the term in a manner similar to the English expression 'to recharge your batteries', meaning to relax in order to restore one's physical and mental energies after hard work. However, in *New China Dictionary of Neologisms*, the term '*chongdian*' is listed as 'to supplement your knowledge and skills by way of study' (Shangwu yinshuguan cishu yanjiu zhongxin 2003: 35).[6] Its inclusion in a dictionary of new terms and phrases confirms that to use the expression 'recharging the batteries' in reference to continuing education or educational reading is rather new in Mandarin Chinese. During my period of field research I realized that many of my young contacts and interviewees were eager to recharge their batteries in the form of language studies or vocational reading.

According to Wang Yalin's 2003 survey of urban leisure, young Chinese urbanites (age 18 to 25) read more during their spare time than do other age groups, and young employees in the private sector devote more time to self-study and reading both during weekends and general work days than does any other group of employees (Wang Yalin 2003: 29, 77, 89). In Quanzhou, this trend among young adults was acknowledged by librarians and booksellers alike. One of the librarians who had been with Quanzhou Library since 1979 had the clear impression that young people in Quanzhou now spent more time reading than they did only few years ago. Even if most of the people who spent time reading in the library were elderly men, the librarian stated that the majority of their borrowers were actually younger people. Vocational textbooks and books on management and entrepreneurship make up a significant portion of the sales in local bookshops. At the same time, the collection of vocational literature also had the highest circulation in Quanzhou Library. As a consequence, the library now strives to supply more books of relevance to employees in local enterprises, especially in the areas of shoe and garment design and manufacturing. 'Young people need to increase their knowledge in their spare time in order to do well in their jobs,' said the librarian. 'They need to "charge their batteries".'

Whether or not the practice of charging the batteries should be regarded as a form of leisure depends on the criteria used to define leisure itself. If we by leisure mean 'spare time', charging the batteries is a leisure activity because it is something individuals do after-hours. However, if we look at leisure as an experience of 'freedom from demand' (Kleiber 1999: 4), this charging of batteries can hardly be regarded as a form of leisure. The need to charge the batteries is a demand from society (the labour market) rather than an experience the individual seeks for his or her own satisfaction. As stated in Chapter 2, this study analyses leisure as practices individuals pursue for the sake of pleasure or relaxation, including both activities that are apparently pointless and those that are decidedly goal-oriented. Therefore, when I insist that charging the batteries is an example of a leisure practice, I do so on the basis of the interviews and observations I made in the field. I found that in spite of the work involved, the new skills and knowledge interviewees gained from goal-oriented reading and self-study was for them a significant source of pleasure and self-esteem. From this perspective, the charging of batteries can be regarded as a leisure practice.

Young employees' increasing interest in self-study and vocational reading should be music to the ears of those who worry about the way Chinese people spend their time. However, the increased interest in self-study does not mean that young employees in Quanzhou subscribe to the leisure ethic in the sense that they want to develop their skills for the benefit of the Chinese nation. On the contrary, when I asked young professionals about their reasons for spending time on educational reading, the stated main objective was without exception the furthering of their individual careers. While some felt a need to increase their knowledge for the sake of new employment prospects, others spent time reading in order to do well in their present jobs. Earning enough to buy a flat or a car or to be able to travel was the rationale behind the choice of taking up more serious reading as a leisure activity.

With its incessant admonitions (Choose healthy leisure! Stay away from Internet cafés!) the PRC leisure ethic can to a certain extent be identified as an aspect of the disciplinary power by which Chinese authorities attempt to produce a 'submissive productive and trained source of labour power' (McNay 1994: 92). However, even if the PRC leisure ethic and the more overarching Chinese discourse of civility and civilization (*wenming*) (Anagnost 1997: Ch. 3) communicate strong imperatives concerning how the individual should spend his or her time and resources, the policies the local government in Quanzhou pursue in the field of leisure do not supply healthy forms of leisure with any efficiency. On the basis of my data I can therefore not conclude that the local government's policies and propaganda cause people in Quanzhou to pursue healthy forms of leisure. Nevertheless, the widespread interest among young white-collar employees for the 'charging of batteries' indicate that many individuals choose forms of leisure which agree with the leisure ethic discourse. Gary Gutting writes that within a disciplinary context, the thoughts of individuals take place 'in a space with a structure defined by a system of rules more fundamental than the assertions of the individuals thinking in the space' (Gutting 1994 in Neuman 2002: 37). In the context of contemporary China, this would mean that if and when people pursue educational leisure activities, they do so because of the structural conditions, not because of violent coercion. In other words, the *wenming* discourse and the many incentives for the population to increase their cultural competence together make up a space where self-study and continued education constitute the normalized trajectory for the urban white-collar worker in particular. In the cities along the southeastern coast of China, the reform-era economy has indeed created a situation where increased skills and education result in upward social mobility. I therefore argue that here, both the material conditions and the standards and values of official discourse serve to confirm the notion that increased qualification leads to better job opportunities and thus an increased quality of life. Under these circumstances, educational leisure becomes attractive in itself and needs but little active promotion and facilitation from the side of the authorities. The fact that none of my white-collar interviewees paid lip-service to the official leisure discourse, but presented their pursuit of foreign languages and vocational knowledge as something they did on their own accord, strengthens the impression that they were not consciously persuaded by any authority to make the 'right' leisure choices. They were simply doing what they perceived as normal from the perspective of young clerks aspiring to a relatively comfortable (*xiaokang*) way of life.

One of the few times I heard the rhetoric of the leisure ethic echoed in an interviewee's statements was when discussing leisure with one of Quanzhou's many migrant workers, a Sichuanese waiter in his early twenties. He had lately become much influenced by a friend who encouraged him to read books and to try to start up an enterprise for himself. At the time, this young waiter was spending most of the hours between work shifts reading, either in his dorm room or in the local bookstores. Before he took up this new habit of reading he was 'having far too much "fun" (*wan*)', he told me. He said that his former lifestyle had become boring to him. It was just 'working, playing cards, drinking, sleeping, working,' he said, adding that he felt he had 'wasted a lot of time' (*langfeile hen duo shijian*). He had now taken to reading reads books on economy, investment and entrepreneurship, and called his self-study an investment in his brain (*dui naozi de touzi*).

This young waiter expressed remorse for his former life of pointless 'fun'. Moreover, the spirit of entrepreneurship which characterized his present lifestyle could very well serve as a model of the leisure ethic were it not for the goal of his efforts. When reading is promoted in the context of the leisure ethic, it is praised as an activity that contributes towards the gross national product and the strengthening of the overall competence of the Chinese population. Even if his actions arguably contribute toward the general 'quality' of the populace, the young waiter's goals were less lofty: he wanted to earn more money for himself, and he dreamt of starting up a business. Similarly, when young white-collar workers in Quanzhou recharged their batteries through self-study, their hope was that this investment in their brains would earn them a better livelihood, or make it possible to maintain a higher standard of living. In this respect, their reasoning follows the 'economistic' thinking upon which the PRC leisure ethic rests, namely the notion of leisure as a resource which ought to be exploited and not allowed to go to waste. The concern of these middle-class youth, however, was not the sacrifice of other, less 'worthy' kinds of leisure for the sake of collective interests, but rather the realization of their own individual dreams. This shows that in the cases where individuals realize the goals of the leisure ethic and the *wenming* discourse, i.e. work to increase their skills and competence, they do so because they perceive it as being in their own, personal interest. In other words, the discourse is not a product of the governmental exercise of power alone, it is also reproduced and modified by individuals on the basis of their own experiences.

Summing up, the examples from Quanzhou show that while the dominant discourse of leisure praises reading and the use of libraries as 'healthy' leisure activities, the local administration does little in the way of strengthening the function of the local libraries as places for leisure. Reading remains a popular leisure activity, but the library is no longer the only 'knowledge treasury' available. The local libraries struggle to maintain updated collections for the benefit of local readers, but the lack of public information, outdated buildings and inconvenient opening hours leave the libraries virtually empty. At present, bookshops with comfortable premises challenge the role of libraries as the chief facilitators of serious reading and self-study. Thus, the rise of the book café exemplifies the process where so-called healthy leisure activities gradually move away from the institutional structures set up by the party-state and enter the realm of the commercial leisure market. The analysis of this process is the focus in the following section, which draws on examples from organized leisure activities in Quanzhou.

The diminishing role of state-organized leisure

Anthropological studies of social life during the Mao era tell us that the brigades and work units organized not only political meetings but also cultural activities

'Healthy leisure' in transition   97

ranging from team sports to film screenings and so-called voluntary work (Henderson and Cohen 1984: 15, 19; Chan *et al.* 1992: 81, 250; Yunxiang Yan 2003: 34).[7] In the 1960s especially, activities were strongly politicized and group-oriented, and attendance was mandatory (Shaoguang Wang 1995: 153). Deborah Davis writes that 'when the workplace lost its obligation to provide recreation activities, the commercial sector went into high gear [...] and the number of commercial venues where residents could relax beyond the purview of their employers and their relatives grew exponentially' (Davis 2000: 12). It is a fact that today, Chinese individuals may spend their private time without much government interference. But in the case of group activities, the official policy is that all groups – be they social organizations or cultural associations – must be registered and approved as a 'popular' organization by the Bureau of Civil Affairs at the relevant organizational level (Saich 2000).[8] The Chinese Communist Party outlined the first regulations for the registration of 'mass organizations' in Yan'an in 1942, and the regulations have been enforced in the PRC since 1950 (Zhang Ye 2003: 6–7). The policy for the regulation of organizations was later revised in response to the popular protests in Beijing and elsewhere in 1989. The continued existence of these regulations is indicative of the level of suspicion the Chinese authorities maintain towards any type of assembly outside the realm of the party-state. As Thøgersen writes, the inclusion of organized cultural activities into the hierarchical administrative framework enables 'the authorities to supervise and control [these activities] and to isolate and strike out against their "unhealthy" elements' (Thøgersen 2000: 136; see also Saich 2000: 132). In Quanzhou municipality, as in all other parts of China, the local representatives of the party-state still preside over a range of organized leisure activities through the network of officially recognized social organizations. Some of these have a history linking them to the propagation of Communist Party ideology, while others are rather recent additions to the officially endorsed cultural scene.

Leisure organizations with party connections

One of the 'popular' organizations certified by local Quanzhou authorities is the Quanzhou Photographers' Association, which organizes approximately 600 active members throughout Quanzhou municipality. Some members work as photographers in the media or in advertising, but most are amateurs who regard photography as their leisure activity of choice. Membership is gained by submitting work to the association board for evaluation. The Photographers' Association belongs to the local Federation of Literature and Art Circles (*Wenxue yishujie lianhehui*) and is officially approved by the municipal Bureau of Civil Affairs (*Minzheng ju*). This administrative connection with the party-state does not, however, entail any involvement by the Communist Party apparatus in the actual running of the association. Since its establishment in 1998, the Photographers' Association has organized a number of large-scale outdoor photo exhibitions that have attracted large audiences. The women's branch of the association has also published the first Chinese volume presenting work by women amateur

98 *'Healthy leisure' in transition*

Figure 5.2 Members of the Photographers' Association in action.

photographers. Its many activities notwithstanding, the Photographers' Association had never received funding from the local government prior to 2007.

In 2006, the Quanzhou Photographers' Association was voted the most active branch of the China Photographers' Association, and thus won the bid to host the Fourth Urban Photography Conference in March 2007. For this conference, the Quanzhou Photographers' Association would have to provide free meals and lodging for more than 100 delegates from all over China. In addition, they chose to organize a short field excursion to a picturesque fishing village just within the Quanzhou city limits, and to hold a public photo exhibition. In order to increase the probability of getting financial support from the local government, the association decided to hold the conference in conjunction with the Maritime Silk Road Festival. During the course of the last few years, the local authorities have transformed Quanzhou's traditional Lantern Festival into the Maritime Silk Road Festival, an annual event aiming to promote Quanzhou as place of interest for tourists and investors. The head of the local bureau of propaganda recognized the sudden opportunity to have Quanzhou portrayed by photographers from all over China, and so the Photographers' Association was allocated 200,000 *yuan* to help cover their conference expenses. Additional funds were raised by way of association members' personal networks among factory owners and entrepreneurs in Quanzhou, a strategy the head of the Bureau of Propaganda himself advised the members to pursue.

The Quanzhou Photographers' Association has no administrative staff and no office space to facilitate the leisure activities they provide for their members or the popular public exhibitions they organize each year. In preparation for the Urban Photography Conference, key members made use of their own workplaces – and a flexible definition of work hours – to carry out the necessary clerical work. In the weeks preceding the conference, the women's branch of the Photographers' Association met in a hotel suite or in the lobby area of a local fitness centre to make preparations for the coming event. The manager of the fitness centre was a friend of one of the members of the association. By providing these women with a place to meet and organize, her fitness enterprise and its services were made known to a new group of potential customers.

The case of the Quanzhou Photographers' Association demonstrates that in spite of its relationship with the local branches of the party-state, the day-to-day activities of the association were facilitated by appealing to local businessmen and small-scale entrepreneurs, and by time and resources donated by the members themselves. The leader of the Photographers' Association put it this way: 'Until now, we've never received a penny from the government. We've relied on society [for support] (*women kao shehui*).'

Associations that have a history of more direct involvement and logistic support from the government currently find themselves in a situation where the local party-state continues to oversee the associations' activities while reducing the support it gives them. This is true for the local Volunteers' Association in Quanzhou (Rolandsen 2010), and also for the Quanzhou Municipal Choir.

Over the years, the Municipal Choir has grown accustomed to logistic and financial support from the local government, but is now struggling to maintain its level of activity without having to 'rely on society'. The choir is a 'popular' association that sorts under the Federation of Literature and Art Circles. In the past, the choir consisted of local cadres and officials, and was organized in close cooperation with the Bureau of Propaganda. At present, the choir consists of about 50 skilled amateur singers from various professions,[9] many of whom have had a musical education. Even if the membership base of the choir has changed in recent years, the bureaus of propaganda and of culture still demand the choir's participation in the shows they stage for local cadres and officials in celebration of national holidays. Most recently, the choir was appointed to participate in a concert of songs glorifying the history and modernization of Quanzhou. Both singers and conductor alike resented having a repertoire forced on them by the government. In addition, choir members were dispirited by the decrease in economic support from the same authorities. One of the tenors, Mr Wu, explained that when he joined the choir in 1998 the singers would often go out together after rehearsals, to eat or to sing karaoke, but that the choir now lacks the funds to sponsor such social activities. As for larger expenses, the choir received 10,000 *yuan* from the Bureau of Culture to help fund its participation in the World Choir Games, an international choir competition held in Fujian in 2006. From the choir's point of view, this sum was far from sufficient; the registration fee for the competition alone was 6,000 *yuan*. In addition, the choir wanted to hire a professional conductor to coach them in the period leading up to the competition. 'How else would we be able to compete?' one of the baritones complained. In the end, the singers themselves had to pay for some of the expenses. 'The challenge for us now,' said Wu, 'is that the chairman of the choir lacks the experience needed to make and maintain social contacts.' By this he meant that the people nominated to promote the choir's interests lacked both the connections and networking skills necessary to procure funding from the relevant departments.

Regardless of whether local government's financial support for the Quanzhou choir has actually decreased, or whether the present funding seems inadequate only in relation to the choir's escalating ambitions, the choir perceives its fiscal situation as significantly altered during recent years. The government's limited financial backing of organized amateur performers and arts associations like the Quanzhou Municipal Choir and the Photographers' Association indicates that, at present, the proliferation of organized, government-sponsored leisure activities is not high on the local government's agenda. The lack of funding is an indication that the government system for the management of popular organizations is undeniably intended to secure the government's control over organized activities. It is no longer a vehicle for the initiation of government-sponsored leisure activities, if it ever was. As pointed out by Tony Saich, the party apparatus does not have the necessary resources to enforce these regulations. Moreover, the successful registration of a 'popular' association demands that members of the prospect association have an intimate knowledge of the party-state apparatus and are willing to go through a considerable amount of paper work. As a consequence, some associations now choose to evade the official registration procedures altogether and operate as unofficial 'forums' or 'clubs' (Saich 2000: 133–5). Quanzhou is now home to several such unofficial groups which provide a variety of organized leisure activities quite openly.

Unofficial leisure organizations

In January 2007, visitors to Quanzhou's major bookshops could pick up flyers inviting 'young officials in all government departments and elite personnel in all trades' to practice their spoken English while 'getting to know new people in a friendly and relaxed environment'. The flyers were designed and distributed by Ms Hua, a young secretary in one of the local government offices. Being single and having few chores and obligations at home, Ms Hua found herself in a situation where she had little to do, and she often felt bored during weekends and afternoons. Wanting to do something active with her leisure time, she started the Professional English Club. The fact that a young, resourceful state employee such as Ms Hua resolved to create her own, unofficial leisure association bears witness to the increasing irrelevance of the official 'popular' organizations, even among white-collar state employees. The Professional English Club had its first meetings in one of the many Quanzhou karaoke parlours, a place to which the club returned for several of their get-togethers. In the beginning, most of the participants were friends and former class mates of Ms Hua. By March, when the club organized an all-day excursion to Qingyuan Mountain, several people from outside Ms Hua's personal network had joined the club. Although the flyer announced that expenses were to be covered by the individual club members, the young businessmen in the group relished flaunting their VIP cards and fought to pay the karaoke bills, as is the custom in Quanzhou. Apart from the members' propensity to speak English, no outward signs revealed the Professional English Club as an organized group. To the clerks at the karaoke parlour, they probably resembled any other party of returning guests. With its plain black-and-white flyers and loosely organized gatherings in public leisure places, the Professional English Club was discreet in its operations, but not in any way secretive. This shows that the lack of official approval did not significantly inhibit the leisure activities organized by Ms Hua and her associates.

Another example of an unofficial organizer of leisure activities in Quanzhou is the Happy Outdoors network, which consists of roughly 200 young adults who take an interest in hiking and mountain biking. These are men and women in their late twenties from various white-collar occupations such as banking, trade, education and the arts. The network started as a web page and chat room hosted by a group of male friends who are now in their early thirties. Their friendship with a local mountain biker, who has gained renown among his peers for his daring and for strenuous expeditions in various corners of China, lends credit to the network as being serious about the outdoors. Most of the members are single, and core members stated firmly that their network would not consider organizing activities suited for the whole family. In its present form, the network is open to anyone who creates a user account on the network's website. Happy Outdoors does not, however, accept students, because the network cannot take the legal or economic responsibility for potential accidents during group activities. Moreover, even though individual members were willing to share or hire out their equipment to newcomers, the considerable cost of mountain bikes and hiking equipment prevented some prospective members from taking part in the network's activities.

The Happy Outdoors presents itself as a virtual network. Their Internet chat room is lively and their web galleries contain pictures of network participants on hikes and outings around Fujian. Happy Outdoors, however, is also a real-life community of roughly 20 people who meet in a local café every week to reminisce about former adventures and plan new trips and activities. In addition to several two-day hiking trips and day trips in the vicinity of Quanzhou, the network participants organize a mountain bike race once a year on the slopes of nearby Qingyuan Mountain. When I asked about the official status of their organization, one of the central people in the group explained that 'it's not an organization, at least not in the way you mean, with an attachment to a government unit and somebody's formal approval. We are basically a web page, a platform for people in Quanzhou who are interested in outdoor activities.' The fact that both newcomers and long-term participants kept using their screen names even when socializing offline confirms the role of the web page in sustaining the Happy Outdoors network. If we look at the activities the Happy Outdoors organize, however, it is evident that this platform functions very much like any other leisure organization: it is an association that brings people together in pursuit of common leisure interests. Several participants stressed that it was the outdoor experiences that bound them together as a community. Some even argued that those who participated in the virtual network and café get-togethers, but who had not yet taken part in any of the outdoor activities, were not to be considered 'real' network participants.

The initiators behind the Happy Outdoors network held it to be important that their activities were not organized *for* the network participants, but *by* the people in the network. The ability of the network to utilize members' joint resources was evident in their third anniversary celebration, which took place in the convention room of a local work unit in March 2007. The venue was made available to them for free, because one of the participants 'knew somebody who knew somebody' in the work unit in question. The anniversary party was announced on the web page, and while some of the initial organizing was conducted over the Internet and via SMS, more than 20 people showed up in the aforementioned café a few days before the event to lend a hand in the preparations. The celebration was in the form of a variety show where participants in the network entertained each other with a choice of performances and games. A 20-*yuan* cover charge paid for snacks, balloons, paper decorations, party whistles, and clappers for the 150 network participants present. The highlight was an elaborate montage of pictures from trips and outdoor activities they had organized during the previous three years, accompanied by music, cheering, and humorous comments.

The Happy Outdoors participants took pride in the non-commercial nature of their network, and some of the long-term participants criticized the sort of hiking clubs that are run for profit by local shops that sell outdoor clothing and camping equipment. I asked one of the most active participants whether they had considered asking local entrepreneurs or businesses to sponsor their activities. She answered that they had never done so, and that they chose to do things on their own and at a low cost. Their non-commercial image not withstanding, the network's reliance on a local café as their physical headquarters meant that they were indirectly supported by a commercial enterprise. The café owner is a friend of one of the founders of the network, and because of this connection he does not demand that the network participants spend money while they are in the café. This generosity was pointed out to me by several of the Happy Outdoors members, and it seemed that in their eyes the close association with an establishment in the local leisure market was not at odds with their otherwise anti-commercial image.

The Happy Outdoors is truly a popular organization, both in the sense that it is run by and for ordinary citizens, and that it exists independently of the government. The fact that they were able to stage their anniversary show in a government work unit and, moreover, that the pictures from their mountain bike competition show local police securing the roads during the biking contest, indicates the kind of leeway unofficial associations enjoy in Quanzhou today. Still, some unofficial associations kept a much lower profile than both the Happy Outdoors and the Professional English Club did. During my stay in Quanzhou I learned of an informal discussion forum managed by a group of friends who met regularly in a café in the new downtown district. At regular intervals they invited a person within their extended network of friends and colleagues to give a talk on a chosen topic. The talks took place in the empty floor of an office building, and all participants paid three *yuan* each to cover the rent. Mr Li had taken part in this forum since his arrival in Quanzhou one and a half years ago. He worked as a sales representative for small enterprises in neighbouring provinces, which meant flexible working hours and ample opportunity to spend time reading and talking to fellow patrons in cafés and bookshops. According to Li, recurrent topics in the forum were how to live one's life, how to do better at work, and how to organize one's business. Some discussion nights were also spent in more open dialogues without a set topic: 'We just meet to discuss things, no matter where the discussion takes us,' he said. They would often talk about their backgrounds, how they came to end up in the situations they were in, and about choices and opportunities. The forum included men and women, and both locals and 'outsiders' (*waidi ren*) like Li himself.

These examples from unofficial leisure associations in Quanzhou demonstrate that in spite of the official policies that demand that all associations register with the local authorities, informal groups subsist and thrive outside the realm of the party-state. Both the Professional English Club and the Happy Outdoors network provide activities that are very much in tune with the official leisure ethic. The fact that they contribute towards 'healthy' practices (language learning and physical exercise) may explain why such communities are allowed a considerable degree of latitude from the political authorities. Conversely, the social criticism that most certainly is voiced in the informal discussion forum may explain why this group keeps a lower profile than the others. The Professional English Club, the Happy Outdoors network and the discussion forum were all unofficial associations, but it is important to note that none of the groups perceived their unofficial status in terms of subversiveness; they congregated for the sake of their own pleasure and the leisure interests they shared.

Towards a public sphere with Chinese characteristics?

At present it seems that unofficial leisure organizations in Quanzhou can perpetuate their activities without any support or certification from the local authorities. Official leisure organizations, however, having been established within the structures of the party-apparatus and having operated in observance of official policies for the management of organizations, have had little choice but to retain their association with the government. The way the Bureau of Propaganda utilized the Photographers' Association and the Municipal Choir to further the interests of the bureau (i.e. the promotion of the Quanzhou brand name) gives the impression that these leisure organizations were being preyed upon. On the other hand, being an officially recognized association brought a certain kind of prestige to the undertakings of the Photographers' Association and the choir. Moreover, this prestige was appreciated by the people involved. Members of the choir were for example proud to be the Municipal Choir, which in their eyes singled them out as more accomplished than choirs at the district (qu) level. This distinction rests on the logic of the administrative hierarchy of the party-state, which the system of 'popular' organizations mimics (Saich 2000: 132). Recognition from higher levels of the organizational hierarchy was also appreciated by the organizing committee responsible for the Urban Photography Conference. To them, the presence of chairmen from the China Federation of Literature and Art Circles and the national level of the Photographers' Association, as well as important personages from Hong Kong, Taiwan and Singapore, was the ultimate proof of their success as an organization (Zhu Huangnian 2007: 1). This kind of token recognition makes little or no sense for groups that exist outside the system of the party-state. As long as being an officially registered association does not entail any real funding, and as long as the local authorities do little to curb their activities, it is likely that the unofficial leisure groups in Quanzhou will preserve their autonomy from the local government.

Much has been written concerning the existence and development of civil society and a public sphere in China.[10] In a discussion of the role of tea houses in the development of a public sphere, Feng Chongyi warns against using a Western model of social development in the analysis of Chinese realities. He recommends that we regard both independent associations and semi-autonomous organizations as a 'Chinese variety of the public sphere and civil society' (Feng Chongyi 2005: 145). I argue that the fact that informal associations such as the Happy Outdoors network and the Professional English Club may actually congregate should not be taken as proof of a growing public sphere, either in a Western sense or one with Chinese characteristics. Mary Rankin describes the 'public sphere' in a broad sense as 'intermediate arenas in which open, public initiatives are undertaken by both officials and the populace'. In Rankin's definition, a public sphere demands a state presence, as well as autonomous or voluntary involvement and legitimizing ideas of the common good. More importantly, in order for the public sphere to be recognized as such, 'some social impact on policy' is required (Rankin 1993:160). Feng Chongyi concludes that although new urban leisure places provide an arena where people can congregate – both randomly and in official and semi-official associations – the party-state's continued supervision of the media ensures that there is no link between the conversations that take place in these public spaces and the Chinese realm of politics and policy-making (Feng Chongyi 2005: 147). For the same reasons, the associations and groups discussed in this chapter can be regarded as participants in a public sphere only in the sense that they exist in the space between the private and the state. So far, this sphere does not, however, facilitate any two-way conversation between the authorities and the people, a fact which I will return to in Chapter 8.

It is possible that the informal debate forum I discussed briefly above can develop into a more formalized group working to further the interests of educated out-of-town employees in Quanzhou. My data from Quanzhou does not, however, indicate any development of this kind. Moreover, although both the Happy Outdoors and the Professional English Club constitute networks of people who could potentially be rallied for the support of civic demands, I find it unlikely that either of the two will develop into advocacy groups of any kind. The thirst for social change is not their *raison d'être*, neither is it the reason these groups exist outside the officially designated category of 'popular' organizations. As I see it, these young people are to a surprising degree disembedded from the realm of the party-state, and they apparently see no reason to engage with the world of government units and official approvals. Even if they are aware of how official organizations should be organized and officially approved – as indicated in the interview with one of the Happy Outdoors senior members, quoted above – these groups clearly hold the bureaucratic structure to be irrelevant to their purpose, which is to provide their members with meaningful leisure activities. Therefore, to analyse these groups as agents in a public sphere we would have to conjure up an interest in social conditions – or as Rankin puts it, ideas of the common good – which is not part of these organizations at the present time.

Despite the difference in their relationships to the different levels of the local government, the official and unofficial leisure groups in Quanzhou had several characteristics in common. They all organized 'healthy' leisure activities, but did so on meagre or inadequate budgets. In the case of the official associations, government funding was granted only in cases where the activity would contribute towards the ultimate agenda of the local propaganda bureau, i.e. the promotion of Quanzhou to a national or international audience. Moreover, with the exception of the choir, which met for regular rehearsals in a local school building, both the official and unofficial groups lived a nomadic existence, floating between commercial leisure places (fitness club, café, karaoke parlour) and venues accessed by way of personal networks. This indicates that while the role of the government apparatus is decreasing, informal relations and agents within the commercial leisure market have become increasingly important in the facilitation of organized leisure. None of the organizations, official or otherwise, had access to office facilities of any kind. Several of the interviewees pointed out that having some kind of administrative headquarters where their steering group could meet, make phone calls, keep their records and papers etc. would be beneficial, but the desire for office space or a headquarters did not mean that the associations or groups wanted a closer cooperation with the local culture bureaucracy. In the case of the Photographers' Association, a fixed place to meet would simply have made the management of their activities easier. Other informants were more concerned with providing their peers with a place to gather and socialize, independent of both the government and the leisure market. This wish was most clearly voiced by a group of young artists who met irregularly in a building where some of them taught children's weekend classes in calligraphy and painting. One of the painters envisioned a kind of cultural centre: 'It would be nice to have a place where artists and people like ourselves could meet and talk about painting and essays,' he said, adding that there should be room there for people to sit down and exchange thoughts, as well as for people to work on their paintings. Some of the others lamented that there were no sidewalk cafés in Quanzhou where friends could meet and talk 'like they do in Europe'. In their eyes, the local cafés were too 'industrialized' (*chanye hua*),[11] and essentially 'places where people go on dates'. They also did not want to form an association (*xiehui*), because in their opinion arts associations belonged to the government. Returning briefly to the question of a public sphere, this group of artists articulated their distance to both the government and the leisure market. It may very well be that their desire for and visions of a space where artists and cultured people can meet may develop into a demand for an autonomous space. I do not believe that this process is significantly hindered by the lack of a physical place to gather – after all, there was already room for the discourse of an independent space, as the above quotes demonstrate. However, the improved facilitation of leisure activities and a place designated for informal gatherings and the exchange of ideas, for example in the form of a cultural centre run by the organizations themselves, would mean an improvement in the current conditions, especially for informal leisure groups.

More than a decade has passed since Wang concluded that the party-state still aims to influence the leisure activities of the population and guide them in the direction of activities that are 'physically healthy, morally correct, socially consolidating, and politically integrative' (Shaoguang Wang 1995: 172). The role of commercial leisure places such as bookshops, cafés and karaoke parlours in the facilitation of leisure activities and the new and altered forms of organized leisure in Quanzhou show that the local government's promotion of 'healthy' activities exists primarily at the level of discourse. The system of registration for 'popular' organizations is the only remnant of the party-state's practical attempts at social engineering through collective leisure activities. Instead, the official leisure ethic endorses 'healthy' activities by appealing to middle-class members' eagerness to recharge their batteries, i.e. to increase their cultural capital as individuals through self-study and educational leisure activities. This shows that facilitating increased cultural competence in the population through healthy leisure is no longer a collective responsibility, but rather has become the ethical duty of the middle-class individual.

Shaoguang Wang has described this movement away from the Party realm as the 'depoliticization' of leisure (Shaoguang Wang 1995: 165; see also Feng Chongyi 2005: 134). The data from contemporary Quanzhou show how organized leisure, which was once shaped by the Party structure, has come to rely increasingly on the structures of the commercial leisure market. This transition does not, however, entail a total separation of leisure from the realm of politics. The party-state's promotion of 'healthy' leisure is essentially a promotion of the consumer lifestyles and cultural preferences of the upper-middle classes in Europe and the US. Leisure pursuits such as photography, singing in a choir, outdoor sports and lingering in book cafés epitomize the enlightened modernity to which the PRC aspires. It is the Good Life as defined by China's political elite. Conversely, the labelling of given leisure practices as 'un-healthy' (*bu jiankang*) serves to mark the popular culture of lower-income groups – and youth especially – as detrimental to society. While the party-state's responsibility for 'healthy' leisure has gradually been transferred to the leisure market and the individual leisure consumer, Chinese authorities still actively regulate what they define as 'un-healthy' and 'chaotic' (*luan*) aspects of popular culture. The party-state's continued attempts at governing and supervising popular leisure places will be analysed in the following chapter.

6 Bad people in bad places?

The preceding chapter concluded that the local government contributes very little towards the facilitation of so-called healthy leisure activities. The resources the local bureaucracy spends on keeping unhealthy and potentially chaotic activities at bay are, however, considerable. It is telling that, apart from its role in Quanzhou's Maritime Silk Road Festival, the local culture bureau's only plans for involvement in local leisure in 2005–2006 were continued surveillance, supervision, and control of the leisure market (*QZSWHJ* 2005: 7–9).[1] This shows that, while the facilitation of leisure activities is no longer regarded as a responsibility of the government, the policing and control of so-called unhealthy leisure practices remains a main concern for the local branches of the party-state. Chinese scholars within the field of leisure studies and consumer culture have described various kinds of leisure practices, such as disco and karaoke, watching DVDs and playing pool and video games, as examples of unhealthy leisure (see for example Zhang Jian 2004: 22; and Fan Xiaoxian and Kong Linghua 2006: 88). As will be demonstrated in this chapter, these are also among the activities local authorities in Quanzhou seek to repress by way of campaigns, surveillance and direct management.

This chapter focuses on two specific leisure places – Internet cafés (*wangba*, lit. 'net bar') and karaoke parlours (popularly called 'KTV')[2] – and the diverging ways in which local authorities, the media and local townspeople describe these places and relate to them. There are certainly leisure activities in Quanzhou – for instance, gambling and prostitution – which could illustrate the workings of the relevant authorities in a much more dramatic and clear-cut manner, but these are illegal forms of leisure. It is difficult but not altogether impossible to study illicit activities in China, as recent studies on prostitution in China show (see for example Hyde 2001; and Jeffreys 2004). I have chosen to focus on less problematic examples of unhealthy leisure primarily because I take an interest in the grey zone where the moral judgments of the official leisure ethic meet popular practices. I have chosen Internet cafés and karaoke parlours as cases because, although the local culture administration disapproves of these leisure places, Internet surfing and karaoke parlours are perfectly legal activities and also extremely popular.

In Quanzhou, chatting and surfing the Internet and playing computer games are all widespread activities among people of different social backgrounds and occupations. Similarly, going to a karaoke parlour is a leisure activity favoured by people from all walks of life. Even so, these leisure places have a reputation as being places of 'chaos' (*luan*). Karaoke parlours are identified by the local administration as facilitators of binge drinking, drug abuse and unlawful spending of public funds, while the Internet cafés are held in contempt because they facilitate 'net addiction' and the spread of pornography and other unhealthy materials among the young. As Thøgersen has shown in his analysis of the commercial leisure culture in Xuanwei, Yunnan, local cadres' attitudes towards leisure establishments are ambiguous: on the one hand it is the responsibility of local cadres to enforce the regulation of illegal and immoral practices, but on the other hand the development of a commercial leisure market creates revenue and is also regarded as a welcome sign of modernization (Thøgersen 2000: 135–6). Moreover, state employees have also invested in restaurants and other establishments in the leisure market (Goodman 2001: 248–9), and, as Thøgersen points out, cadres often frequent commercial leisure places as patrons (Thøgersen 2000:135; see also Jeffreys 1997: 49–50). This was also the case in Quanzhou, where local cadres and their juniors in the local administration frequently used karaoke parlours as venues for socializing. As we shall see in the following, both cadres and well-educated white-collar employees are known to frequent places which in the official leisure discourse are labelled as chaotic or unhealthy.

In this chapter, I argue that the dominant leisure ethic in China reveals a pattern where the types of leisure associated with the lifestyles of the middle classes and well-to-do are held to be commendable, while the activities available to people of a lower status and income level are regarded with suspicion.[3] Thus, karaoke is only 'chaotic' when it is practiced by young men with a low level of education, and Internet surfing and computer gaming are more likely to be considered 'unhealthy' if they take place in an Internet café rather than in a middle-class home. The manner in which the local authorities manage and control this part of the commercial leisure arena reveals the party-state's bias against – and also the strong incentive to influence and control – the leisure practices of underprivileged citizens in general, and youth in particular.

'Luan': keeping chaos at a distance

In my description and definition of the official PRC leisure ethic in Chapter 3, I stressed the importance of the expressions 'healthy' and 'unhealthy' as a dichotomy in scholarly writing about leisure. The concept of healthy leisure is closely knit to the authorities' overall goal of increasing the education level of the populace and thereby China's relative economic strength and competitive power in the international market. In short, the underlying logic of the official leisure ethic is that healthy leisure serves the goals and policies of the party-state, while unhealthy leisure may give rise to social chaos (*shehui hunluan*) and ultimately threaten the party-state's legitimacy.

In everyday speech the term '*luan*' refers to all things chaotic, and people in Quanzhou use the term to describe everything from disharmonious interior decoration to sexual promiscuity and the lack of management in a workplace. Most often, however, the term is used to express a sense of distaste and pass a moral judgement on a practice or place that is considered a potential source of disorderliness. I found that middle-class townspeople and elderly citizens especially use the term '*luan*' to express a growing fear of social disruption in their local communities. This sentiment can be illustrated by the example of Mr and Mrs Gao, a couple in their late sixties who have lived in Quanzhou all their lives. As many of the inhabitants of their generation, the Gaos found that Quanzhou had changed a lot, and not always for the better. One of their worries was the deterioration of the neighbouring East Lake Park. Mr Gao complained that the park had become too commercialized, saying 'It is all right to sell fruit and some refreshments [in the park], but now it is all about money.' Then his wife chimed in: 'It has become quite *luan* there.' There were many rumours about the activities going on in and around Quanzhou's parks during night-time, and friends constantly advised each other to be careful when moving about town in the evening. In Quanzhou, this perceived development towards a state of social chaos was sometimes attributed to the policies of economic reform and the resulting changes in the social structure. More often than not, however, the perceived danger was simply blamed on the many out-of-town workers, the *waidi ren*.

Farquhar and Zhang found a similar fear of chaos (*luan*) among elderly people in Beijing, where their interviewees expressed scepticism towards social and environmental changes in their local neighbourhoods. Many among them also recalled the earliest decades of the Mao era as 'more orderly and more deeply gratifying than the present' (Farquhar and Zhang 2005: 309; see also Farquhar 2002: 41). I do not consider such statements as expressions of nostalgia for the days of Maoist rule, but rather as a sign of insecurity among those who have profited from the reform policies (i.e. the urban populace along the east coast who got the chance to 'get rich first'[4]). These statements signalize uncertainty among those who live in relative comfort as to how long the process of social and economic differentiation can go on before the less privileged lose patience and chaos sets in. In this matter, the urban middle class and the central authorities undoubtedly have a shared interest in a continuation of the relative social stability Communist Party rule has provided throughout the reform era.

Farquhar and Zhang state that the 'avoidance of public chaos' has informed much of the party-state's policy making in the reform era (Farquhar and Zhang 2005: 310). The level of force used to curb the student and workers' protests in 1989 is one example of the value Chinese authorities place on social order. Another is the authorities' campaigns against 'superstitious' activities, also defined by the government as campaigns for the prevention of social chaos (*luan*) (Chen *et al.* 1995: 357), or the recent show of force against protesters in Tibetan areas. I argue that the regulation of the commercial leisure industry is yet another arena where the prevention of chaos is at the forefront.

The fear of chaos and its influence

At the macro level, the term '*luan*' invokes a general fear of social disturbance, but the perceived spread of chaos also has consequences at the level of the individual. Consider the following examples of tactical manoeuvres individuals employ in order to keep chaos at arm's length.

Ms Wang manages a newly established fitness club in Quanzhou, catering exclusively to women. She offers classes in callisthenics and posture, which she argues will assist her customers in building self-esteem and in making good first impressions on their own business clients. I asked Ms Wang whether her classes would not also be suitable for men. She responded that she had considered including male participants but had decided against it. She explained the 'women only' angle partly as an attempt to offer something different in the local leisure market, and partly as an attempt to separate her fitness club from dance halls (*tiaowu ting*) and other similar establishments where women and men mingle. According to Ms Wang, dance halls constituted a potential for 'social chaos' (*shehui hunluan*) and she feared that a mixed-gender fitness club would give potential customers the wrong impression. The propriety that separated her business from the '*luan*-ness' of dance halls was evidently more important to her than the potential of increased profit.

The logic underlying Ms Wang's reasoning is that certain places or activities cause people to lose their self-control and sense of propriety, and, moreover, that the mere association with things '*luan*' could tarnish the reputation of her business. Several practices in Chinese society reveal a similar belief in the power of negative and positive influences and show attempts to escape or even utilize such influences. One example is the notion that young students will benefit from boarding in a teacher's home, as in the following case of the middle school student Little Ping:

A few years back, when his parents returned to university to get their MA degrees, Little Ping – then a primary school student – boarded with one of his teachers. He did his homework and had his meals there, and shared a bedroom with other students of his own age. I asked Ping's father whether living with a teacher had meant that Ping received extra tutoring. He answered that there were so many students living in the teacher's household that there was no opportunity for tutoring. The father was nevertheless confident that the exemplary virtue present in a teacher's household would somehow rub off onto his son. According to Børge Bakken, education through imitation or emulation of model behaviour is the basic principle of socialization in Chinese society (Bakken 2000: Ch. 4 especially). Judging from the above example, no teaching or intentional action on the part of the teacher was needed for the transmission of knowledge or a cultured *habitus* to take place. The father held that his child could benefit simply from residing in the same physical space as the teacher. This case illustrates the notion that physical proximity or a shared physical environment facilitates a transmission of good habits.

Little Ping's father had made arrangements so that his son would come under the good influence of a teacher. Similarly, Little Ping's parents did their best to ensure that their son did not become associated with people whom they suspected of having a bad influence on him. This effort was evident in the parents' recurrent admonitions to Little Ping to stay away from Internet cafés. Little Ping had a computer with Internet access in his bedroom and, while he was given ample opportunity to surf the Internet at home, he was strictly forbidden to go to Internet cafés. When I asked him why he was not allowed to go to Internet cafés, his explanation was as follows: 'If you go to the Internet cafés you can develop some bad (*buliang*) habits and lifestyles. You know, the people there can influence you so that you yourself become a bad person (*huairen*).' A similar 'chain narrative of danger' (Bakken 2000: 319) can be found in a 2005 propaganda poster warning against the menace of video games (see Figure 6.1).[5]

The headline reads 'Clinging to video games made him a criminal', and the message is communicated in the form of a cartoon short story as shown on the following page. The cartoon tells the story of Little Huang, and it goes like this:

1   When Little Huang was in junior high, he often secretly played video games, even though the school stressed time and time again that playing video games was forbidden.
2   Because he did not feel like going to class and because his results were very poor, he did not want to go to school anymore, so he quit school before finishing his junior high courses.
3   After quitting school, he spent whole days in the video game arcade. Later he acquired a 'friend' at the entertainment centre and the two of them often went there together.
4   In just a few days, their pockets were empty.
5   [They] wanted to have fun but had no money. What to do? This gave them a crooked idea. One afternoon, they went to a private house, they checked that no one was home, and then Little Huang acted as lookout.
6   His friend climbed through the window and into the house, and stole 500 *yuan*, a watch and two stamp albums. After sharing the profits, they returned to their squandering in the arcade.
7   Throughout a period of almost a year they committed crimes together several times. They stole 10,200 *yuan*, 123 Hong Kong dollars, 600 *yuan's* worth of government bonds, gold and silver jewellery, video recorders, bikes etc., adding up to a total of 21,000 *yuan*.
8   They used the profits from the sale of stolen goods to finance their gambling. But the next time they committed a crime, they were arrested by Public Security officers.
9   Little Huang was in the flower of youth,[6] but because he played video games he ended up on a path of crime. His is a thought-provoking example.

The examples of Little Ping and the fictitious Little Huang both serve to demonstrate the perceived importance of distance and proximity to negative and positive role models: proximity to people who enjoy high moral standing can result in the transmission of positive qualities. Likewise, association with bad people and

Figure 6.1 'Clinging to video games made him a criminal'

114 *Bad people in bad places?*

the places they frequent constitutes a risk of contamination. The propagandistic moral tale about Little Huang exhibits the perceived influence of a chaotic environment at the level of the individual. Little Huang's presence in the arcade and his socializing with other patrons there constitute the first links in a chain of destructive events which, over time, turn him into a criminal. This anecdote brings us to the question of the actual source of contamination: is it the leisure *place* (the arcade), the leisure *activity* (playing video games) or the *people* (the friend) that is *luan*? Let us first proceed to the general notion of physical places as *luan*.

Chaotic places: the production of space revisited

In a study from coastal Fujian in the 1990s, Sara L. Friedman shows how karaoke parlours, restaurants and factories in the area earned a reputation as 'chaotic spaces' among local people (Friedman 2006: 170). If we return to the central claim made by Henri Lefebvre that spaces are not 'empty mediums' but socially produced (Lefebvre 1991: 87), it follows that restaurants or karaoke parlours cannot be chaotic in and of themselves. Lefebvre writes:

> To picture space as a 'frame' or container into which nothing can be put unless it is smaller than the recipient, and to imagine that this container has no other purpose than to preserve what has been put in it – this is probably the initial error. But is it error, or is it ideology? The latter, more than likely. If so, who promotes it? Who exploits it? And why and how do they do so?
>
> (Lefebvre 1991: 94)

Here, Lefebvre argues that the definition of what a space is or means is an exercise of power; it is part of the ideology that serves the interests of the power holders. Friedman's study centres on friendship ties in a community where men and women have traditionally lead separate social lives. Her analysis shows how social and economic change caused tension between those who wished to preserve the patterns of gender separation and those who were more open to new practices. Friedman argues that in this case, the traditionalist mainstream had the power to define karaoke parlours, restaurants and factories as chaotic spaces. And, that their definition was a product of the impressions they had of these places as arenas for cross-gender socializing and even prostitution.[7] What makes Friedman's example intriguing is the counter-strategies applied by a group of young women who enjoyed spending time in these so-called chaotic places. Friedman writes that by focusing on the activities in which they themselves were engaged and by recounting among themselves how many times they had been to a given karaoke parlour or restaurant, the women 'sought to reclaim them as leisure spaces available to all' (Friedman 2006: 192). They rejected the definition of karaoke parlours as places of prostitution by representing their own activities at the local karaoke place as 'honest fun – singing and eating' (Friedman 2006: 192). Through their practices and the strategy of a counter-narrative, these young women produced their own 'connotative discourse' (Lefebvre 1991: 56) about karaoke parlours and restaurants as places of 'honest fun'. Friedman's example strengthens the claim that places are neither chaotic nor ordered in themselves, but that such characteristics (negative or otherwise) are attributed to places through discourses and practices. Thus, when Chinese authorities use the discourse of the leisure ethic to characterize a video game arcade, an Internet café or a karaoke club as *luan*, it is really the practices and the patrons in these places that are labelled as chaotic. In other words, their patrons are singled out as harbingers of social instability. In Quanzhou, the local government – assisted by local media – relied on this aspect of the leisure ethic in their governance and control of local Internet cafés.

Internet cafés as chaotic leisure spaces

Net surfing and the playing of online games have become part of Chinese mainstream leisure. While middle-class citizens are encouraged to consume the services of state-run telecom companies and connect their home computers or mobile phones to the Internet, the party-state apparatus keeps a close watch on the numerous Internet cafés that cater to a less privileged segment of the populace (CNNIC 2008: 30).[8] Judging from local print media and propaganda posters, the authorities' stated intent is to prevent fire hazards, curb Internet addiction and hinder youth from being exposed to unhealthy online material such as pornography and violent and addictive computer games. By examining the local government's supervision of Internet cafés and how their interventions are presented in the local media, and moreover, by analysing local middle-class citizens' perceptions of Internet café customers, it becomes evident that the chaos associated with Internet cafés stems not from the café itself, nor from unhealthy websites. *Luan*-ness is perceived as an attribute of the typical Internet café customer: the young, uneducated male.

The regulation of the Internet café market

The establishment of Internet cafés or cyber cafés is an international phenomenon, and businesses of this sort provide people with Internet access in public places in countries all over the world (Stewart 2000: 320; Mutula 2003). Chinese Internet cafés operate under close governmental supervision: all Internet cafés must acquire a license from the local cultural bureau and the Administration of Industry and Commerce at the relevant level. These departments are also responsible for the monitoring of Internet café activities, with assistance from the fire department and public security bureaus. From the perspective of the Chinese government, Internet cafés make up 'an arena that requires government supervision' (CNNIC 2008: 29). It is a well-known fact that Chinese authorities seek to control the activities of Chinese netizens by censoring the types of information that may be posted and distributed on the Internet. But, this is only one of several reasons why Chinese authorities insist on the close supervision of the Internet café market.

As of December 2007, China had a total of 210 million Internet users,[9] which places China second only to the US (215 million) (CNNIC 2008: 10; Hwang 2008). The Internet penetration rate in China is 16 per cent (CNNIC 2008: 11), compared to 69.7 per cent in the US (May 2007), 68.2 per cent in Hong Kong (Feb. 2005) and 7.0 per cent in India (Nov. 2008).[10] What is special in the Chinese case is that, compared to countries with higher Internet penetration, a large number of netizens' Internet access takes place in local Internet cafés (CNNIC 2008: 28). In the PRC only 67.3 per cent of Internet users have access at home, while 33.9 per cent of Internet users use Internet cafés.[11] And in the Chinese countryside, 48 per cent of Internet users rely on Internet cafés to go online (CNNIC 2008: 29). Moreover, in the period from 2002 to 2008, the number of Chinese citizens who have Internet access at home increased by 35.7 per cent, but the increase in Internet café customers in the same period was 60.9 per cent (CNNIC 2008: 28). This shows that Internet cafés are important facilitators of online access throughout China and that this appears to be a stable trend.

For the fee of a couple of *yuan* per hour, Chinese Internet cafés provide their customers with a desktop computer and most often a headset and a web camera to facilitate the full use of online content. The fact that several customers use the same computer, and therefore also the same IP address, during the course of a day means that it is difficult for the authorities to obtain exact information about the pages and sites visited by the individual. Only a few years back, Internet café customers had to produce an ID in order to go online. Customers' names were written down on a list at the counter, along with the number on the designated computer. In this way the customers' identities and the relevant IP address could be recorded and presented to government inspectors upon request. With the new system of net bar membership cards, the registration of users and the monitoring of their pre-paid access are made easier. Still, it is always possible to ask for a visitor's pass with a temporary log-in, and I myself experienced that it was possible to borrow a friend's membership card and log in without questions being asked. In addition, the numerous unofficial, 'black' Internet cafés (*hei wangba*) do not observe these regulations at all. The loopholes in these registration routines that make it possible to surf from an IP address anonymously, are one of the reasons the Internet café sector, and the unregistered 'black' cafés especially, are regarded with suspicion by the relevant government departments.

A second reason for the government's interest in this segment of the leisure market is the fact that Internet cafés are a lucrative business: each day, an average of 40 million Chinese visit Internet cafés, and the annual production value of China's licensed Internet cafés has surpassed 25.6 billion *yuan* ('Quanguo wangba' *DNZB* 7 April 2006, A2). In his analysis from Xuanwei, Yunnan, Stig Thøgersen brings to attention the diminishing influence of the party-state on the local culture sector. Thøgersen shows that the role of the authorities in the 'entertainment market' is reduced to that of 'taxation and control' (Thøgersen 2000: 135; see also Goodman 2001: 247). My data from Quanzhou cannot support a thorough assessment of the local authorities' yield from taxation of local leisure businesses. The data do show, however, that the national policies of active interference in the development of the Internet café business give the local branches of the culture bureaucracy the tools to monitor and control the 'chaotic' segment of the leisure market, as well as the opportunity to protect its strongest and most well-connected operators. In 2003, the central government ordered the local authorities to stop issuing licences to independent (*danti*) Internet cafés. Subsequently, the running of Internet cafés was handed over to ten select national chains supplemented by up to three local chains in each province. The ministry also set a target quota for the development of the Internet café market: one café per 10,000 people. The change in management policy is said to have been initiated in the wake of an accidental fire in a Beijing Internet café in 2002 (Zhao Jicheng 2006: A4, *HXDSB*). The authorities' stated goal was to increase security by eliminating 'scattered, chaotic, low-quality and small' (*san, luan, cha, xiao*) Internet cafés from the market ('Liansuo wangba' *Information Times*, printed in *DNZB* 7 April 2006, A2). In effect, the policy meant a move towards a state-endorsed monopolization of the official segment of the Internet café business. The concentration of Internet café management in the hands of a few chains at the national and provincial levels was undoubtedly productive for the investors involved. It seems, however, that the 2003 restrictions on the issuance of Internet café licenses failed to foster a more effective control over the cafés in general. By March 2006, the ten national chains were in charge of no more than 10 per cent of the total number of approved Internet cafés, and only five of the nationwide café chains had developed businesses in multiple locations ('Liansuo wangba' *DNZB* 7 April 2006, A2). Meanwhile, operators in the market complained that the national chains were allowed to retain their special status despite their poor performance, and that there was no opportunity for existing independent cafés or province-level chains to make bids for national chain status ('Liansuo wangba' *DNZB* 7 April 2006, A2).

According to a report from the Quanzhou cultural bureau, control units are regularly dispatched to check up on both officially approved and black Internet cafés. In 2005, 253 violators were prosecuted and 56 black cafés were dismantled within Quanzhou municipality (*QZSWHJ* 2005: 8). Commenting on a crackdown on Internet cafés in the district level town of Jinjiang in 2007, the local head of the Department of Culture and Sports confirmed that the 'eruption' of black cafés was indeed a result of the slow development of the legitimate Internet café market. He nevertheless maintained that once the quota of one café per 10,000 people is reached, the black enterprises will disappear (Chen Lengleng 2007: A7, *HXDSB* 26 January). The government blueprint for orderly café management and approval did not purge the market of its black cafés. On the contrary, limiting the Internet café business to a small number of chain operations made it almost impossible for local, stand-alone Internet cafés to obtain licenses from the culture bureaucracy. It is therefore likely that the unequal opportunities in the market caused an unintended increase in the number of illegal establishments (Zhao Jicheng 2006: A4, *HXDSB* 7 April).

The third reason for the Chinese authorities' restrictions on Internet cafés is concern about the effect of surfing and online games on segments of the populace, most notably young students. The harmful effects of excessive computer use and the possibility of addiction to online services have caught the attention of researchers and authorities in other Asian countries, as well as in other parts of the world (Gross *et al.* 2002; Johansson and Götestam 2004; Ng and Wiemer-Hastings 2005; Fackler 2007). But in the Chinese context, the negative aspects of Internet surfing are not always linked to the abuse of the medium itself. In Quanzhou, the unhealthy consequences of Internet use were associated mainly with the Internet cafés and their clientele.

Limiting young students' Internet (ab)use

Chinese legislators use concern for public security to justify the government's monitoring of Internet cafés. In Quanzhou, local newspapers reported that the authorities carry out Internet café inspections in order to prevent fire hazards and make sure that the cafés do not open their doors to minors (See for example Tang Qirong and Weng Hongxiang, *DNZB* 6 April 2006, A8; Chen Lengleng, *HXDSB* 26 January 2007, A7). Thus, in the case of Internet cafés, maintaining public security does not only entail surveillance of online activities, it involves inspections of the physical space as well as the customers who make use of it. The strategies employed by the authorities reveal that their main priority is not to ensure that café managers provide customers with a safe environment. Judging from reports on the local government's control of the Internet café market, their main concern is to keep middle school students away from the cafés.

Parents with whom I discussed middle school students' use of Internet shared the government's scepticism towards the cafés. In several families there was an ongoing debate over how many hours the young people could be online each week, whether Internet surfing should be restricted to weekends only, and whether or not the children could go online when home alone. My general impression was that parents had strict rules for how their children could spend their time during the afternoons, but that these regulations were not always enforced. These types of discussions are not particular to families in China; parents worrying over their children's Internet habits can also be observed in other societies where Internet access in the home has become widespread (for an example from the US see Gross *et al.* 2002: 75). What is special in the Chinese case is that Internet cafés and the perceived danger of frequenting these places enter into parent-child discussions of Internet use. This may be explained by the fact that Internet cafés are more widespread in China than in other countries (CNNIC 2007: 36). According to CNNIC statistics from 2007, an average of 66.2 per cent of young Internet users in China have online access at home, 29.1 per cent can use the Internet at school, and 48.4 per cent of youth in the same group visit Internet cafés frequently (CNNIC 2007: 55). This means that Internet cafés are more popular among youth (48.4 per cent) than among the average Internet user (33.9 per cent). The numbers also show that even those with online access at home also use the Internet in places where they can escape the supervision of teachers or parents, i.e. the Internet cafés.

The popularity of online leisure activities among middle school students is described as problematic both in official reports and in the party-state's propaganda materials. The 2007 CNNIC report states that 'if students are online too long, their studies will suffer' (CNNIC 2007: 56).[12] Moreover, the report concludes that youth who spend more than 20 hours online each week should be warned by the school authorities, and that special attention should be given to those who spend more than 40 hours per week on the Internet. *Reuters* in Beijing reported, that according to the government think-tank China National Children's Centre, '13 per cent of China's 18 million Internet users under 18 were Internet addicts' ('Worried China...' 7 March 2007). Also, in the spring of 2007, propaganda posters in Quanzhou warned youth against black Internet cafés and the threat of Internet addiction. According to official statistics cited on these posters, 17.7 per cent of young boys and 10.4 per cent of young girls in China suffer from Internet addiction.[13] A recent study from Norway conducted by behavioural psychologists suggests that 8–10 per cent of Norwegian youth (ages 12 to 18) have Internet dependency, and that this estimate is consistent with research results from studies in Australia and the US (Johansson and Götestam 2004: 45). Johansson and Götestam's study concludes, however, that there is a low correlation between the number of hours spent online and the development of Internet addiction.[14] The Chinese sources consulted tend to focus on the number of hours youth spend online as the root cause of Internet addiction. In addition, both the 2007 CNNIC report and the survey results provided on the above-mentioned propaganda posters suggest that addiction is a looming threat towards the sound development of all middle school students. However, if we look closer at the amount of time the average Chinese Internet user and the average Chinese student spent online in 2007, CNNIC estimates an average of 18.6 online hours per week for Chinese Internet users in general, and fewer than 12 hours per week for students (CNNIC 2007: 37).[15] This means that students as a group are no closer to becoming Internet addicts than is the average net user. The exaggerated concern for young people's (ab)use of the Internet is also evident from the national legislation that states that Internet cafés are not allowed to operate within 200 metres of any school campus ('Liansuo wangba' *DNZB* 7 April 2006, A2). It is also telling that whenever school holidays are approaching, the Bureau of Culture, articles in local newspapers and public propaganda posters all highlight the need for extra surveillance of Internet café activities (*QZSWHJ* 2005: 8; Ceng Xiaoqin, *HXDSB* 15 March 2006, A13). These strategies reveal the authorities' incessant concern with both the manner in which young students spend their time and the environment in which young students engage in leisure activities.

In the frequent news articles that report on the local government's campaigns to curb chaotic conditions in local Internet cafés, the cafés in Quanzhou are described as dungeon-like firetraps where youth are tricked into passivity in front of computer screens. Consider the picture (Figure 6.2) and the description

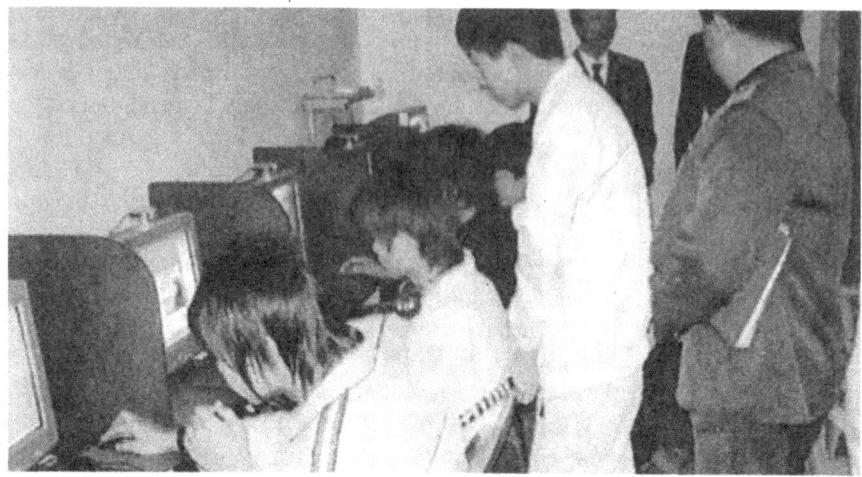

Figure 6.2 Youth in one of Quanzhou's 'black' Internet cafés.

of two black Internet cafés on the outskirts of Quanzhou, taken from a newspaper article entitled 'On the Spot: Internet Cafés Crowded with Children':

> Through a windowpane plastered with newspaper scraps, one could see ten to twenty computers in a room of less than twenty square metres. The seats in front of the computers were filled with Internet surfers whose expressions revealed their absorption. Some among them looked like students. All sorts of wires were strung across the room, creating a great hidden security risk. [...] In the dim Internet café, the air was stale with smoke, and the space was crowded to capacity. The narrow passageway could only accommodate one person passing at a time. Some children who seemed to be about sixteen years of age were playing popular online games in deep concentration. When they spotted the law enforcement unit, they hastily stood up and left.
>
> (Xie Weiduan, *DNZB* 22 March 2006, A5)

The expressions 'playing [...] in deep concentration' (*jujinghuishende wanzhe*) and 'absorption' (*shenqing zhuanzhu*) in these quotes serve to highlight the lack of self-control the journalist attributes to the customers. A similar vocabulary is used in the aforementioned propaganda posters, where students are said to be 'wallowing in' (*chenmi*) and showing a 'blind love for' (*milian*) online games. The difference in the media's portrayal of online gamers in Internet cafés and young adults who play computer games at home is evident in the following excerpt from the same newspaper. As part of a Consumers' Day special, the paper brought attention to the plight of Mr Lin, a local online gamer who was the victim of an online robbery where he lost virtual armour and weapons worth more than 1,000 *yuan*. The pictures in the article (Figure 6.3) show Mr Lin in his

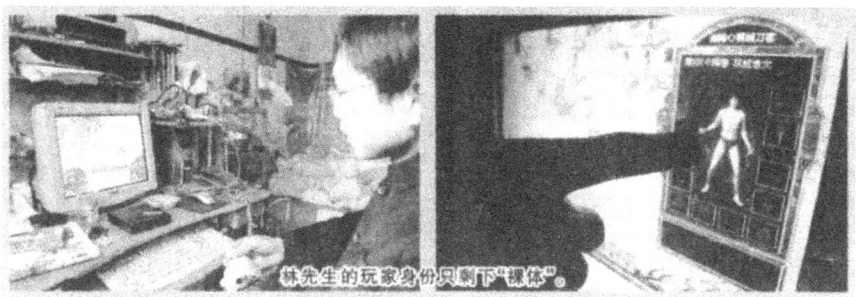

Figure 6.3 Mr Lin, the time-honoured online gamer.

home office, and a shot where Lin points out his robbed online alter ego on a computer screen:

Mr Lin was introduced to the readers as follows:

> As many of Quanzhou's time-honoured online gamers, Mr Lin started playing online games several years ago, and has spent considerable energy and money doing so.
>
> (Pan Deng, *DNZB* 15 March 2006, A13)

The vocabulary used in the latter article expresses a neutral attitude towards the way Mr Lin has chosen to spend his energy and money. Moreover, being an adult gamer, he is not 'immersed' or 'absorbed'. He is called a 'time-honoured online gamer' (*zishen wangluo youxi wanjia*), which conveys the impression of a venerable person engaged in a well-respected pursuit. The illustrative photos used in the two articles also reveal the difference in the journalists' angles. The warning in the text about children in Internet cafés is flanked by a photo of youth in school uniforms gathered in front of computers in an Internet café. Mr Lin is portrayed sitting in front of his personal computer in a cosy home office. A similar distinction between respectable Internet surfing and the act of being present in an Internet café also exists in everyday speech. Whereas the middle class 'go online' (*shangwang*) at home or in the office, impressionable youth are said to 'fool around in Internet cafés' (*pao wangba*). This distinction serves to emphasize the fact that it is not Internet surfing in itself (the leisure practice) that is associated with a lack of self-governance and lax morals, but rather it is the Internet café (the leisure place) and the clientele (the group of people) associated with this place that are regarded as harmful for impressionable youth.

Guidance and self-governance

In the Chinese context, self-governance is regarded as a moral virtue, and a person's lack thereof signals not only immaturity but also moral dubiousness

(Bakken 2000: 103–4, 343–4). It is not only in the media that youth are described as lacking in self-control, it has also been a recurrent topic in research on juvenile delinquency in China (Bakken 2000: 343–4) and in writing that promotes leisure education (see for example Zhang Jian 2004: 210, 215). A recent example can be found in the 2007 CNNIC report, which states that young Internet users lack a 'definite world view and values', and that they have 'insufficient self-control capability' and therefore need 'guidance' concerning the content they access online and how to govern their time (CNNIC 2007: 52, 56).[16] As argued in Chapter 3, the PRC leisure ethic is promoted by Chinese authorities in order to guide the populace in their leisure choices. In this context, the Internet café – on a par with the video game arcade – is an immediate threat to the moral order the Chinese authorities promote. Seen from this point of view, games and other online activities threaten to draw young people's attention away from more goal-oriented pursuits. These young people are, after all, the ones who shall 'shoulder the construction and development of the country' (CNNIC 2007: 52). As mentioned above, Internet addiction among young people receives increased attention outside China too. In November 2007, the *New York Times* reported the concerns of child psychiatrists and counsellors in South Korea, where the government has funded a number of counselling centres and hospital treatment programs as well as a rehabilitation centre *cum* boot camp where young 'compulsive Internet users' are exposed to 'military-style obstacle courses' and 'therapeutic workshops' (Fackler 2007). It should therefore come as no surprise that a training camp in Hebei claims to bring youth out of Internet addiction by way of a special training program. Here, youth are taught to earn money the hard way by peddling flowers and newspapers around the town of Shijiazuhang. According to the aforementioned propaganda posters, these activities 'let the children experience the hardships their parents go through to earn a living', and 'these children will henceforth stay away from Internet cafés, and study in earnest'. According to the same poster series, a hospital in Shandong successfully rehabilitated 30 Internet addicts in 2006 and helped them on their way to pass college entrance exams.

In China, the Internet café is considered a twofold danger to middle school students. First, the attraction of the cafés draws students' attention away from their studies and thereby disrupts them in their task of developing skills that can contribute towards the development of the Chinese nation. This latent downward trajectory is epitomized in the propaganda cartoon about Little Huang who left school, headed for the games arcade and stumbled onto a path of crime. Second – as stated by Little Ping above – Internet cafés represent the liability of indirect and direct association with a chaotic environment populated with bad people. Chinese educators and psychologists stress that proper guidance for middle school students is provided at school and in the home, where teachers and parents serve as role models and can assist the student in the process of socialization (Huang Heqing 2001: 24, 26; Hong Ming and Wang Hongli 2002: 754; Sun Hui and Wang Shujuan 2003: 59). The idea that Internet surfing is less harmful if it is practiced in the home means in effect that net surfing is regarded as less detrimental for the offspring of upper-middle-class parents. These are parents who can afford a PC and an Internet connection at home. Moreover, these are parents with a higher-than-average level of education and thus expected to be good role models and guides for their children.

In China the cost of a computer and maintaining an Internet connection at home is considered expensive, and it is telling that the income level of Internet café customers is lower than the income among Chinese Internet users in general (CNNIC 2008: 30), and that very few of the respondents in the *Far Eastern Economic Review*'s 2003 survey of the Chinese elite report having made use of Internet cafés (Croll 2006: 96–7). The scarcity of home computers emphasizes the importance of Internet cafés – officially approved or otherwise – as providers of popular leisure activities to citizens in lower income groups.

In an interview in the *Beijing Times*, Zhang Xinjian of the national Ministry of Culture calls for the government to change its tactics vis-à-vis Internet cafés from prevention to facilitation, stating that

> [...] what the government needs to do is to create places where young people can develop in a healthy manner (*jiankang fazhan*), and not merely tell young people where they cannot go.
> (Gong Gao *HXDSB* 17 February, A30)[17]

Examples of government initiatives that make the Internet available to youth in a healthier setting are rather scarce. The propaganda posters in Quanzhou did, however, refer to two projects, one in Chengdu and one in Changsha, where specially approved 'green' Internet cafés (*lüse wangba*) have been established. Here, middle school students whose parents have given their consent can access the Internet in an environment that encourages civilized (*wenming*) and healthy (*jiankang*) Internet habits. The Party apparatus has also sought to utilize young students' interest in computer games by way of providing alternative, healthy computer games. One example is the 2006 production and promotion of *The Lei Feng Game* (*Lei Feng youxi*), a computer game where players gain points by repairing army trucks, instructing comrades-in-arms in the spirit of Chairman Mao and fighting landlords, rightists, spies and imperialist elements (Xiu Sheng, *HXDSB* 16 March 2006, A4).[18] The government-sponsored online game *Chinese Hero Registry*, where players 'gain points by getting appreciation letters for doing good deeds, such as helping old ladies home in a rainstorm and stopping people from spitting on the sidewalk', (Ni Ching-Ching 2005) is another case in point. This shows that, from the point of view of the party-state, new kinds of leisure practices are not regarded as detrimental in and of themselves. They are only harmful if they serve to take attention away from the young individual's prime duty, which is to educate him or herself and ultimately contribute toward the development of the larger collective.

Quanzhou Internet cafés, both 'black' and official, were frequently caught servicing juvenile customers. Because of this malpractice and the underlying suspicion that Internet cafés give impressionable youth access to online resources without there being proper guidance, these cafés have earned a reputation as places of chaos. This reputation also included Quanzhou's Internet café clientele, who had come to be stigmatized as poorly educated, lacking in self control, and as youth of low cultural competence (*suzhi*). As we shall see in the following examples from the Quanzhou library and one of the local bookshops, Internet café customers as a group were considered essentially different from the more typical patrons, the readers.

The chaotic Internet café customers

The Glorious Bookshop, one of the longstanding book cafés in Quanzhou, underwent a series of transformations during my period of fieldwork. When I first visited the bookshop in 2005 it comprised an Internet café a book café, and a substantial bookshop. When the shop reopened after the New Year holidays in 2007, the Internet café was gone, replaced by a fashionable menswear outlet, and the bookshop and book café were relocated to the top floor of the building. The in-store Internet café had been one of the novelties of the Glorious Bookshop when it opened in 2001. 'At that time people were very curious about computers, and there were not so many Internet cafés as there are now,' said Mr Sun, who worked in the bookshop in its early days. The original plan had been to provide two or three computers where readers could access online resources such as the Digital Library of China (*Zhongguo shuzi tushuguan*). In 2002, however, when the investment group that owned the bookshop acquired a license to run a province-based chain of Internet cafés, the wall towards the neighbouring garage was torn down and the space was converted into a sizeable Internet café area.

According to Sun, 'the air and the environment was much better in our bookshop than in a regular Internet café'. But while Mr Sun perceived the in-store Internet café as an integrated part of the healthy bookshop environment, Mr Xu, the present manager, regarded the experiment as more problematic. He stated that 'there was a conflict between the Internet café and the bookshop'. According to Xu, himself a man in his thirties, this conflict was caused by the Internet café customers, whom he described as 'young people who made a constant racket and who were mostly interested in computer games'. Xu held that bookstore readers, in contrast, were fond of tranquillity and that readers were bothered by the behaviour of the Internet café customers. 'The Internet café customers did not care about the wishes of the readers. So the loss of the café was a good thing for our reading clientele.'

The notion that Internet café users are essentially different from readers was also evident in the way the local library staff talked about visitors to their electronic reading room (*dianzi yuelanshi*), the library's own Internet café area. As was the case in the Glorious Bookshop, the idea behind the library computer room was to give readers access to e-books and other electronic reading materials. 'The fact is,' said the library director, 'people who use our electronic reading room do not really employ these resources. Instead they chat, they look for news and they watch movies. They treat it as if it were a regular Internet café.' The library computer room opened in 1998, and has extended its opening hours to half past eleven at night. Despite this, there has been a steady decline in the number of visitors, according to one of the librarians. She holds that 'people who hang around in Internet cafés find our opening hours too limited'.

In these accounts, the Internet café customer is cast in the role of the uncultured, uncontrollable 'other' who disturbs the tranquillity of the respectable reader. He belongs in the Internet café, a limitless environment where there is no closing time and where it is possible to be noisy and inconsiderate. With his 'disorderly' practices, the Internet café customer fails to conform to the '"consensuses" or conventions' (Lefebvre 1991: 56) of the healthy spaces libraries and bookshops attempt to generate. Moreover, the Internet café customers' leisure preferences are presented as unsatisfactory and inferior to those of the more cultured reader. When given the opportunity to read, the Internet café customer will instead choose games, movies, and online chatting. Thus, the Internet café customer is regarded as the embodiment of low cultural capital, poor taste and low class status – in other words, he is regarded as a person of low cultural competence (*suzhi*). These notions are further strengthened by official surveys stating that the fact that 60.4 per cent of young rural students (compared to 43.9 per cent of urban students) surf in Internet cafés is a problem that 'deserves the attention and guidance of the competent authorities' (CNNIC 2007: 55–56). Moreover, official propaganda materials highlight that middle school students in vocational schools are more likely to become Internet addicts than are students in regular schools (*Wangluo wenming* propaganda posters, Quanzhou 2007). In China, vocational schools are generally regarded as less prestigious, and as providers of a type of education that is more fitting for students of poor quality, i.e. rural youth (see for example Zhang Xiaofeng and Fan Guorui 2002: 53). Thus, Internet cafés have come to be associated with the 'inappropriate other' (Gyan Prakash in Anagnost 1997: 77), in this case the younger segment of the floating rural population, distinguishable from the urban middle class by their low level of education, unstable work relations and general 'poor quality'. This image is strengthened by media reports in which Internet cafés and other 'middle- and low-level places of entertainment in areas where town meets country' are described as 'breeding grounds for criminals' (Lian Yuji, *HXDSB* 28 November 2006, C4).

In Quanzhou, Internet cafés have come to be regarded as places of disorder where young students risk being exposed to unhealthy (*bu jiankang*) materials, bad (*buliang*) habits, and bad people (*huairen*). These examples from Quanzhou suggest that the Chinese media's portrayal of forces of *luan* is part of the Party's hegemony-building effort, as argued by Anagnost. On the one hand, writes Anagnost, any article describing *luan* practices will be 'eagerly read by educated urban residents who absorb this powerful lesson in a state of shocked titillation'. At the same time 'the display of these forces of *luan* as barely controlled threats to the social order also builds hegemony for the party as the only alternative to chaos' (Anagnost 1997: 96). In *The Exemplary Society*, Bakken likens the Chinese

126 *Bad people in bad places?*

process of socialization to 'a theatre in which the minority of upper and lower levels parade virtue and vice for the wavering but educable majority of the middle' (Bakken 2000: 92). Bakken's metaphor is descriptive of the way 'chaotic' Internet café customers are presented in the official reports, media, propaganda texts and everyday expressions analysed above; they are paraded as a warning to students and their parents of the dangers of association with all things *luan*.

Karaoke rooms as segregated social spaces

While the Internet café is most often portrayed as a place of chaos, karaoke parlours enjoy a more ambiguous reputation. Quanzhou's local papers often convey an image of karaoke parlours as prime sites for drug abuse and night-time brawls (Yan Peng *et al. DNZB* 15 February 2006, A8). This, however, does not prevent the general middle-class audience from socializing in the very same karaoke parlours. Karaoke is an import from the Japanese leisure market that became popular in China during the late 1980s and early 1990s (Feng Chongyi 2005: 148, note 1).[19] In Quanzhou, this leisure activity is referred to as '*qu KTV*' or '*qu K*' ('go out to KTV'), '*qu changge*' or even '*qu K ge*' (lit. 'go out to sing'). It is an activity enjoyed by middle-class people of different ages and vocations.

Quanzhou has a choice of karaoke parlours that cater to the various customer segments, ranging from the extravagant services of the Quanzhou hotel, where

Figure 6.4 Singing – or at least mouthing the words – together at the karaoke parlour.

the fee for the karaoke room is said to be 6,000 *yuan* a night, to the branches of a local karaoke chain where a few hours in a karaoke room cost less than 100 *yuan*. Karaoke parlours consist of a number of separate rooms, each containing couches and tables, one or more large TV screens, microphones, and a computer from which to choose songs. Whereas the Internet café is a limitless space open for association with chaos and 'bad' people, the karaoke parlour offers separate rooms for each party of guests. The most comfortable rooms are equipped with a small bathroom, which adds to the sense of privacy. This separation into closed-off rooms makes it possible for the urban middle class to perceive the karaoke space as inviting and orderly, and 'theirs'. Thus, the presence of chaotic 'others' in a parlour can be regarded as a mere anomaly. By considering in detail the variety of ways in which karaoke is enjoyed – from binge drinking to reminiscing about one's youth – this section shows that, through their diverse practices, the different audiences generate their individual sense of the karaoke parlour as leisure space.

The multiple meanings of karaoke

Some interviewees in Quanzhou held that karaoke parlours were only for the very young, or considered them as establishments that catered only to young men with no responsibilities and too much money to spend. These opinions were typically held by men in their thirties who had recently left their bachelor lifestyle behind, or by middle-aged men who preferred the tranquillity of the tea house to bustling karaoke parlours. In recent years, the everyday practice of drinking and serving tea has become transformed into a prestigious leisure activity in Quanzhou. Knowledge and appreciation of fine teas has come to be considered a mark of cultural distinction. Some of the local tea aficionados regarded karaoke as an unsophisticated and rather uncouth form of leisure. Through conversations and observation, however, I found that there was no clear-cut distinction between the tea house and karaoke clientele. In fact, some ardent karaoke parlour customers proved to be as well versed in tea culture as in the art of karaoke.

As an example, in celebration of her fortieth birthday, Ms Zhang invited four of her closest friends and their children (aged nine to 14) to dinner at her favourite restaurant in Quanzhou's Gourmet Street. The guests were women with university-level educations, all employed in various local cultural institutions. The meal was followed by a visit to one of the nearby karaoke parlours. Zhang's friends had brought a layer cake that they enjoyed inside the karaoke room, to a choice of evergreens and pop hits. Some weeks later, the same party, minus the children, gathered for a foot massage and a snack before proceeding to a discreet and distinguished tea house, where they sampled and discussed choice teas from a local mountain region. This example serves to demonstrate the ease with which middle-class customers switch between different leisure establishments and engage in both popular and high-brow activities. An International Women's Day lunch party hosted by one of the local government bureaus is another example of the degree to which karaoke is embraced by well-educated women. After a hearty meal in one of Quanzhou's up-market restaurants, the party continued in the neighbouring karaoke parlour. The group sat down in a karaoke room and continued to snack and drink while singing along to Hong Kong and Taiwanese pop hits from their student days. A woman of minority descent sang a song inspired by her native place, and a colleague who had once received musical instruction was asked by the boss to entertain with songs in semi-operatic style. A younger woman who had recently been transferred from a military academy pleased her superiors with several numbers from the selection of military tunes, including 'We, the Soldiers' (*Zan dang bing de ren...*). The ability to contribute a well-executed karaoke number is also admired and appreciated in social settings outside the karaoke parlour itself. As an example, during the festive reception held in connection with the Urban Photography Conference, the most notable conference participants were asked to contribute a song of choice. Local wedding receptions also sometimes entail guests offering up karaoke performances in honour of the newlyweds.

The utility of the karaoke routine as a way to pay one's respects to a host or show off one's talents to colleagues and superiors shows the recognition of karaoke as a form of social exchange. These semi-official performances differ, however, from karaoke as it is typically practiced by parties in Quanzhou's karaoke parlours. Here, karaoke is seldom a performance given by an individual facing an audience. More often than not, it is a collective form of music appreciation in which a group of people sit together facing the screen, singing or at least mouthing the words of the song. Some karaoke parties revolve around the opportunity to sing the songs that carry a special meaning to the people present, for the sake of a shared memory or the shared love of a given song or popular performer. In other cases, the karaoke room itself is the main attraction. Ms He, a homemaker and amateur artist, stated that she and her friends 'go to KTV not so much for the singing, more because it is a place to get together, to talk, and be together with friends'. A similar point was made by a group of former classmates, now in their late twenties, who had gathered in a local café. One young man held that going to a karaoke parlour was just the same as going to a café: 'It is mainly a place to get together – that is to say, no one goes to the coffee house for the sake of the coffee...'. The importance of the karaoke parlour as a place to gather with friends was also confirmed by interviewees active in the local associations, such as the Municipal Choir, the Volunteer's Association and the Professional English Club. When members of these associations wanted to socialize outside of their regular events and activities, they often met at a karaoke parlour or a café, partly because they had nowhere else to meet. Moreover, compared to Quanzhou's bars and cafés, the low-end karaoke parlours are the most reasonably priced establishments in the Quanzhou leisure market. Regular weeknights are often heavily discounted, and the thriftiest customers even bring their own snacks and alcohol rather than buying from the in-house shop. In addition, the karaoke room provides a level of privacy that can hardly be matched by any other leisure place – or public spaces, for that matter – in

Quanzhou. Judging from my observations in the local karaoke parlours, these were not places where people would mingle as they do in local bars and discos;[20] customers arrived in parties and socialized behind closed doors. A party might be joined by latecomers, however, and spontaneous invitations could be sent to friends and friends of friends via SMS. Karaoke parlours provide an affordable place for friends to meet in privacy. And as we shall see in the following, the element of privacy has become an object of contention.

The privacy of the karaoke room

In March 2006, a new set of national 'Regulations for the supervision of public entertainment places' received much attention in the local Quanzhou media. The new regulations entailed a restriction in opening hours (all establishments should be closed between at 2.00 a.m. and 8.00 a.m.) and an end to the admittance of unaccompanied minors into karaoke parlours. Several newspaper articles also described a novel mode of supervision the local authorities would bring into play, namely the direct transmission of surveillance footage from the entrance and exit points of leisure establishments. These recordings would then be monitored by the municipal cultural bureau, which in the new regulations also gained the authority to shut down leisure establishments.[21] A representative from the Bureau of Public Security explained to local journalists that these new methods of surveillance would assist the authorities in protecting the local citizenry by preventing prostitution and drug abuse in karaoke parlours, dance halls and other entertainment places 'where such offences as fighting, brawls and theft are over-represented' (Yan Peng *et al. DNZB* 15 February 2006, A8). In her study of the policing of the Chinese karaoke market, Jeffreys notes that, during official inspections, the staff often exploit the labyrinth-like layout of the karaoke parlour to 'delay the police investigators and warn potential suspects' (Jeffreys 1997: 52). From the point of view of the police, electronic surveillance tapes may mean the end of such obstacles. However, in an interview in the *Beijing Times*, Zhang Xinjian, head of the Department for the Culture Market (*Wenhua shichang si*) at the Ministry of Culture, stressed that the increased surveillance would be in the interest of the public.[22] The extended surveillance measures in karaoke parlours were further justified with reference to similar surveillance practices in Taiwan, Japan and Germany, and the use of surveillance tapes for the police and fire departments (Gong Gao *HXDSB* 17 February, A30). When questioned about the need for increased use of video surveillance in places of entertainment, Zhang argued that '[e]ntertainment places are public places of consumption, so there is no infringement on consumers' privacy there. Moreover, it can be of use to prove whether [officials] spend public funds on entertainment' (Gong Gao *HXDSB* 17 February, A30). The fact that many karaoke parlours in Quanzhou already have video surveillance in place, and some businesses have also installed window panes in the doors of each room so that waiters can keep an eye on the customers' activities, means that the new regulations will not radically alter the existing conditions in the karaoke business

(Yan Peng et al. *DNZB* 15 February 2006, A8). This indicates that the extensive media coverage of these 'new' initiatives mainly to show off the local administration taking strong measures to secure 'the healthy and orderly development of the culture market' (*QZSWHJ* 2005: 7).

In the above interview, Zhang Xinjian from the Ministry of Culture also argued that '[l]ate opening hours can harm people's physical and mental health and their work and life' (Gong Gao *HXDSB* 17 February, A30). A critique of nightlife as a waste of energy and resources can also be found in Fan Xiaoxian and Kong Linghua's 2006 article about consumer culture, where they stress that fashionable nightlife habits are damaging to the body (Fan Xiaoxian and Kong Linghua 2006: 88). A similar point is made in sociologist Wang Zhongwu's article on consumption and modernization, where he warns against the physical consequences of 'reckless waste and extravagant consumption' in restaurants and other nightlife establishments (Wang Zhongwu 2005: 125). It is a fact that lifestyle ailments are an increasing problem in China and that excessive drinking and drug abuse is both a social problem and a health risk for the individuals involved. My point here is to show how these facts are rhetorically incorporated into the official leisure ethic discourse. Karaoke parlours and other businesses that comprise the nightlife segment of the leisure market are consistently described by administrators and social commentators as sites of 'bad habits and corrupt customs' (*louxi*) (see for example Wang Zhongwu 2005: 125, 126). These indirect appeals for the public to practice self-discipline and temperance in their leisure are based on an instrumental leisure ethic, where leisure is regarded primarily as a means to restore people's work capacity. Within this discourse, karaoke is acceptable only as long as it offers the workforce an opportunity for recreation, not exhaustion. The fact that cadres employed in the Party and government administration not only enjoy more leisure time during weekends and holidays than do others but also spend more time and resources eating out and going to entertainment places than any other social group in China (Wang Yalin 2003: 87–8) is never discussed in these contexts. The leisure ethic and its appeal to exercise restraint in one's leisure life is addressed to the general workforce. The leisure practices of the administrative elite are, however, conveniently ignored.

In the interviews and quotes above, government representatives and scholars describe the culture market as a space infested with petty crime, prostitution, health hazards and embezzlement. The message is that these disorderly activities warrant a stronger degree of control and inspection from the local authorities. This perception of the Quanzhou leisure market was not necessarily shared by karaoke customers. One of the local newspapers printed a small *enquête* where townspeople were asked to comment on the new legislation. One woman was said to welcome the new opening hours, as she had lost many nights of sleep because of noise from a neighbouring karaoke parlour. A second woman wanted entertainment places to remain close to the residential areas in the city centre, as this would be most convenient for her as a regular karaoke customer. She also expressed a strong dislike for increased surveillance in entertainment places, and was critical of both video surveillance and the possibility of installing window panes in the doors of each karaoke room. This, she said, would make her feel very uncomfortable (*bu zizai*): '[i]t would be like sitting in a shop window for everyone to see. There would be next to no privacy (*tai meiyou yinsi le*)' (Yan Peng *et al. DNZB* 15 February 2006, A8).[23] In the same article, a representative from the local bureau of culture was asked to comment on this woman's statement. He responded in a manner similar to that of Mr Zhang in the Ministry: 'What takes place in these spots is mass entertainment, which does not involve personal secrets. Moreover, the footage will only be shown to trained personnel in the Bureau of Culture [...]. We cannot call this an infringement of privacy (*qinfan yinsi*).' My data from conversations and participant observation in Quanzhou's karaoke parlours show that the karaoke room is cherished by customers precisely for the kind of privacy it provides. Although socializing does take place in private homes in Quanzhou, several of the interviewees who were in their twenties either lived with their extended families or boarded in simple rooms that could not easily accommodate visitors. These young adults expressed that it would not be practical – and it would make them uncomfortable – to invite their peers to socialize in their homes. As a consequence, karaoke rooms were appreciated as one of the few places where a party of friends could meet in private to socialize. On the whole, it seems that '*qu* K *ge*' really means 'to go out together' and that the act of singing actually plays a secondary part in the karaoke experience. This notion was evident when Mr Lu, a graphic designer in his mid-twenties, brought me along to a karaoke parlour on a late Thursday evening. In my field notes I recorded the following:

> [...] We took the elevator to the fifth storey of the Happy Day karaoke parlour and entered the familiar labyrinth of hallways lined with numbered doors, one for each karaoke room. When we reached our destination we found the party was already well under way. Twelve young men in their early twenties were standing and sitting around a group of imitation leather sofas. The table was littered with spilled drinks, little plates of snacks, and five empty bottles of fake brand liquor. The room was lit by blurred video images on three large TV screens. Two of the young men joined in a melancholy Chinese pop ballad, screaming into the microphones with none of the others paying attention. Some were engaged in a drinking game. A girl was asleep on the sofa [...].

This scene was analogous to the description Lu gave me of a regular night out for him and his young friends. First they – both men and women – would meet for dinner in a restaurant, and then they would proceed to a karaoke parlour where they would 'drink and talk until someone pukes or falls asleep. We really don't sing that much,' he said. 'For us, the KTV is basically a place to drink beer. You turn on the music, shut the doors and then nobody can disturb you.'

See no evil, hear no evil

The opportunity to socialize behind closed doors makes the karaoke room an insulated space where the activities of other customer parties can go unnoticed, or at least be ignored. I found it remarkable that – with the exception of Mr Lu – none of the middle-class townspeople with whom I went to karaoke parlous ever mentioned the crime and chaos which were so prominent in the media's portrayal of these entertainment places (for examples, see Fu Jian *HXDSB* 18 November 2006: A5; Yan Peng *et al. DNZB* 15 February 2006, A8; Gong Gao *HXDSB* 17 February, A30). When I referred to news reports of recent crackdowns on drug abuse and other violations of the regulations for leisure spaces, my companions often reacted with incredulity. When I recounted to more reserved karaoke customers my own observations of rowdy karaoke parties and excessive drinking at their favourite karaoke parlours, the reaction was either that such activities were very rare, or that they had heard of such behaviour, but only in 'other places'.

The spatial organization of the parlour makes it easy for a group of people to envision or 'produce' the kind of space they themselves prefer or at least accept. The doors serve to shut in the goings-on of a private party, but also serve to shut out the practices of others. This may explain why the local administration's professed need for increased monitoring of local karaoke parlours was met with little or no understanding by many customers. They did not recognize their own experiences and practices in the government *cum* media descriptions of the karaoke parlour as a chaotic space.

In his 2000 case study from Yunnan, Thøgersen analyses local culture in terms of four cultural spheres: official culture, intellectual culture, commercial culture, and indigenous traditional culture. Thøgersen concludes that none of the four spheres of culture exists in isolation (Thøgersen 2000: 141). This is also true in the case of Quanzhou's leisure culture; some activities can be said to be associated with certain groups, such as tea tasting with intellectuals and educated entrepreneurs, and card games with the uneducated and unemployed. At the same time, there is an abundance of examples where the leisure practices of the individual diverge from what is expected from his or her social standing. Moreover, the cases analysed in this chapter show that people from different parts of the new middle class (i.e. those who have a middle-class[24] income, occupation or level of consumption) (Zhou Xiaohong 2005: 1–8) often engage in the same leisure activities. Importantly, however, the ways in which different people engage in a given practice do serve as a more detailed marker of social status. Surfing the Internet at home rather than in an Internet café is one such example, and using the karaoke room as a place to talk and sing together with fellow middle- or upper-class citizens, rather than taking part in a 'chaotic' drinking binge as less 'cultured' customers might do, is another. Sometimes, however, these divergent karaoke cultures clash in one and the same person. This was the case when Mr Lu brought me along to the Happy Day karaoke parlour, as described in the excerpt above.

Within minutes of entering the room, Lu wanted to leave, and as we made our way out of the building he told me over and over that 'these people are just too crazy'. In an effort to distance himself from the party, Lu repeatedly informed me that the only person he knew there was his boss' driver. He also said that 'guys like these earn comparatively well and have few responsibilities, so they don't care much about the way they spend their time or money'. When we arrived, the party had already consumed a thousand *yuan's* worth of fake brand liquor and the room they had chosen would cost them a further 100 *yuan* per hour. Lu went on to say that the young men in that room 'have little or no education; some of them have not even finished primary school'. He expected that the party would proceed to a hotel somewhere where the young men would pick up prostitutes. Lu said that he himself did not want to be part of that.

It may be that Lu was truly embarrassed to be associated with these activities, both those we observed and those he expected to occur. Or it may have been that my presence as a foreigner or as a woman made him want to dissociate himself from the people and the activities we had encountered, however briefly. I nonetheless find it noteworthy that Lu linked the excessive drinking we just witnessed (and also took part in) to people of low culture and little education, while at the same time regarding it as perfectly normal for himself and his closest friends to 'drink and talk until someone pukes or falls asleep'. My point here is not so much to demonstrate Mr Lu's contradictory streak, but rather to bring attention once more to the way moral judgements are made on the basis of social status. In the privacy of the karaoke room, a variety of parties gather on any given weeknight for a combination of drinking, snacking, chatting and singing – an activity they call '*qu* KTV'. While the leisure activity is essentially the same, the boss's driver who is drunk at a karaoke parlour is judged differently from the low-level official who has toasted too many of his superiors in the room next door. While the former is considered *luan* and an example of unhealthy leisure, the latter signifies mastery of a code of behaviour among officials and businessmen. As in the case with Quanzhou's Internet cafés, karaoke is only unhealthy when practiced by people of a low social standing.

The importance of first-hand experience

In the case of the Internet cafés, it seems that the official leisure ethic's description of the Internet café as an unhealthy place and its clientele as *luan* rings true to middle-class parents, as well as to the interviewees in the book trade. Here, the leisure ethic with its focus on education as the road to prosperity is very much in tune with the values and experiences of Quanzhou's middle classes. This again poses the question of the extent to which Quanzhou inhabitants are influenced by or adhere to the PRC leisure ethic. If we compare the two cases analysed in this chapter, we find that the government's suspicion of Internet cafés is consistent with prevalent attitudes among the middle-class city population. When it comes to the official depiction of karaoke parlours as chaotic spaces, however, the official stance does not seem to influence the attitudes of middle-class patrons towards these establishments. The inconsistent measure of effect that the official leisure discourse has in these two cases may be explained by the impact of first-hand experience. Quanzhou's middle-class residents know the karaoke parlours from personal experience. They have been there, they have had fun there, and, in the same way as Friedman's interviewees did, they can recount their experiences there as 'honest fun'. This explains why the media's portrayal of karaoke parlours as places of violence and drug abuse was met with incredulity by regular customers: the media images did not mirror their own personal experiences. As for the Internet cafés, the adult middle class in Quanzhou is not part of the clientele, which means that they lack first-hand experience with the Internet café as a place of leisure. Middle-class interviewees' perceptions of Internet cafés were based mainly on hear-say and reports in the local media, and they had no personal counter-narrative to inform them in their assessment of the café environment. This shows that the official discourse of unhealthy and healthy leisure has a stronger impact when judgements are not measured against personal experience. As long as the administration's approach to the Internet café business focuses more on control than on facilitation, the stigmatization of Internet cafés and their users will remain unchallenged.

The analysis of Internet cafés as chaotic leisure places shows that that the official discourse of chaotic and unhealthy leisure disguises questions of social class, taste and morality. While middle-class inhabitants of Quanzhou shunned the places they held to be chaotic and warned their children to keep bad influences at a distance, they often engaged in the same activities in more healthy spaces, i.e. in their own homes. The fact that members of the local middle class held the same opinions of Internet cafés as those expressed by governmental departments and the local Party-dominated media cannot, however, be taken as proof of a general consent among middle-class consumers to the local administration's policies vis-a-vis the culture market. As the analysis of karaoke as a leisure activity indicates, middle-class customers pay little heed to official warnings against karaoke parlours as places of unhealthy leisure, since they have their own experiences as a point of reference. Conversely, the fact that well-educated white-collar employees do not patronize Internet cafés makes them less prone to scrutinize the official portrayal of the cafés and their clientele as *luan*.

The analysis shows that it is not the intrinsic quality of the leisure activity that distinguishes the healthy from the unhealthy. Rather, it is the level of cultural competence that sets the uneducated and chaotic karaoke customer or Net surfer apart from the civilized and self-disciplined urban middle-class leisure consumer. With its dichotomy of healthy and unhealthy forms of leisure, the PRC leisure ethic serves to divert attention away from questions of social class and social inequality among the urban population. These findings support Anagnost's suggestion that in post-Mao China the discourse of class has been supplanted by a discourse of civility – and the lack thereof.

The examples in this chapter also serve as illustrations of the Chinese authorities' idiosyncratic approach to the culture market and the leisure activities it provides. On the one hand, the party-state seeks to govern the influence of popular culture on the populace. The government's hands-on supervision of the leisure market, bolstered by the propagation of a serviceable leisure ethic, can be seen as a means towards this end. On the other hand, the leisure market's various outlets, including restaurants, karaoke parlours, tea houses, spas and health clubs, have 'come to be seen as powerful symbols of modernization' (Thøgersen 2000: 135; see also Feng Chongyi 2005: 134). To many Chinese, having both time and money to spend on leisure is proof of their ascent into the relatively comfortable (*xiaokang*) standard of living. Seen from this perspective, a prolific leisure market serves to legitimize the party-state policies of economic growth by fulfilling the population's expectations of a modern urban lifestyle. This calls for a closer look at changes and continuities in the consumer practices of the Chinese city population.

7 Consumption as a form of leisure

It was Saturday morning in Quanzhou, and I was accompanying Ms Zhang on her weekly round of grocery shopping in a three-storey mall a few blocks from the walled community where she lives. At 40, Ms Zhang is the manager of a government work unit in the culture sector. She has a busy work schedule and prefers to leave an opening on Saturday mornings to do the grocery shopping for

Figure 7.1 Migrant worker with a taste for middle class-style consumption.

the week to come. First we browsed the clothes stores on the ground floor, where she looked for a sweater to wear for the New Year's celebration. We then took the escalator up to the grocery department, where she pointed out to me the quality of the supermarket's interior, that it was open, clean and practical. She also talked about the prices, which she found to be affordable, and the quality of the vegetables and meat, which were reputed to be superior. Ms Zhang browsed the shelves at a slow pace, inspecting all famous brands for bargains. Whereas she considered her daily shopping for additional vegetables and condiments to be stressful and boring, shopping in the mall was to Ms Zhang a personal treat: doing her shopping in this particular mall gave her a sense of peace (*anjing*), she said. The spatial qualities of the supermarket and the way she could do her shopping there – at her own pace and in a tranquil mode – made the mall a relaxing and leisurely space.

During the weeks leading up to the Chinese New Year, I had several opportunities to join Ms Zhang and some of her girlfriends, all in their early forties, in the continued search for the perfect New Year's sweater. They would try out countless garments in department stores and independent boutiques, all the while bantering humorously with the saleswomen and sharing advice concerning which styles were in fashion and which colours suited whom. They also discussed what would constitute a bargain in their case. 'You should not buy this sweater simply because it is affordable,' one of them said to Ms Zhang. 'You have so many sweaters at home and there's no point in buying one you will not use. Better buy one you really like.' In response to this reasoning, Ms Zhang replied that 'at our age and at our wage level we should buy clothes that are approximately in the price range of three to five hundred *yuan*'.[1] Over the weeks, one sweater turned into several, and Ms Zhang also bought a pair of pants and a winter jacket, some sweaters for her son and also for her brother, whom she said 'trusts my taste and always enjoys a gift'.

Ms Zhang's shopping practices epitomize the significance of shopping among the Chinese middle class: the mall and the shopping street function as places of leisure, places to socialize and confirm social bonds through a shared shopping experience or through the purchase of gifts. Moreover, Ms Zhang's willingness to spend a considerable sum on a sweater she did not really need serves to illustrate the fact that the Quanzhou middle class is far removed from the 'low income and low consumption, planned distribution and shortage' that characterized everyday life under Maoism (Lu Hanlong 2000: 131). This change in purchasing power and retail supply in the reform era has been described by Western scholars in terms of a 'consumer revolution' or even a 'second liberation' of the Chinese people (Davis 2000; Madsen 2000). Elizabeth Croll writes that in the 1980s

> [t]he new world of goods encouraged *new practices*,[2] the chief of which was the transformation of shopping from a small corner or utilitarian corner of domestic life into one of the most compelling of leisure occupations.
>
> (2006: 40–1)

But to what extent does this shopping-as-leisure constitute an essentially *new* phenomenon? The introduction of economic reforms in the late 1970s and early 1980s brought increased spending power to many Chinese, and the ensuing spending on consumer durables such as refrigerators, washing machines, bikes and motorbikes has meant significant changes in people's everyday lives. Contemporary Chinese consumer practices and attitudes towards consumption should be considered, however, not only in terms of social change, but also from the point of view of continuity. The analysis of window-shopping later in this chapter shows that it is a kind of leisure practiced even before the coming of the market economy. This means that it is the prevalence of consumption *cum* leisure rather than the phenomenon in itself which is a novelty.

A second objective of this chapter is to discuss the argument made by, among others, Elizabeth Croll and, most explicitly, Jing Wang, that the Chinese government has used and still utilizes consumer policies as tools for the pacification of the Chinese populace (Jing Wang 2001a; 2001b; Tomba 2004: 3; Croll 2006: 30–1). I agree with both Croll and Jing Wang in their analyses of the legitimacy of the party-state, which they regard as closely linked to the authorities' ability to generate economic growth and increase people's living standards as promised. It is certainly in the interest of the Chinese party-state that the growth of the national market is fuelled by private spending. Nevertheless, I find that Jing Wang underestimates the agency of the Chinese consumer when she claims that government campaigns are successful in their drives to make citizens spend more money on the 'rational recreations' promoted by the same authorities (Jing Wang 2001a: 40). This may have been the case in the late 1980s and early 90s when the authorities evidently feared the rise of a critical middle class, as demonstrated in the campaigns to promote 'spiritual civilization'. However, as we shall see in the following, the relationship between the party-state and the growing middle classes has turned out more harmonious than the authorities expected. In the previous chapters, my analyses of examples from Quanzhou show that the use of official campaigns to guide or determine the practices of the populace is rather limited. I argue that this is also true in the case of consumption. By focusing on individual consumers and their outlooks and practices, this chapter concludes that attitudes towards consumption and commercialism among the Quanzhou middle class are shaped just as much by the embodied experiences of individuals and the values of the cultured middle class as they are shaped by the party-state's attempts at social engineering.

Changes and continuities in Chinese consumption

> 'Restrain extravagance, worship frugality' (*yi she chong jian*).
> (Wang Zhongwu 2005: 124, with reference to Yu Chengdiao 1999)

These are the terms used by sociologist Wang Zhongwu in his description of what he calls the Chinese 'traditional consumer culture' (*chuantong xiaofei wenhua*) (Wang Zhongwu 2005: 123). Wang writes that in the Confucian mainstream tradition, frugality was promoted as a virtue. According to Wang, the perceived respectability of a simple and even impoverished life may have proved instrumental to the power holders in ancient China; it was an ideology that assisted the rulers in their attempts at governing a territory populated by poor peasants. Wang Zhongwu writes that this traditional concept of consumption was a hindrance to the development of modernity in China (Wang Zhongwu 2005: 123).[3] He goes on to argue that the transition from the people's struggle to secure food and clothing (*wenbao*) to the spread of a relatively comfortable standard of living (*xiaokang*) has been fuelled by a change in mentality. He perceives this as a change from the 'traditional' focus on thrift and frugality to a 'contemporary' kind of consumer culture where people 'know how to earn and spend and strive to increase their quality of life' (Wang Zhongwu 2005: 124). I find that Wang's application of the term 'consumer culture' to describe social phenomena in a vaguely defined Chinese past is problematic for several reasons. First, 'consumer culture' as a social phenomenon is usually linked to the development of an industrial economy and the mass consumption that followed in its wake (Campbell 2000: 52, Ewen: 2000: 186; Fan Xiaoxian and Kong Linghua 2006: 87). Here, Wang Zhongwu is in danger of taking contemporary practices as a norm and thereby considering pre-modern people 'to be merely prevented from behaving like us because of the lack of an industrial economy' (Campbell 2000: 52). Second – as Wang himself does point out – there was no real market for the sale of products and services in ancient times and thus no cultural consumption in the strictest sense. Third, Wang does not take into account the buying and selling of commodities of foreign origin in China in the late nineteenth- and early twentieth centuries. In *Exotic Commodities*, Dikötter describes the spread of consumer objects from thermos flasks to bicycles and cameras in the time before the establishment of the People's Republic. Dikötter stresses that while 'things foreign were often displayed to indicate social status by modernizing elites, many also found their way into the daily lives of ordinary people' (Dikötter 2006: 1). This means that the consumption of goods both for practical use and as symbols of status is not an entirely new phenomenon in China (Latham 2006b: 231). A similar string of continuity can be followed in the alternation between frugal and colourful clothing since the end of the imperial era. In Qing times, wearing dark-coloured clothing was a sign of decorum and modesty, and there was also a system of distinct colour codes (yellow for the emperor, purple for officials, etc.). The Republican period saw both a spread of diversified clothing styles and the popularization of multi-coloured garments and accessories (Dikötter 2006: 196–202). After the 1949 revolution, the blue or green Mao uniform became a symbol of the frugal and egalitarian values of the Communist party-state. However, even during the Cultural Revolution, when 'efforts to be fashionable were viewed as signs of reactionary values or bourgeois taste', women in Shanghai added little touches of colour to their uniforms (Lu Hanlong 2000: 132). Moreover, official propaganda posters in the early 1970s depicted women with 'pretty bows in their hair, or colourful and patterned blouses peeping out from under their Mao jackets' (Evans 2006: 177–8).

So when Croll describes the transition from 'blue garb to a variety of dress colour and style' in the early stages of the reform period, this should be read as the culmination of a gradual *re*introduction of colourful fashion, rather than the appearance of something new. These examples indicate that the difference between the consumption of objects and clothes in the present and consumer practices in the past is more a question of degree than of essence. In other words, the significance of adornment and fashion styles and the purchase of consumer items to show off one's status are not particular to contemporary China. Rather, it is the spread of varied consumer opportunities to a larger amount of the population which is characteristic of this time and age.

In the above-mentioned article, Wang Zhongwu makes a valid point when arguing that the development of the Chinese consumer culture is not merely a question of changing economic structures but also a change in the dominant attitudes towards private consumption. Wang describes this as a change from a 'traditional' to a 'contemporary' attitude towards consumption, with Deng's introduction of reform policies as the turning point. Judith Farquhar challenges this historiographic stance by taking into account the continued influence of moralist asceticism and the strictly-enforced distribution policies during high-Maoism on the consumer practices we find in China today (Farquhar 2002: 15). The denial of individual desires under Maoist collectivism – a time when, in Farquhar's words, 'it was not acceptable to introduce individual appetites, or their indulgence, into discourse' (Farquhar 2002: 3) – must be taken into consideration when we seek to understand Chinese people's current attitudes towards consumption. It is against the background of the ideologically grounded denunciation of private consumption during the 1950s and 1960s that the contemporary attitudes towards consumption stand out in relief.

The renewed acceptance for consumption

It is customary to represent consumption in the reform era as consecutive waves of 'three big items' (*san dajian*), from the wristwatch, sewing machine, and bike of the late 1970s via the gradual introduction of the colour TV, refrigerators, and washing machines in the 1980s, to stereos, air conditioners and microwave ovens in the 1990s (Lu Hanlong 2000: 136; 'Xin "san dajian"...' xinhuanet.com 2005; Croll 2006: Ch. 2 and 3; Meng Lei 2007: 22). The popularity and spread of these consumer items not only demonstrates the increased spending power among – first and foremost – the urban population. It is also tangible proof of the changes in attitudes towards private consumption in the Chinese Communist Party. Whereas anti-consumerism had dominated the Party ideology during the Mao era (Madsen 2000: 317), and a majority of goods and edibles had been distributed to the urban population by way of the *danwei* system (Lu Hanlong 2000: 129), the reform era saw the return of consumption (as well as food production) to the level of the individual household.

Reading through issues of the local Party newspaper, the *Fujian ribao*, from the early days of the reform era, the change in the Communist Party's official attitude towards private consumption is striking. Here, commercials for consumer items made their first appearances in the spring of 1980. On pages that until recently had been occupied by calls for birth planning, the mechanization of agriculture, and exegesis of the Four Modernizations, the editors suddenly made space for black-and-white photos of Swiss wrist watches accompanied by the following caption:

> Eternal beauty. Complete satisfaction.
> (Advertisement in *FJRB* April 2 1980: 4)

The same paper printed the following advertisement for a Hong Kong brand of tape recorders:

> Returning home to visit relatives? Looking for gifts for relatives and friends? A Kangyi brand [tape recorder] is the optimal choice.
> (Advertisement in *FJRB* April 2 1980: 3)

Advertisements such as these indicate that the satisfaction of consumers' desires was considered legitimate in the official media already in the early 1980s. However, between 1981 and 1984, the Communist Party initiated campaigns to curb the materialist tendencies that Party authorities termed a form of 'spiritual pollution' (Friedman 2006: 231). Ann Anagnost describes how the Party's ideological leadership perceived the 'pursuit of material development independent of ethico-moral development' as a trend which would 'lead to the brutalization of life and social disorder' (*luan*) (Anagnost 1997: 84). The campaigns addressed Party members and intellectuals especially (Friedman 2006: 231), but Croll reports that, in the early days of reform policies, ordinary people also showed a reluctance to brag about new purchases, as they were afraid that policies would suddenly turn and that 'they would become the object of criticism rather than admiration' (2006: 37). As will be discussed in more detail below, I found that there was a prevalent concern about the detrimental effects of consumerism among Quanzhou's more cultured inhabitants. Among the Quanzhou middle class in general, however, I got the impression that the pursuit of the 'three big items' of the present decade, i.e. higher education, apartments,[4] and cars ('Xin "san dajian"...' xinhuanet.com 2005; Meng Lei 2007: 22), was widespread and also accepted. The general attitude was that a good match in marriage involved an apartment and a car, and that the next step in material comfort would be a villa (*bieshu*) in one of the developing suburbs along the coastline. In 2005, advertisements from local real-estate developers glorified the lavish lifestyles of the rich and famous, using slogans such as

> Luxurious housing is the symbol of status, the family banner.
> (Chinfit Real Estate Chinfit Mountain Villas, prospectus: 43)

and

> Live a celebrity-style life in nourishing waterside villas.
> (Fujian Jinwei jituan. Kingwei Waterside Villas prospectus: 2)

In Quanzhou, living in a villa is a dream for many but an opportunity only for the few. The existence of both a popular desire for upscale living and a local market that caters to dreams of material comfort demonstrates the extent to which the satisfaction of the individual consumer's demands has become both acceptable and legitimate in contemporary China.

The scope of cultural consumption in China

The previous chapters have concluded that the commercial leisure market has taken over much of the role the Party apparatus previously played in leisure facilitation and, moreover, that the Quanzhou middle class has acquired the habit of spending both time and money in commercial leisure venues such as karaoke parlours and book cafés. In Quanzhou's old town centre, Confucius himself has now been made the equivalent of a patron saint of commerce. The lanes circling the Confucian temple have been remodelled into the Confucius Temple Antiques Market (*Fuwenmiao guwan shichang*), where vendors offer souvenirs, trinkets and curios from all over China to tourists and locals who come there for window-shopping. There is no doubt that consumption has surpassed both Confucian frugality and Maoist self-denial as the chief virtue in contemporary China.

Jing Wang has argued that in present-day China, leisure and consumption are so closely linked that leisure in effect equals consumption (Jing Wang 2001a: 40; 2001b: 78). Taking Beijing in the late 1990s as her case, she states that the consumption of entertainment and cultural events has increased to the extent that the 'distinction between the realm of culture and the realm of economic activity' has withered (Jing Wang 2001b: 84) and culture has become 'an economic activity in itself' (Jing Wang 2001b: 83). These generalizations about leisure among urban Chinese consumers are challenged by data from other studies. In Wang Yalin's authoritative survey *Chengshi xiuxian* (Urban Leisure), a mere 10 per cent of the respondents in Tianjin had been to a commercial leisure venue during the month in question (Wang Yalin 2003: 57). This finding can be explained with reference to at least two factors. First, the selection of commercial leisure activities in China remains rather modest, and this, of course, has consequences for the actual number of leisure consumers (Wang Yalin 2003: 57; see also Ma Feifeng 2002: 14; Zhang Taiyuan 2007: 107). Second, Wang Yalin's Tianjin survey was conducted in 1998 and much has changed in the Chinese leisure market during the last ten years. Nevertheless, Wang Yalin's findings draw attention to the fact that the consumption of commercial leisure and entertainment is common only among the more affluent segments of the population. In the countryside in particular, cultural consumption is restricted by such factors as a relative stagnation in the rural service sector, a lack of places to congregate, and very limited surplus income. Several Chinese scholars have concluded that although the party-state has succeeded in creating a consumer society among the urban population, the spread of cultural consumption among the general populace in China is still rather limited (Ma Feifeng: 2002: 14; Jun Liping and Li Jing 2002: 27). That the level of Chinese consumers' demands is overestimated is also one of the central points in Elizabeth Croll's recent writing about Chinese consumers (2006: xii). It is a fact that the majority of Chinese citizens have little or no access to leisure venues and only a few *yuan* to spare. Even so, I agree with Jing Wang in her claim that 'regardless of the spending power of individuals, [Chinese people] participate in consumerist culture, and their lives are affected by it' (Jing Wang 2001b: 84). When we consider the amount of attention that consumer items and commercial leisure venues receive in the national media and in everyday conversations throughout China, consumption in itself – and also as a leisure activity – has become a significant aspect of everyday life for people in all income groups.

Consumer policy and consumers' agency

In his introduction to *Consuming China*, Kevin Latham writes that during the course of the last 25 years, the 'asceticism of revolution [has been] replaced by the economic driving force of consumerism' (Latham 2006a: 1). As the above analysis indicates, the political authorities' renewed acceptance of private consumption has opened up for a reinvigoration of popular consumer practices in China. Jing Wang and, to a certain extent, also Elizabeth Croll and Luigi Tomba explain this change in practices as a result of social engineering on the part of the Chinese government (Jing Wang 2001a, 2001b; Tomba 2004: 3; Croll 2006: 30–1). But can the new significance of leisure consumption among the populace be attributed to the government's pro-consumer policies and propaganda alone? This brings us back to the discussion in Chapter 3 concerning Lefebvre's theories of the production of space. Can technocrats simply project their visions of a certain space onto the real world and thus govern and dominate the everyday practices of the population? In other words, can the Chinese government utilize consumption – in this case the consumption of leisure activities in the culture market – as a means of dominance?

The limited use of consumer policy as a form of social engineering

The scholar who has most explicitly scrutinized the instrumental value of the leisure market for Chinese authorities is Jing Wang. She analyses the Chinese cultural economy as a 'ruling technology', used by the local party-state to make the middle classes invest their resources in cultural capital (Jing Wang 2001b: 71). In two articles from 2001, Wang has analysed the impact that the introduction of the two-day weekend and the Labour Day holiday have had on the Beijing 'cultural economy' (*wenhua jingji*) (Jing Wang 2001b). Wang's case study describes how, at the introduction of the two-day holiday in 1994, the local propaganda department in Beijing carried out a nine-month campaign that propagated the guiding principles for 'leisure culture' (*xiuxian wenhua*) (Jing Wang 2001b: 71). Visiting museums, going to movies, participating in sports, sightseeing, learning English, taking driving lessons and learning how to use computers were among the activities the local government promoted as 'rational' leisure. According to Wang, Chinese authorities promoted the consumption of 'rational recreation' (Jing Wang 2001a: 40) because consumption of this kind will eventually enhance the cultural competence of the populace and thereby increase the potential for national economic growth.

Jing Wang's analysis of the propagation of 'leisure culture' in Beijing focuses on the local leisure space as it is conceived and 'conceptualized' (Lefebvre 1991: 38–9) by local-level technocrats. The Beijing authorities' promotion of useful, rational leisure activities as described by Wang exemplifies the kind of utilitarian leisure ethic I analysed in detail in Chapter 2. In my analyses of the ways Quanzhou inhabitants make use of leisure spaces in their local communities, I have found, however, that ordinary people often defy the recommendations propagated by the government. This is true of customers in Quanzhou's karaoke parlours, and it is also the case for those who use 'secret' back roads to get free access to the popular recreation area at Qingyuan Mountain, as we shall see in the following chapter. Wang, on the other hand, alleges that the Chinese authorities have managed to realize 'the disciplinary potential of a consumption-based notion of leisure' (Jing Wang 2001b: 78), and states that the propaganda campaign in Beijing caused 'a sudden outburst of leisure activities that demonstrated the residents' revived interest in haute culture' (Jing Wang 2001b: 78). These claims are, however, not sufficiently documented in her writing.[5]

The analyses of the relationship between the official discourse of leisure and the leisure practices of people in Quanzhou suggests that there is no immediate link between what the government propagates and what the populace decide to do in practice. I also find that where the official leisure ethic and the priorities of the consuming middle class do correspond – as is the case with the promotion of self-study and the denunciation of web surfing in Internet cafés – the correspondence is incidental rather than the result of the individuals' adherence to official policies, as shown in Chapters 5 and 6. I do not doubt that the local government's initiatives to fill Beijingers' leisure lives with constructive activities attracted numerous leisure consumers. The 'sudden outburst' of interest Wang detected does not however necessarily prove the efficacy of the government's campaign as a 'ruling technology'. The local government may have endeavoured to – in Lefebvre's term – 'produce a space' for rational leisure practices, but in Wang's case study there is little proof of the citizens being subjugated by the government's attempt at social engineering.

In Chapter 4 I argued that the success of a leisure place or event rests in part on levels of attraction and convenience, and I believe that this observation is relevant also in Wang's case from Beijing. In the mid-1990s, the two-day weekend was in itself a novelty (attraction) that gave citizens the opportunity to spend their time in different ways than before. This, paired with the propaganda campaign that provided information about leisure activities – new and old – served to make leisure places and leisure activities more accessible (convenience) to the public. It is therefore just as likely that the new interest in leisure activities among the Beijing population was provoked by increased access to leisure and the effect of improved public information. In sum, I argue that Wang overestimates the efficacy of government propagation for the spread of consumption in China, and, moreover, that this position has ramifications for her analysis of consumer agency in contemporary China.

Consumers and advertisers as agents in the market

In the above section, I questioned the extent to which official propaganda campaigns can cause consumers to alter their habits of leisure consumption. Although I question the power of the party-state propaganda, I do recognize the role of consumer policies in the facilitation and governance of the Chinese market. I agree with the position held by Croll, Tomba and also Jing Wang that it is in the interest of the Chinese government to facilitate increased spending by the middle classes (Jing Wang 2001b: 75; Tomba 2004: 5, 10; Croll 2006: 30–1). Similar arguments have been made by Chinese scholars who regard the development of cultural consumption (*wenhua xiaofei*) as beneficial for both the economic development and the continuance of social stability in the People's Republic (Wang Zhongwu 2005: 125; Meng Lei 2007: 26). One of the indicators of the Chinese government's interest in boosting private consumption is the incessant focus on consumer products and consumer issues in the state-dominated print media and broadcasting.

In the case of Quanzhou, the local media plays a vital role in making consumer practices and the new rhetoric of consumer rights known to the public. Space given to stories concerning consumers' complaints and the coverage of the International Consumers' Day (*Guoji xiaofeizhe quanyi baohu ri*) in local newspapers in Quanzhou is substantial. The local TV station also has a daily show that reports on a range of consumer-related news – from oil prices to the latest in fashion – and there is a weekly show that focuses solely on car owners' issues. It may be that by casting the middle-class consumer as an influential agent in a market prone to offer fake goods and flawed services, the official media succeeds in diverting attention away from the economic and social depravity experienced by significant parts of the population, as Jing Wang suggests. Wang stresses the fact that the party-state utilizes the discourse of consumer rights to bolster its political agendas (Jing Wang: 2001b: 73). In the case of Quanzhou, however, I found that commercial agents were equally skilled in their manipulation of 'consumers' interests'. For example, a major Chinese wine producer used the 2006 Consumer's Day as an opportunity to flaunt the company's awareness of consumers' rights in an advertisement that filled half a newspaper page and was disguised as a regular article among the general editorial content. The title was 'March 15[6] is here again: What do you know about wine?', and the ingress read as follows:

> It is March 15 once again and consumer's rights are getting stronger by the day. The [consumer's] right to know is regarded with importance by all big factory owners.
>
> ('3.15 you dai...' *HXDSB* 15 March 2006, A5)

Although the 'article' contained a guide to recognising fine wines (famous wine districts, the concept of vintage, etc.) along with a list of awards won by the company for its consumer awareness, this is an example of how Consumers' Day is used as an excuse for poorly concealed advertisement. Other factories and shops attempted to make Consumer's Day into a day for consumption by announcing a range of 'March 15 offers' ('3.15 you dai...' *HXDSB* 15 March 2006, A5). These examples show that both the party-state (through the media) and commercial enterprises are eager to entice the wage-earning middle class to spend their money on consumer items. Moreover, it is evident that the rhetoric of consumer's rights is deployed by both the government and major corporations as a means to increase private consumption.

In her analyses of consumption policies in China, Jing Wang takes this point much further by claiming that the Chinese government utilizes the satisfaction of consumer demands as a means of pacifying popular dissent, and that the authorities propagate consumer rights as a substitute or *faux* democracy. Wang writes:

> As China recovered from the trauma of 1989, the collective project in which the Chinese public was invited to participate was not a political utopia of any sort (socialist or liberalist), but the making of an egalitarian consumer public theoretically unmarred by vertical hierarchies, in short, participation in the democratic consumption of leisure culture.
>
> (Jing Wang 2001b: 73)

If we follow Wang's logic, this would mean that the new influence Chinese individuals have gained in the role of consumers satisfies their wishes to such a degree that their appetite for democratic rights is ruined. Here, I find Fewsmith's analysis of the relationship between the Chinese party-state and middle class more instructive (Fewsmith 2007). With reference to Li Chunling's surveys of the Chinese middle stratum, Fewsmith concludes that middle-class people's interest in political participation is low not because they are bamboozled by the government but simply because, during the reform period, 'the interests of China's middle class have paralleled those of the state' (Fewsmith 2007: 6–7). For the sake of the development of a domestic market and social stability, the Chinese authorities wish the population in general to aspire to the level of consumption, skills and education the Chinese middle class has already attained. This, of course, is an encouragement to people in the middle-class segment who have not only got 'rich first', but who have also got a good education and thus were the first to be 'cultured' (*you wenhua suzhi*). From this point of view, I agree that the satisfaction of consumer demands and the spread of consumer culture among an ever-increasing part of the population serve to legitimize the power of the Communist Party (see also Croll 2006: xiii). Even so, I find that Jing Wang's analyses are guided by a too-narrow focus on the institutional aspect of consumption, i.e. consumer policies and official campaigns. By stating that the Chinese authorities are in the process of 'redefining residentship or citizenship as an activity of consumption' (Jing Wang 2001b: 80), Wang denies any agency on the part of the consumer as individual. She thereby ends up doing what Daniel Miller warns against in his analyses of consumption: namely, portraying the consumer as being weighed down by dominant discourses 'generated by forces such as state power and capitalism, which merely employ the individual as legitimization for their project' (Miller 2001: 64). My point here is not to claim that consumption is in any way a liberating practice. It has been suggested that the individual can identify his or her position in society by way of consumption, and that consumption provides the individual with a sense of the power to make his or her own decisions (*zizhuquan*) (Chen Pingyi and Zheng Yangfu 2007: 150; Mort 2000: 272). These positive side effects of the practice of consumption may be perceptible at the level of the individual, but, from the point of view of consumer theory, the individual can never make decisions that are entirely free from the production of wants that are promoted through both government policies of production and the logic of the market (Galbraith 2000: 218; Galbraith in Campbell 2000: 54, 57). I still argue that the individual consumer does play his or her own role (however minuscule) in shaping the market, and that this was evident among my interviewees in this study.

Among my interviewees and contacts I observed a keen awareness of consumers' rights in terms of return policies and warranties, as well as an obsession with food hygiene and safety. Because of the prevalence of production flaws and fake merchandise in local shops and markets, middle-class consumers regarded a favourable return policy as a significant part of a good bargain. As for food safety, this awareness was spurred by the experience of the SARS outbreak in South China in the winter of 2002 and early 2003, and by the many food scandals that have marred Chinese markets in recent years. Although the Chinese media sometimes publish reports concerning food safety, the everyday gossip over local food scams and the possible health risks caused by chemicals in farm products were equally important for the choices made by Quanzhou's middle-class consumers. It was not government propagation alone, but also the rumour of poor hygiene in local food stores that made consumers like the aforementioned Ms Zhang purchase most of their meat and poultry in high-class supermarkets. And it was not advertisements alone but also a spreading sense of distrust in the factory-like production – mixed with a touch of vanity – that made tea enthusiasts in Quanzhou buy their teas from select small-scale producers. Quanzhou consumers made practical use of their knowledge of market conditions, but this can hardly be described as participation in a *faux* democracy. Whatever satisfaction the local consumers may have experienced from their influence in the market was overshadowed by the frustrations and anxiety that caused them to be cautious in the first place. Judging from my field research in Quanzhou, the choices local consumers make, both when they buy services in the commercial leisure market and when they consume regular commodities, are not guided by government propagation but rather by levels of income, knowledge of the local market and by the tastes and values they maintained as (aspiring) middle-class consumers.

It must be said in Jing Wang's defence that her analyses of Chinese consumption are primarily concerned with the consumption of culture. There is certainly a difference between the purchase of tea leaves or chicken fillets and buying a theatre ticket. Even so, Wang herself deploys a definition of leisure that is purely economical. According to her, the Chinese state has succeeded in utilizing leisure culture as 'a site where new ruling technologies can be deployed and converted simultaneously into economic capital' (Jing Wang 2001b: 71–2). Here, she not only exaggerates the party-state's ability to govern the Chinese leisure space in accordance with its plans and concepts, but ignores the fact that cultural capital, as it is defined by Bourdieu, can only with difficulty be converted into economic capital (Bourdieu 2006: 9–10). If we define 'leisure' narrowly as practices within the space of the culture market (*wenhua shichang*) (*QZSWHJ* 2005: 7), the term does refer to the purchase and consumption of a (popular) cultural event or experience. However, by analysing these practices simply as acts of consumption, i.e. as cultural consumption (*wenhua xiaofei*) (Zhang Taiyuan 2007; Chang Qinyi *et al.* 2007) in a cultural economy (*wenhua jingji*) (Jing Wang 2001b: 71; 2005b: 19), it is easy to overlook the value of leisure as a practice-based experience, i.e. as it is practiced and enjoyed by the consumers themselves. As argued in Chapter 2, when the analysis of leisure starts from the level of everyday practices, the epitome of leisure is not capital, but fun (*wan*). When leisure takes the form of consumption – as is certainly the case in the following analysis of window shopping – it is an exchange of commodities for money. But, importantly, for the consumer, the act of consuming can also carry additional value in the form of enjoyment, social exchange, and ideally a sense of satisfaction.

Shopping as a meaningful leisure activity

In the previous chapters I have argued that commercial leisure places such as bookshops and cafés are gradually taking over the role of the Communist Party apparatus in the practical facilitation of leisure activities. Although I would not go as far as Jing Wang, who claims that Chinese leisure now equals consumption, it is a fact that the leisure activities of the middle class often involve the purchase of a service, be it a foot massage, the lease of a karaoke room, or a serving of hot beverages in a book café. One of the practices that most clearly typifies this amalgamation of leisure and consumption is window shopping, a prevalent leisure activity among Quanzhou's inhabitants, and an activity I will analyse in more detail here. Window shopping is not merely a way to while away time between appointments, or a substitute for the making of actual purchases; window shopping is a meaningful leisure activity in itself, as the following examples from Quanzhou will demonstrate.

Shopping for fun

Although it was pointed out to me on several occasions in Quanzhou that the Mandarin term '*guangjie*' (lit. 'stroll [through the] streets')[7] does not refer to shopping – neither literally nor in practice – I have chosen to translate it into English as 'window-shopping'. I argue that as a practice, *guangjie* does not differ significantly from what can be observed in malls, shopping streets or bazaars in any major city in the world. Even so, one of the young women who took me out to *guangjie* put it this way:

> Westerners can admit that they are just window-shopping, but to Chinese, this would be a loss of face (*diu mianzi*). It would be like admitting that 'I have no money, so I can only browse and cannot buy anything'.

My observations from numerous strolls through the streets of Quanzhou with young girls and women indicate that some form of purchase is usually made when one is out to *guangjie*, but that the volume or cost involved is inconsequential. A cup of bubble tea,[8] a hair ornament or a token present for a friend are typical examples of purchases Quanzhou women might make when they are not looking for anything in particular but just out for a little stroll (*guang yixia*).

Local *guangjie* practices are shaped by the contexts of time and place. Whereas indoor shopping opportunities are more widespread in cities further north and east, Quanzhou with its warm climate is well suited for street vending and outdoor night markets. The Minnan area is also proud of its bountiful range of local night-snacks (*yecan*), which shoppers enjoy on the spot or while strolling the busy streets in the old town quadrangle. A stint of window-shopping often takes place after a meal, visit or meeting. It can also be an occasion in itself that brings friends, colleagues and class mates together, especially during weekends.

Elizabeth Croll describes Chinese women's window-shopping practice as a form of appreciation and daydreaming:

> [As] a form of recreation, shopping [...] has become both a means and an end in itself with visits to up-market department-store displays, tableaux or dream worlds visited and gazed upon, much as in museums, not so much of past record and achievement but of future lifestyles arousing curiosity, desire, anticipation and dream if not retail therapy.
>
> (Croll 1997: 4)

Croll's description brings to mind the sense of restorative calm that Ms Zhang said she felt whenever she was browsing at her local mall. Although I sometimes observed, and also received accounts of, people going window-shopping alone, the leisurely browsing of shopping street boutiques and malls was typically a social occasion. Wang Yalin's survey shows that Chinese women spend more time window-shopping than men do (Wang Yalin 2003: 74). However, in Quanzhou I often spotted window-shoppers – both male and female – in pairs or small groups, walking arm in arm, discussing the merchandise and enjoying the *renao* which is so typical of Chinese streetscapes and which the shoppers themselves are part of. This shows that window-shopping is a leisure practice among both sexes and, depending on the occasion, it can take the form of either individual recreation or a social event.

Although window-shopping as a phenomenon is often linked to the economic developments of the last ten or 15 years in China, Quanzhou people's *guangjie* habits stretch further back in time, as demonstrated by the following reminiscence of Quanzhou life in the late 1970s related to me by Mrs Ma, who was a young mother at the time:

> I worked in a government-run textile mill, and would often have to take some sewing work home with me. During summer vacations my sons would also do some sewing at home in order to finance their school fees for the coming semester. One evening when I came home form work and was very tired, my two boys asked me: 'Oh, can't we please go *guangjie* together this evening, all three of us'. I said to them that 'No, we cannot. We have to finish these clothes by tomorrow, and you know that.' But the boys kept asking and I told them once more that it was impossible. Then the boys showed me that they had already finished all the sewing by themselves. And so we all went out to *guangjie* together.
> (Informal interview, Quanzhou, 15 September 2005)

Whether or not the boys expected that a stroll through the streets with their mother would also mean the purchase of some small indulgence is impossible to discern from the story. It is evident, however, that the opportunity to *guangjie* was considered a treat by these schoolboys. There are clear differences in the experiences of Mrs Ma's two boys during the early days of consumerism and the sort of leisure shopping experienced by children of the contemporary Chinese middle class. Children both now and in the past may have looked forward to window-shopping with a similar kind of anticipation, but the range of commodities, the variety of streetscape spectacles and the frequency of window-shopping stints have increased significantly with the rise in personal income and expenditure. Davis and Sensenbrenner's study of children and consumption in the late 1990s indicates that while shopping had become a significant leisure activity among Chinese children, it was also typical that their parents – who had been deprived of material comforts during their own childhoods – often took 'vicarious pleasure' in shopping for their own children (Davis and Sensenbrenner 2000: 72, 79; see also Croll 2006: 172). This shows that attitudes towards consumption depend not only on the present-day income levels of the individual or the individual's parents, but also on experience of poverty and deprivation in the recent past (Croll 1997: 6, 8; Jing Wang 2001b: 79; Farquhar 2002: 28). As we shall see in the following, the bodily experience of affluence and scarcity separate generations in terms of attitudes towards consumption.

Looking at consumption across the generation gap

In *Appetites*, Judith Farquhar argues that Chinese consumer practices are influenced by more than changes in dominant mentalities (frugality, asceticism) and official policies (collectivism, economic reform); consumer practices are also shaped by people's memories and bodily experiences of deprivation and comfort (2002: 54). For contemporary youth, the memories of material deprivation are part of a family narrative of life as it was in an unspecified 'before' (*yiqian*) – before the liberation (*jiefang*) or before the reform and opening up (*gaige kaifang*) – when meat was hard to come by and people often went hungry. For the parent and grandparent generations, the scarcities that characterized life 'before' are more than just a narrative, they are an embodied experience that still has consequences for people's values and outlooks in the present. An illustrative example can be found in Huang Shumin's *The Spiral Road*, where Party secretary Ye, who was in his late teens during the Great Leap, scolds the author for letting a bowl of steamed buns go to waste, saying:

> Only a plateful of food? Do you know how many lives this plateful of food can save? Do you know how much hunger people in our generation have suffered? I wish heaven would condemn all those who waste food to live through the Great Leap forward!
>
> (Huang Shumin 1989: 56)

According to Farquhar, people's bodily experience of the shortages during the first decades of the People's Republic and, moreover, the guilt people felt when secretly indulging in modest pleasures during times of strictly enforced (re)distribution of food and other resources, informs contemporary Chinese consumer practices to a surprising degree (Farquhar 2002: 54). Her findings are supported by Jing Wang's suggestion that 'the average citizen in China indulges in the excess of consumption in much the same fashion as do post-war Americans and Europeans haunted by memories of wartime scarcity' (Jing Wang 2001b: 79). However, in addition to triggering overindulgence, memories of past scarcity can also explain why consumers exercise special caution in the present. As an example, at the end of the 1990s, the crumbling of the state-sponsored social security system and the unemployment experienced by laid-off workers from the many state enterprises created not only rising expenses for households all over China but also a rising sense of economic insecurity (Jun Liping and Li Jing 2002: 27; Croll 2006: 62–3). It is probable that the recent memories of scarcity and deprivation informed people's choices to spend less of their income; by the end of the decade, 'saving took precedence over spending' in China (Croll 2006:

66). Moreover, many communities have experienced the disappearance of collective resources, as in the many cases where communal land has been sold to private enterprises (Hansen 2007: 10, 17–18). Experience of corruption and embezzlement has also made many Chinese reluctant to trust their funds to such institutions as banks and providers of health and life insurance (Liu Yuanli 2004: 161). This is another example of how experience from recent history causes continued caution among Chinese consumers.

While contemporary Chinese consumer practices are to a certain extent shaped by past experience when necessities were in short supply, it is important to keep in mind that these consumer practices are equally influenced by current experience of relative comfort (*xiaokang*). The new familiarity with a comfortable standard of living leads to a different view of normality, as illustrated in the above example of Ms Zhang who found that a three to five hundred-*yuan* sweater is now a legitimate object of desire for a woman of her social standing and income level. The diverging definitions of normality among the different generations can also be seen in Yunxiang Yan's article 'Rural youth culture in North China' (1999). Here, Yan describes a situation where rural youth have taken up what the elder generation perceive as an abnormally lavish consumer lifestyle. Village youth, however, regard their own consumer practices as normal, arguing that the problem lies with the older villagers who – according to local youth wisdom – 'simply do not know how to live a good life' (1999: 79). In Quanzhou, on the other hand, I overheard parents accusing their offspring of not recognizing the joys of making New Year purchases (*nianhuo*).

The weeks leading up to Chinese New Year are the peak season for local shoppers who – as in the above mentioned case of Ms Zhang – look for that perfect set of new clothes that traditionally marks New Year's Day (*chuyi*). At this time of year, clothes purchases for children (and husbands) was a recurring topic when women met. Prior to the New Year in 2007, I noticed that many people commented that, now that people get new clothes so often, the significance of new clothes for the New Year has been lost. As one woman put it; 'New Year used to be special because of the meat and the other delicacies one could not usually afford. And, there would be new clothes, which all children would love. Now, there is not so much difference between Spring Festival and other days of the year. I don't have that New Year feeling this year.' Sentiments like these were common among young adults, especially parents, who saw their children reacting to the New Year purchases with indifference. Although some daughters were happy to receive new clothes and accessories for the holidays, I also observed how a 13-year-old boy told his parents that he did not want any new clothes for New Year. Like many teenage boys, he did not want his mother to dress him up. He was a devoted basketball fan, and felt both comfortable and perfectly fashionable in his school uniform, which was a track suit and trainers. His mother described his attitude as unappreciative.

When talking about the New Year, adults who are now in their late thirties and early forties recalled their childhood holidays as a time for family visits, traditional lion dancers, a lot of fire crackers and 'all kinds of *renao*'. These

Consumption as a form of leisure 153

reminiscences were often accompanied by criticism of the contemporary New Year celebration, with the inevitable CCTV[9] New Year gala and the rush of impersonal New Year rhymes that ticked into their mobile phones via SMS on New Year's Eve (*Chuxi*). For ten-year-old Meimei, however, the highlights of the 2007 *Chuxi* was exactly the CCTV gala, which she looked forward to with intense expectation, as well as the big bag of sweets she had been given by her parents.

Nostalgia for a time before consumerism is typical of people in their late thirties, writes Judith Farquhar, adding the ironic comment that '[no] one I have talked to, however, longs for a return to political infighting or Lei Feng-style guilt over crusts of rice' (Farquhar 2002: 41). Chinese parents' reminiscences of a simpler, less-commercialized New Year celebration are probably akin to the perceived loss of a 'true Christmas spirit' among adults in the Christian culture sphere. It is likely that these are both local versions of a general sentiment among parents in their thirties and forties who have idealized the celebrations and joys of their own childhood to the extent that contemporary festivities seem empty and bleak in comparison. Nevertheless, the consequence is that in their nostalgic search for that 'New Year feeling' in the boutiques and malls of Quanzhou, parents tend to overlook the possibility that their children are as excited about the contemporary celebrations (the TV gala, family excursions to parks and squares, having visitors, getting their New Year money gifts (*yasui qian*), eating snacks and not going to class) as they themselves were during the celebrations when they were children.

According to Meng Lei, Chinese media broadcast an image of the middle-class consumer as a person who exists in a state of euphoria and contributes towards the economy while finding self-fulfilment: 'I consume, therefore I am!' (*wo xiaofei, gu wo zai*) (Meng Lei 2002: 24). Consumption as a form of leisure has certainly become an intrinsic part of the middle-class lifestyle as it is practiced in Quanzhou, and the prevalence of window-shopping is but one example of the intermingling of consumption and recreation that takes place in the local cityscape. I would not, however, describe these consumer practices in terms of 'euphoria' or even as an 'embrace' of consumption. On the contrary, I find that middle-class consumers in Quanzhou perceive consumption with distinct matter-of-factness. If consumption in the past was a minefield of guilty pleasures, as described by Farquhar (2002), contemporary shopping is invested with a neutral sense of entitlement: 'I shop because I can'.

The cultured middle class's attitude towards consumption

Jing Wang has argued that the current 'obsession with mass consumption' in China indicates 'that it will be some time before Chinese consumers or even their critics (i.e., elite humanist intellectuals)' take up any form of criticism towards the way leisure has become part of the market domain, and the way leisure is regarded first and foremost as a source of revenue (Jing Wang 2001b: 79). I never detected any explicit criticism of the role consumption has come to

154 *Consumption as a form of leisure*

play in everyday life among my interviewees and contacts in Quanzhou. Among the cultured middle class,[10] however, there was a strongly articulated critique of what were regarded as signs of 'commercialization' (*shangpinhua*) and the tendency to seek profit (*zhuan qian*) in all matters. As we shall see in the following, these cultured consumers were critical of the conspicuous consumption they attributed to their cultural 'others', more specifically the emergent class of entrepreneurs (*qiyejia*). At the same time, they spent a considerable amount of resources on the kinds of leisure they themselves held to be commendable.

The cultured middle class

As discussed in the introductory chapter, the definition of the Chinese middle class(es) varies depending on the choice of criteria (education, profession, income, self-definition). In the following, the 'cultured middle class' is a broadly defined segment of the general middle class, whose members are be distinguished by their cultural capital, most concretely their university degrees and/or employment in the local culture administration. In Quanzhou these were low-level cadres in the culture sector, artists both amateur and professional, teachers in urban high schools and colleges, and holders of university degrees employed in other sectors. These people were often described by their peers as people of culture (*you wenhua, suzhi gao*). In other words, the consumers I will focus on in the following are part of the contemporary middle class, whose distinguishing feature is their cultured sentiments, or *bildung*. The members of this cultured middle class, however, are not intellectuals in the sense of scholars' (*xuezhe*) 'engaged in independent thought and the creative life of the mind' (Ogden 2004: 112). Rather, they were examples of the contemporary intelligentsia (*zhishi fenzi*), whom Ogden describes as 'a heterogeneous group of experts, scholars, advisors, propagandists, managers and technocrats' (Ogden 2004: 112). Members of the cultured middle class in Quanzhou did, however, place themselves in the role traditionally reserved for the Chinese intellectual elite, namely acting as 'the political and social conscience or moral vanguard of the community' (Schwartz 1996 and Tu, W. 1989 in He Baogang 2004: 263), who regard it as their 'duty to educate or enlighten' ordinary people (He Baogang 2004: 266).

The cultured middle class is of special interest in the study of leisure consumption because it embodies the characteristics that the party-state has set up as ideals of civility (*wenming*). Its members are well-educated individuals whose values and consumer practices match the official leisure ethic in many respects. They despise commercialization and promote education and the arts. In this respect, members of the cultured middle class in China hold opinions reminiscent of the cultural highbrows described in studies of mass culture and elite culture in Western societies (Gans 1974; Peterson 1992: 245). However, as Richard A. Peterson argues, elite audiences can no longer be said to despise mass culture, nor do they show an exclusive preference for elite culture. On the contrary, in terms of cultural consumption, contemporary highbrow audiences are usually 'omnivores' (Peterson 1992: 245). They have knowledge of, and also participate in and consume, a variety of leisure and art forms regardless of the distinction between 'popular' and 'elite' culture (Peterson 1992: 252). Recalling the example in Chapter 6 where Ms Zhang and her women friends were equally comfortable sampling high-quality teas and frequenting karaoke parlours, it is evident that cultural omnivores also exist in China. The cultural competence of the said women transcended the boundaries of 'high' and 'low' culture, a characteristic shared by many of my interviewees in the cultured middle class. I found, however, that their ability to enjoy and digest multiple forms of culture, of which their leisure practices bore witness, was frequently downplayed. Typical cultured middle-class consumers did not consider their own spending and investments – however prolific in objective terms – as examples of a consumerist lifestyle. Rather, it was characteristic of cultured consumers to highlight the cultural value of their own consumption while criticizing examples of hedonism and wastefulness among the population in general, and amid uneducated entrepreneurs in particular.

Interviewees from the cultured middle class regarded conspicuous consumption as a moral problem – a problem that did not concern them, only the uncultured *nouveau riche*. The types of leisure spending in which the cultured middle class themselves engaged, however, they characterized as forms of culture rather than forms of consumption. This reasoning is parallel to the logic of the PRC leisure ethic, where ordinary people's leisure is regarded as a potential source of chaos, while the leisure practices of the privileged are exempt from scrutiny. I argue that by playing down the economical aspect of their own leisure activities, members of the cultured middle class seek to maintain a distance from the commercial leisure market they hold in contempt, while at the same time enjoying the sorts of leisure that agree with their cultural tastes. It is their status as civilized (*wenming*) cultured (*suzhi gao*) people that makes members of the cultured middle class immune to the critique of consumption they themselves tend to voice.

These contradictory attitudes towards consumption became evident during the Urban Photography Conference in Quanzhou in March 2007. The conference brought together amateur photographers from all over China, most of them bringing their expensive brand-name camera equipment. Although one objective for the conference participants was to take photos of the Quanzhou cityscape, the chance to flaunt their photo equipment among their peers was certainly another. The keynote speaker at the conference, an art photographer of renown, accused the amateur photographers of pursuing photography as a form of conspicuous consumption, saying:

> Some people take photography seriously and call themselves photographers. These are the people who show respect for photographic skills. Then there is the group who regard photography as a kind of leisure. They treat cameras as a kind of toy (*wanju*), and while they can't afford to play around with a car (*wan xiaoche*), they can afford a cool camera.
> (Informal interview, Quanzhou, 4 March 2007)

This art photographer equated the cultured middle class's interest in photography with the conspicuous consumption among the car owners of the economic middle class, insinuating that the hobby photographers were more interested in impressive photo equipment than the art of photography itself. The fact that a majority of the conference delegates went sightseeing in Quanzhou rather than taking part in the panel sessions during the conference supports his stance. In informal interviews, however, amateur photographers expressed a common concern regarding the spread of small digital cameras in the general population. They saw this as a threat to the kind of photography practiced by themselves as a form of cultured leisure. For example, one of the local photo enthusiasts lamented how photography had now become part of the mass culture (*dazhong wenhua*). He likened the popularization of photography to the situation in the Chinese publishing business where 'almost anybody can get a book published these days'. He himself had published several volumes of calligraphy, but evidently did not regard himself as one of these neophyte 'anybodies'.

A similar disdain for newcomers to the world of cultured leisure activities was expressed by a group of middle-aged employees in one of the local government units in Quanzhou. Sitting down for an informal chat and a few cups of exclusive[11] tea in the conference room, the talk around the table unsurprisingly turned to the topic of tea and tea culture. I introduced the question of whether or not the local tea culture was becoming commercialized (*shangpinhua*). Heads nodded around the table, but one person responded that commercialization was not really the issue. According to him, the real problem was that 'there is now very little culture left in the tea culture – there are so many uncultured people among tea drinkers' (*hen duo he cha de ren meiyou wenhua*). These expressions convey an understanding of cultural value as determined by scarcity. Within this paradigm, the popularization or 'massification' of forms of cultured leisure causes a kind of inflation where the relative cultural value is lost in the process. In this case, tea consumption is considered to lose its cultural value when practiced by the 'uncultured'. This understanding of culture explains why an entrepreneur spending his money in a tea house is suspected of showing off to his clients, whereas a man of culture spending the same amount of money is described as practising a cultured form of leisure. The entrepreneur is accused of using tea culture as a means to make money, while the cultured consumer is regarded as one who seeks culture for its own sake. Seen from this point of view, the leisure consumption of the cultured is therefore to a lesser degree tainted by the 'uncleanliness' (Veblen in Peterson 1992: 245) of the popularized and commercial.

Stig Thøgersen has observed attitudes towards commercial culture among the '*wenren*' in Xuanwei County in rural Yunnan. These were the teachers, amateur artists and cadres in the culture sector, 'a local civilizing elite who represent Chinese high culture and hold a responsibility for raising the cultural level of the local population' (Thøgersen 2000: 132). Thøgersen writes that these *wenren* had a tendency to expound on 'decadent urban lifestyles', specifically corruption, and to the worship of money and fashion (2000: 132). In his study from

Hainan, Feng Chongyi also writes that '[i]ntellectual circles often seem to hold negative views about the current trends in China's commercial nightlife' (Feng Chongyi 2005: 144). What I found noteworthy in the discourse of consumption among the equivalent group of cultured people in Quanzhou was that there was very little criticism among them of the market or consumption as such. Rather, it was people's motivations that were scrutinized and evaluated. As we shall see in the following, this tendency can be traced in the attitudes towards commercialization among Quanzhou's reading public, and in the way a local tea house is (re)presented to its cultured customers.

Separating culture from commerce

As mentioned in Chapter 5, readers in Quanzhou tended to criticize the local library staff for taking too little responsibility in their role as purveyors of culture. As one local MA student put it:

> If you go to a bookshop, the people who work there really take an interest in books, not only in making money. In the library, however, those who work there do so simply for their wages. It is part of the government; they are mere administrators (*zuo guanli*).[12]

Ironically, it is the public library, represented by its staff, rather than the commercial booksellers that is accused of money worship. The quote also shows that it is not the act of making money that is the object of criticism but doing something for the sake of money. When interviewing bookshop managers, I found that they presented themselves as a type of culture worker who – in contrast to librarians and clerks in the state-owned *Xinhua* bookstores – had an 'understanding of readers'. They identified strongly with the first generation of independent booksellers (*minying shudian laoban*) from the 1990s, who in their eyes successfully combined social values with commerce. This first generation of *laoban* was described to me as lovers of literature (*benshen ai shu*) whose main concern was to give more people access to books and reading. This kind of *laoban* would talk with the customers and make friends with them. To them, money was secondary, and this was a virtue which the contemporary bookstore managers claimed to aspire to themselves.

The bookstore managers I interviewed were certainly avid readers, and they spent much of their time on the premises conversing about books with customers and acquaintances. But even if they portrayed themselves as patrons of literature, they did not hesitate to admit that they earned far more from selling beverages and snacks in their book cafés than from the sale of literature. When I asked about the function of the book café, bookstore managers explained them first and foremost as a way to cater to readers' needs to sit down and browse the books in comfort. Second, the book café was described as means to save the bookstores from liquidation. This claim was usually bolstered with reference to the truism that 'there is no money in the book trade'. The image of the bookseller as a person who is primarily a bibliophile rather than a salesman fits well with the ideals of the cultured middle-class customer. Within this paradigm, the leisure shopping of the cultured consumer – in this case the purchase of a book or snacks and drinks in the book café – is elevated from the level of base commerce to that of cultural refinement. It is no longer simply consumption; it is culture(d) consumption.

The manager of Quanzhou's most prominent tea house sought to develop a similar rapport with the cultured consumers in the town area. Mr Pang, who is a man in his thirties, has converted a run-down courtyard mansion into an impressive-looking tea house where a variety of customers come to see young waitresses perform brewing ceremonies, and to sample local specialty teas. On a busy night there will typically be parties of old friends relaxing together after dinner, groups of businessmen about to close a deal, and the odd table of card-playing students. Mr Pang depicted his tea house as a project to help the restoration of local architecture, and as a vehicle for the spread of tea culture. During my interview with Mr Pang, he presented himself as a champion of culture and downplayed the business aspect of his tea-house establishment. He even cast himself in the role of a teacher of cultural competence, stating that 'I will not sell expensive teas to people who don't know what they are doing. First,' he said, 'I will teach them how to enjoy the tea in question, and only then will I sell them the most expensive varieties.' Mr Pang also claimed that the reason his establishment was thriving was that he was not in business for the sake of money. He accused other tea houses of thinking only about their earnings and of 'wanting more than their share of the cake. I myself want only a tiny portion of the cake,' he stated, adding with pride that he had more than 600 VIP cards spread around town. Mr Pang's professed non-commercial attitude to the tea house trade resonates with the anti-commercialist values of the cultured middle class. Moreover, Pang defined tea culture in opposition to other kinds of popular leisure activities. By defining tea drinking as a cultivated and cultivating practice, Mr Pang sought to remove his tea house from the realm of the uncouth commercial leisure market. In an elaborate 30-page advertisement brochure with tasteful colour photos from the tea house, Pang writes:

> When [this] tea house was established in 1998, the local leisure consumption had a blind spot: karaoke was already yesterday's news, in many bars there was too much of a hubbub, and Western fast food only seemed fresh and new the first time people tasted it. When the teahouse was presented to the public, it filled this empty shelf perfectly.
> (Gu Cuo Tea Culture Company, no date, 18–19)

The image Pang has created for his tea house also echoes the logic of the official leisure ethic, which is critical of leisure places that are suspected of disorderliness and promotes such qualities as discipline and moderation:

> [...] what separates [a tea house] from other, noisier kinds of leisure is that through the slow sipping and tasting of tea one may discipline one's tem-

perament (*peiyang xingqing*), mould one's personality (*taoye qingcao*), and achieve carefree and happy enjoyment.

(ibid.)

The above two quotes demonstrate the ease with which the dominant leisure ethic blends with the ideals of a cultured middle-class lifestyle. As shown in Chapter 6, the official attitude towards the 'hubbub' and late opening hours that are associated with such leisure spaces as bars and karaoke parlours is that they pose a threat to 'people's physical and mental health and their work and life' (Gong Gao *HXDSB* 17 February, A30). As a consequence, leisure activities that secure the recreation of the workforce's spirit and which in addition serve to mould and discipline the character or raise the people's level of cultural competence (*wenhua suzhi*) are promoted by the authorities as commendable, healthy forms of leisure. In this respect, the official leisure ethic works in unison with the preferences of cultured middle-class consumers, who favour educational and cultured forms of leisure consumption (photography, reading, tea tasting etc.) and are quick to express their distaste for conspicuous consumption. We cannot, however, infer from this that the preferences and consumer practices of the cultured middle class result from the successful propagation of a PRC leisure ethic. On the contrary, I argue that the official leisure ethic proposes that all Chinese citizens should emulate the lifestyle of the cultured middle classes. This is evident in the 'spiritual civilization' campaigns initiated by the government in the 1980s to prevent moral decline and fend off materialist tendencies (Friedman 2006: 232). It is present in the campaigns described by Jing Wang, where local authorities sought to ignite an interest in 'leisure culture' among the Beijing population. Moreover, it is manifest in the promotion of educational forms of leisure such as reading and going to museums, as described in the chapters above. The cultured leisure consumption of the well-educated middle class epitomizes the ideal way of life as it is envisioned by Chinese authorities on behalf of the Chinese citizenry.

During the reform period, the Communist Party has communicated a mixed message concerning consumption. On the one hand, the party-state has encouraged private consumption because trade in commodities, services and entertainment contributes towards the growth of the Chinese economy (Jing Wang 2005b: 19; Feng Chongyi 2005: 135). On the other hand, the Party fears the negative effects of a materialist consumer culture on a population where the level of cultural competence is perceived to be low (and possibly declining) (Chang Qinyi *et al.* 2007: 123, 125). Therefore, private spending on 'unscientific' and 'unhealthy' practices such as elaborate burial rites and religious festivals and night-time leisure are regarded as examples of bad consumer habits (*xiaofei louxi*) (Wang Zhongwu 2005: 125; Fan Xiaoxian and Kong Linghua 2006: 88). From the point of view of the official leisure ethic and the scholars who write within this paradigm, these practices are considered counterproductive in the quest for a well-educated (even 'scientific') and rested workforce. Chinese scholars who analyse the consumer culture in China tend to agree that the best way to prevent the tendency towards hedonism and conspicuous consumption among those who have money to spend is to channel their consumption towards the cultural market (Ma Feifeng 2002; Wang Zhongwu 2005; Chang Qinyi *et al.* 2007; Chen Pingyi and ZhengYangfu 2007; Meng Lei 2007; Zhang Taiyuan 2007). In this way, their consumption can cause the national economy to grow while at the same time increasing their cultural competence. This, I argue, is why neither official propaganda nor scholars within the field of consumption in China express any significant criticism of the commoditization of leisure culture or of consumption in itself.[13]

In this chapter I have argued that there is no immediate causal relationship between consumption as it is envisioned, planned and propagated by political authorities in China and the consumption practices and attitudes towards consumption among the general middle class. I have presented examples of how people in Quanzhou talk about consumption – as well as how they spend their money on a choice of leisure activities – in order to demonstrate that the consumption that takes place in a local setting is invested with a variety of meanings that cannot be reduced to a simple response to government policies. In her claim that the Chinese government utilizes leisure consumption as a form of 'bread and circuses' for the pacification of the populace, I find that Jing Wang gives far too much credit to the party-state's ability to govern people's lives, while at the same time underestimating the level of agency on the part of people in general. Although Quanzhou people's experiences of hard times in the past and their new familiarity with material comfort are results of historical changes in the political and ideological climate in the People's Republic, their consumer practices are also shaped by factors such as personal or family income, level of education, and – in the case of the cultured middle class especially – anti-commercialist values.

When analysing leisure and consumer practices in China, the increasing differentiation in terms of income levels and access to leisure activities and free time on a national scale must be taken into consideration. In this study, however, which focuses specifically on conditions among middle-class citizens in a medium-sized town, it is also important to point out the different practices and strategies that surface among those who are relatively prosperous. Tendencies towards lavish spending and conspicuous consumption are very visible in Quanzhou's streetscape, where bright red Audis and BMWs announce the financial status of economic winners as they pass by. In this chapter I have also sought to bring attention to the strategies of 'obscured consumption', which can be observed among the cultured middle class. By redefining their purchases as acts of culture, these cultured consumers pursue their interests in expensive photo equipment or fine teas without being suspected of conspicuousness. This means that leisure and consumption have become closely linked even in the practices of the cultured middle class, the social segment that is most prone to criticize what they regard as a rising materialism and money worship in Chinese society.

8 Contested leisure space

In the previous chapters I have demonstrated the limited influence the government's idealized visions of leisure space have on people's actual leisure practices. The cases from Quanzhou tell us that ordinary people find ways to practice – and even organize – a variety of leisure activities without being in direct opposition to official policies and regulations. In this chapter, however, I will focus on one particular leisure place, Qingyuan Mountain, which became a stage

Figure 8.1 A woman making her way up the stone path at Qingyuan Mountain.

162 *Contested leisure space*

for open confrontation between townspeople and the local administration in the winter of 2005. Drawing on the theoretical works of Michel de Certeau and James C. Scott, I analyse this incident as an example of how antagonism between power-holders and subordinates breeds resistance in the form of popular tactics and a hidden transcript.

There are three identifiable groups that have vested interests in the Qingyuan Mountain area: the local government unit that manages Qingyuan Mountain Scenic Reserve (*Qingyuanshan fengjing mingsheng qu*), one of the major tourist spots in the municipality; local townspeople and tourists who use the mountain as a place for recreation, socializing and physical exercise; and the vendors, farmers and transportation workers who make their living from the leisure activities on the mountain. My analysis of the diverse activities – from conservation to popular leisure to commerce – that take place on the slopes of Qingyuan Mountain shows that these groups have a common interest in the preservation of the natural and cultural resources the area has to offer. This shared interest is clouded, however, by a conflict over how and for whom the area should be utilized. It is not the multiple qualities of the Qingyuan Mountain area that make the mountain a contested space, but rather the lack of understanding and communication between the people who use the area as a place of leisure and those whose job it is to govern it.

Qingyuan Mountain

The Qingyuan Mountain Scenic Reserve is a nature reserve on the northern outskirts of Quanzhou city. The reserve encompasses 62 km^2 of hills and mountains, the tallest at 498 metres above sea level. The nature and culture reserve was established in 1979, which is quite early in the Chinese context. This was right after the Cultural Revolution and at a time when cultural heritage and environmental protection was regarded as less important by local and national authorities than is the case today. Qingyuan Mountain became an administrative unit under the local municipal government in 1979, and the area was in the second batch of Chinese scenic areas to receive a status as National Key Point Scenic Areas (*Guojia zhongdian fengjing mingsheng qu*) in 1986. The Qingyuan Mountain Managerial Board (*Qingyuanshan fengjing mingsheng qu guanweihui*), a government unit that runs the reserve, conducts studies, and manages projects to ensure the protection of local flora and fauna. Qingyuan Mountain is also the site of numerous cultural relics, mostly in the form of stone inscriptions. Over the years, the Managerial Board has carried out significant restoration work to conserve and restore pagodas and stone carvings within the reserve at a total cost of two to three hundred million *yuan*. Entrance tickets are sold at each of the two gates at the foot of the mountain and at a smaller gate close to the villages on the Eastern slope. In 2007 the price of a single entrance ticket was 30 *yuan* and a yearly pass was 80 *yuan*. The board sells 600,000 tickets each year, yearly passes included.

Most of the leisure and sightseeing activities take place on the southeastern slopes of the mountain range, close to the city of Quanzhou. The major tourist attraction is the 5.6-metre-high and eight-metre-wide stone sculpture of *Laojun*, or *Laozi*, the master of Daoism. The area is also cherished as a space for recreation by local townspeople, who often gather around Tianhu Lake, a reservoir where small open-air kitchens serve vegetables and hot water, situated approximately a forty-minute walk from the foot of the mountain. Visitors bring their own tea and usually a deck of cards. To spend the afternoon playing cards and drinking tea by Tianhu Lake is the most popular leisure activity among local visitors to Qingyuan Mountain, be they families or groups of students, retirees, white-collar employees, or migrant workers. During weekends, the paths are crowded with families and students, but people also find their way up the mountain on regular weekdays during lunch breaks or at sundown. The most devoted climbers make the trip at least once a day. Some people also come to make offerings or to seek guidance from the Daoist master or the Buddhist monks in the temples on the hillside. While tourists flock to see the *Laojun* sculpture by the main entrance, local visitors enter via the two smaller ticket booths close to the public bus stops, or they find alternative, unofficial routes that take them to the recreation areas for free.

Qingyuan Mountain as a place of leisure

Throughout the cultural history of China, mountains have been significant as sites of pilgrimage and places for the literati to withdraw to in order to cultivate the art of poetry and enjoy leisurely companionship in an often idealized natural environment (Morrison and Eberhard 1974: vii, xviii). Mountain walking (*pashan*, lit. 'mountain climbing') is a leisure activity that has gained a tremendous following in China over the last 20 years. *Pashan* is enjoyed by young and old, is a social activity, and is also appreciated for the health benefits involved. In Quanzhou, *pashan* first became popular in the 1980s, primarily among retirees from the local government administration. These aging cadres were in relatively good health and found *pashan* an enjoyable way to spend their time in the mornings and early afternoons. Among the elderly in cities like Xiamen and Fuzhou and in smaller towns like Quanzhou and Anxi – all places where mountains are easily accessible to the town population – mountain walking has become an addition or alternative to such morning exercises as *taijiquan* and folkloristic dances, and a cherished leisure activity among townspeople in general.

The many ways to pashan

From the point of view of local visitors, Qingyuan Mountain is first and foremost a recreation area where they can enjoy both the natural environment and the services offered by outdoor kitchens and vendors. Although *pashan* is basically a form of exercise, the term is also used with reference to a wide range of leisure practices where the only common aspect is the fact that they take place on the slopes or at the top of a mountain. In the case of Qingyuan Mountain, the area is enjoyed at all hours by people from all walks of life. Young taxi drivers go there in the early evening when the day shift is over to relax and play cards or *majiang* with friends. Some come to the mountain during their noontime break, when they buy their lunches from the outdoor kitchens and eat in the shadows of the lush trees. Large groups of employees from local enterprises or administrative units walk the mountain together as a form of bonding exercise. At times, participants in the Happy Outdoor network take their bikes up the winding mountain roads, and the local Youth Volunteers' Association organizes trips to the mountain for their members as a social happening outside of their regular activities. And, as mentioned above, the area around Tianhu Lake is also popular after nightfall, especially among young couples who arrive by motorcycle taxi or occasionally in private cars to enjoy the romantic sight of city lights and the discretion darkness offers. During weekends, young students climb the mountain paths in groups, carrying backpacks or plastic bags brimming with snacks and fruit to enjoy once they arrive at their destination somewhere at the top of the mountain. Saturday and Sunday are also favourite days for families – grandparents and infants included – to make their way up the stone-paved stairs that lead to the recreation area at Tianhu Lake. Most visitors wear some form of leisure wear, but brand-name track suits and running shoes are worn only by a few. On several occasions I passed middle-aged women climbing the stairs in high heels and skirts. This shows that *pashan* is not primarily a kind of sport, but rather a leisure activity that can be enjoyed by different people in a variety of ways.

Once the mountain top is reached, most visitors sit down for refreshments or a whole meal, either at rickety plastic tables provided by the small outdoor kitchens in the forest near Tianhu Lake, or at the more permanent eating area by the lakeshore. Stir-fried vegetables, *doufu* and fruit are the most popular snacks, and most parties pay to have hot tea water boiled on paraffin burners by their tables. Visitors are usually welcome to bring their own food and tea leaves. Some parties spend hours chatting and playing cards, and one Saturday I even met a group of students singing English-language pop songs accompanied by guitar. The three 'golden weeks' – Spring Festival, Labour Day and National Day – are the peak seasons for visitors to Qingyuan Mountain. In addition, local religious festival days – especially Tomb Sweeping Day (*Qingmingjie*) – bring a larger number of visitors than usual. On regular weekdays one can observe visitors bringing incense, flowers and food offerings to the various Buddhist shrines on the mountain, and the Daoist master receives people in need of geomantic advice to improve their home interiors or building projects.

Most local visitors to the mountain arrive by public bus routes that take them either to the foot of the mountain or to the villages halfway up the mountain road, which ends by the antennae station on the hilltop beyond the lake. Motorbike drivers run informal transport services along this road. At weekends, when the drivers are sure to get customers for the return fare, it is also possible to get to the mountain by taxi. The mountain is also a popular leisure place among the privileged in Quanzhou who can afford a private car, or command a driver from their work unit. My experience was that among the well-to-do, *pashan* did not really involve any hiking at all.

Figure 8.2 A lunch of tea and vegetables at Qingyuan Mountain.

Qingyuan Mountain as a place of recreation

Mr Luo, an accomplished painter and a Quanzhou media personality, had promised on several occasions to *pashan* with me at Qingyuan Mountain. One Sunday morning at 7.30 we took off in his polished sedan. Along the way we picked up a few of his friends, among them a painter who had brought both his sketch book and a folding chair. I had prepared for a strenuous walk in the forest, and the sight of artist's tools raised my anticipation of the scenery we would pass through on our way. Much to my surprise, neither painting nor actual hiking took place that morning. Mr Luo did not stop his car at the foot of the mountain but proceeded along the winding road leading to the villages on the eastern slope. There, he drove straight past the ticket booth and parked his car at the very top of the mountain. We then got out of the car and walked for two minutes until we reached a paved terrace where we could sit down for a full breakfast and tea prepared by a local peasant woman. One of the dishes was fried eggs from free-range hens, and my fellow visitors praised the quality of the produce. They also stressed how much healthier it was to eat on the mountain rather than down in the city. As we drove back down mountain, my companions pointed out to me mountain brooks with water they claimed was unharmed by chemicals. Moreover, Mr Luo kept the windows of the car open the whole way down so that we could enjoy the quality of the mountain air. To my companions that morning, this was *pashan*. A car ride and an open-air breakfast was their way of enjoying the outdoors.

On several occasions during my stay in Quanzhou, I was invited along on similar 'hiking' trips to Qingyuan Mountain. A handful of businesses – all accessible by car – cater for this group of leisure consumers, who appreciate free-range chicken, the clean air and the supposedly superior quality of vegetables grown on the mountain. In Quanzhou this kind of 'eco-friendly' leisure consumption was in vogue among the monied, and at times a meal on the mountain replaced the run-of-the-mill banquet that was otherwise a means to impress business associates and connections from near and far. I find it ironic that customers of these 'eco-friendly' eating places were also among the visitors who caused much of the pollution in the mountain reserve, namely those who arrived by car. The Qingyuan Mountain Managerial Board plans to limit the number of cars that enter the reserve. In my experience, however, the parties arriving by car were particularly skilled at talking their way past gates and ticket booths. It is therefore unlikely that restrictions against private vehicles on the mountain will prevent these resourceful people from enjoying fresh air from the comfort of their car seats.

Qingyuan Mountain as a source of wellness

Healthy eating, exercise and clean air are qualities that are not only appreciated by the well-to-do. Among local visitors of various social backgrounds, Qingyuan Mountain and *pashan* in general were regarded as sources of physical well-being and good health. The vegetables grown on the mountain slopes were held to be healthier that those on offer at the city markets. There was a widespread belief that there are fewer insects in the mountains and that farmers therefore do not need to apply pesticides in the agricultural process. Qingyuan Mountain also has a reputation among the local townspeople for its clean air, but the fact that the recreation area is situated so close to the city and its industrial production plants means that pollution is probably also significant in this area.

Pashan as a form of physical exercise was mentioned by many, and young women especially talked about the slimming effect of mountain walking. One woman argued, however, that as long as *pashan* was in fact a combination of hours of nibbling and snacking with a mere half-hour of exercise, the effect would be significantly diminished. Even so, the perceived health benefit of going to Qingyuan Mountain was one of the reasons why several local work units handed out yearly passes to their employees. One local bank even paid an additional 100 *yuan* to those among its employees who signed their names on a designated list at the mountain, as a proof of having used the yearly pass at least once. Asking employees in different units about these practices, it became clear that initiatives such as these were still quite rare. The issuing of yearly passes depended very much on the person in charge in the work unit and his or her commitment to the physical well-being of the employees.

The function of mountain sites as places of exercise and healthy foods is part of a general trend of health awareness in contemporary China. Commercial health-related businesses such as saunas, fitness and beauty centres, spa centres, and yoga studios have been part of the Chinese leisure market since the mid-1990s, and their popularity among the middle classes is increasing (Feng Chongyi 2005: 135). The costs of such health-enhancing activities are significant and therefore not available to most consumers. For example, a yearly pass at a yoga studio costs approximately three thousand *yuan*, and at fitness centres the yearly pass is approximately one thousand *yuan*. As a leisure and recreation area, Qingyuan Mountain, however, provides local townspeople with opportunities for physical exercise regardless of income level. The relatively low cost, especially for those who use the 'secret' paths past the ticket booths, adds significantly to the popularity of the area as a place of leisure.

Leisure means livelihood at Qingyuan Mountain

The leisure activities that take place on the slopes of the mountain generate employment for vendors, drivers and providers of various services to Quanzhou's leisure seekers. At the foot of the mountain there is a choice of permanent kiosks where visitors can buy film rolls and refreshments. The Board collects some of its income from hiring out these business spots to private operators. In the vicinity of Tianhu Lake, modest outdoor kitchens and the more presentable lakeside snack restaurant provide employment for a handful of people who cook and serve meals. As mentioned above, similar eating places of variable quality can be found along the road leading up to the lake. These are operated by local farmers, who serve locally grown 'eco-friendly' vegetables and meat dishes from free-range poultry. These were all permanent businesses which probably also operated in agreement either with the reserve administration or the local village authorities. There were, however, numerous vendors along the various paths visitors follow up the mountainside. While some of them, as if by magic, sold boiled tea, eggs and vegetables out of electric rice-cookers in the middle of the forest, others offered water bottles or fruit from simple cloth bundles or plastic bags that they carried on their backs along the steep paths. The further removed from the ticket booths and permanent food stalls, the more vendors there would be. These vendors were often elderly women. It was explained to me that many of them lived in the farming villages on the mountain, and that the unofficial trade in refreshments to hikers had become their main source of income. Another group of people who make a living from the increase in leisure seekers at the mountain is the unlicensed motorbike drivers who drive visitors up to Tianhu Lake, especially in the afternoon and evenings.

As we shall see in the following, the reserve's finances depend on revenue from ticket sales to tourists. The majority of the customers of the informal workforce at Qingyuan Mountain are however, local visitors. For vendors, restaurateurs, drivers and others who make their living at the mountain, it is vital that the stream of visitors to the recreation areas at Tianhu Lake continues. These commercial activities are part of the harmful exploitation of the natural reserve, but at the same time, the reputation of the vegetables grown and poultry raised at Qingyuan mountain as clean and healthy is also part of the capital with which the various service-providers are entrusted. Consequently, the preservation of the natural resources at Qingyuan Mountain is also in their interest.

Qingyuan Mountain from the perspective of the management

The Qingyuan Mountain Managerial Board, which is in charge of the day-to-day administration of the area, has a composite mission. On the one hand it is the responsibility of the Board to oversee the preservation of cultural relics and the natural environment within the borders of the protected scenic area. On the other hand they are charged with running the area as a tourist site and a place of leisure for both tourists and local townspeople. A detailed analysis of the plans and priorities of the Board, and of the municipal government that oversees their funding, reveals a pattern where concern for the tourist industry is given priority over concern for both nature preservation and local townspeople's leisure interests.

Funding and priorities

The Board's director, Mr Hu, supervises the work of the 106 employees who carry out the restoration and preservation of the cultural relics, ensure protection of the natural resources, and carry out sanitation and security work within the reserve area. Although the administration is responsible for planning, management and security, Mr Hu held the preservation (*baohu*) of the nature reserve and its cultural relics to be their number one priority. The way the scenic area is funded, however, makes it difficult for the Board to follow up on this priority. Unlike Quanzhou's West Lake Park, which is a leisure area under the direct administration of the municipal government and where all expenses are therefore covered (*quan'e bokuan*), the Managerial Board at Qingyuan Mountain only has a portion of its expenses covered (*cha'e bokuan*) by the local government.

Contested leisure space 169

The income from ticket sales at Qingyuan Mountain goes directly to the Municipal Department of Finance (*Shi caizhengju*). The Board in turn receives subsidies (*butie*) from the finance authorities to cover management and preservation projects. In practice, this means that the preservation effort at Qinguyan Mountain rests in part on its success as a tourist spot, measured by the number of tickets sold. In their report from a 2005 study of the management of Qingyuan Mountain and Wuyi Mountain reserves, the Beijing Municipal Bureau of Landscape and Forestry encourages the Board to adhere to the principle that environmental benefits are priority number one, and that benefits for society (*shehui xiaoyi*) and economic profit (*jingji xiaoyi*) is the secondary goal (Li Xin 2005). As long as the funding for the scenic area is linked to the Board's ability to generate revenue from ticket sales to tourist and local visitors, however, it will be difficult for Mr Hu and his administration to live up to these ideals.

Environmental protection

As pointed out by among others Daily and Ellison, there is not necessarily a contradiction between sustainable management of natural resources and economic profit (Daily and Ellison 2002). In the case of the Qingyuan Mountain reserve, the influx of visitors to the area has had consequences for the environment, mainly in terms of pollution and noise from transportation on the road which winds its way up to the Tianhu Lake area. According to Mr Hu, the reserve management's recent survey of the biological conditions in the area indicates, however, that their preservation work has had an effect: the variety of species of trees, plants, birds and animals is increasing. Mr Hu wants to continue this positive trend by limiting access to the scenic area for private vehicles. A new 'ecological parking lot' (*shengtai xing tingchechang*) with room for 153 cars and 11 buses has recently been built at the foot of the mountain (Lin Fulong 2006). According to the plan, the trees and vegetation surrounding the parking lot will not only provide shade but also alleviate the exhaust emission from the vehicles. Moreover, in the future, private cars and motorbike taxis will be replaced with a shuttle bus service from the parking area to the lake at the top of the mountain. During my last period of field research, construction of the Qingyuan Mountain Tourist Centre (*Qingyuanshan youke zhongxin*) started up next to the parking area. This centre is expected to cost 13.5 million *yuan* and is funded by the municipal government (Lin Fulong 2006). Tourists will be given access to a rest area, and there will be a hall for performances and screenings that will seat 250 people. According to Mr Hu, the idea behind the centre is to introduce tourists to the natural environment, cultural relics and places of historical interest that the park area contains.

My impression from the interview with Mr Hu was that he regarded Qingyuan Mountain first and foremost as a natural reserve. He wanted to strengthen the understanding of the need for environmental protection among both visitors to the area and those who make their living within the reserve. According to Hu, there had been a long-term ban on forestry and hunting in the reserve. He also stated that in 1992 the Board had put an end to the commercial exploitation of natural resources that had been going on since the 1960s. The 2005 report from the Beijing Municipal Bureau of Landscape and Forestry, however, calls for the 'immediate shut down of the seventy-three quarries in the reserve'. The planned tourist centre with its 'ecological' parking spaces may serve to strengthen the image of the reservation management as environmentally concerned. But the report from the Beijing Municipal Bureau of Landscape and Forestry indicates that Mr Hu's administration still has a way to go when it comes to limiting the commercial exploitation of resources in the reserve.

The preservation of cultural relics

Qingyuan Mountain is the site of numerous cultural objects: the stone monuments from the Song and Yuan dynasties, and calligraphic carvings from Yuan, Ming and Qing being the most famous. In addition, the temple structures on the mountain bear witness to the religious pluralism practised in Quanzhou during the Tang Dynasty. The protected area encompasses cultural relics of importance to Confucianism, Daoism and Buddhism, as well as Manichaeism and Islam (Huang Shuikan 2005: 96). Until the establishment of the Board in 1979, the pagodas and cultural relics were watched over and maintained by local village communities and religious authorities. The Cultural Revolution meant the destruction of many of Quanzhou's historical relics, but several of my interviewees in the culture sector claimed that the damage in Quanzhou was less severe than in other cities. This was explained with reference to two factors: first, that local people hid cultural relics from the political authorities that sought to eradicate religious practices. Second, according to local lore, the Old Mayor (*Lao shizhang*) personally talked local Red Guards out of destroying the Kaiyuan Temple and other cultural treasures in Quanzhou. Mr Hu was one of several interviewees who related to me the anecdote of the Old Mayor's stance against the Red Guards. He argued, however, that the greatest damage to cultural relics in the area in the 1960s and 70s was due to long-term neglect, and that his unit was still working to alleviate this damage.

At the time of my interview with Mr Hu, the Qingyuan Mountain administration was in the middle of a four-year survey of cultural relics within the reservation area. I learned that they had also started the process of attracting donations for the preservation of cultural objects, and that they sought economic support for this work from the local department of religious affairs (*zongjiao bumen*). The Board envisioned a system where the religious affairs department would bring in donors and the park administration would provide regulations and planning. Mr Hu saw this as an extension of the existing practice where people donate money for the reconstruction of local temples. He also stressed the function of such contributions for the individuals involved, namely to secure the donor's own standing with Buddha and Guanyin. The board of management was apparently eager to cooperate with the structures of organized religion. The fact that the Qingyuan Mountain is also the site of a large number of family tombs and therefore plays an important role in local ancestral rites was considered a problem – rather than a cultural enrichment – in the eyes of the administration. Every year, Tomb Sweeping Day brings numerous locals to the mountain slopes, where they place offerings and set off fire crackers by their ancestral tombs. The resulting litter and fire hazard was regarded as a serious threat to the nature reserve, and was also the topic of several articles in printed media in the days leading up to the festival (Lin Jiahua *DNZB* 22 March 2006, A3). The Qingyuan Mountain administration wants to move all tombs that are not of historical interest away from the reserve. Director Hu anticipated that this process will eventually give rise to strong reactions among local townspeople, quoting a local ditty which states that

> [f]or an administrator, the second most difficult task is to move people's houses. The most difficult task is to move the houses of the dead.

The director's attitude reveals a hierarchical appraisal of local cultural heritage: the pagodas, monuments and inscriptions that belong to the officially recognized Buddhist and Daoist communities are held to be worthy of protection, and their followers are wooed as prospective donors and partners in the protection of cultural heritage. Family grave sites and the intangible ancestral rites that are part of the popular cultural tradition, however, are regarded as aspects of local culture that can be removed from their original environment without significant loss to the common cultural heritage. What the moving of tombs will bring in terms of popular resistance lies in the future. The spontaneous acts of resistance and various ways of 'making do' that local people have employed when their leisure practices have been threatened – as will be analysed in the second part of the chapter – provides an indication of the kinds of 'tactics' that may be brought into play the day family tombs are to be moved.

Tourists and local visitors

Qingyuan Mountain's main places of interest are concentrated at the foot of the mountain, not far from where the new tourist centre is being built. Although there are pagodas, inscriptions and other sights of cultural and natural interest along many of the forest paths on the mountain, few tourists venture beyond the easily accessible area close to the gates. Local visitors, however, take little interest in the sights. They aim for the recreation areas at the Tianhu Lake and spend as little time along the way as possible. It is therefore probable that the new tourist centre will be of little interest to regular, local visitors to Qingyuan Mountain. If we use Lefebvre's theories and look at the tourist centre as an example of a 'conceptualized' space (Lefebvre 1991: 38–9), the kinds of visitors the administration envision are tourists who arrive as a group in chartered buses, or drive to the mountain in their private cars. The fact is, however, that the majority of the visitors to Qingyuan Mountain are local townspeople who get there by public transport and therefore do not need parking spaces, 'ecological' or otherwise.

When asked to expand on what part of the population the tourist centre hoped to attract, Mr Hu responded that in his eyes the term *'youke'* (tourist) refers to both tourists and local townspeople, and furthermore that he did not care whether the visitors to the centre actually entered the reserve or not. The objective of the centre, he said, was to spread information about the reserve and its contents. Director Hu was clearly committed to raising people's consciousness concerning the preservation of nature and culture. He compared the scenic reserve to cultural institutions like the Louvre in Paris, where – he argued – people are more than willing to pay to get a glimpse of the cultural treasures on display. 'This reserve is not a welfare establishment' (*bu shi fulixing de difang*), he said. 'What's holding us back is that we're not spreading information (*xuanchuan*)[1] well enough. This place is about preservation, it is about the safeguarding of [our] resources (*ziyuan baohu*).' According to Director Hu, people in Quanzhou lack a thorough understanding of what Qingyuan Mountain contains as a nature reserve and a cultural heritage site. I reached the same conclusion on the basis of my interviews; local people never talk about Qingyuan Mountain in terms of a natural or cultural reserve. I find it rather unlikely, however, that the construction of a tourist centre can assist Hu in his quest to raise the local people's awareness of the environment or their heritage. Apart from a few articles in local newspapers, there was little information available to the general public concerning the plans for the tourist centre. I asked several people about their attitudes towards the plans, but none of my interviewees or contacts had any knowledge of them, and most of them had not even noticed the building site. On one occasion I pointed out the site to a fellow hiker as we were approaching the mountain by bus. When I told her what I had read about the tourist centre, she said that she could not see the need for such a place: 'Isn't the mountain fun enough in itself?' This statement communicates a view of Qingyuan Mountain that is typical among Quanzhou's inhabitants: it is a place to have fun.

All in all, the plans that are made for the maintenance and development of the reserve cater first and foremost to tourists, while the needs and wishes of the local visitors seem to be completely overlooked. In this regard, the local government's investment in the Qingyuan Mountain Tourist Centre is reminiscent of the 'image projects' in the museum sector, as discussed in Chapter 4. Impressive buildings were erected, but at the same time the museum directors were given meagre funds for maintenance or the development of exhibitions. Moreover, little was done to make the museums accessible to the local townspeople. In the case of the tourist centre, the municipal government has initiated and financed an impressive building complex, but the reserve administration still lack the funds needed to maintain and preserve the resources in the reserve. Furthermore, the centre is not built with the interests of the returning local visitor in mind. It is a display built for occasional tourists, so that they can enjoy the cultural relics and natural wonders of Quanzhou without setting foot in the actual reserve.

From the point of view of the Board, Qingyuan Mountain is primarily a preservation area and a resource to be exhibited to transient visitors. For local townspeople, it is a place of leisure. In my experience, what local visitors wanted from the Qingyuan Mountain administration was that some of the paved paths that were currently in disrepair be restored for the sake of safety, and that paper scraps, bottles and other kinds of litter be removed by the reserve's sanitation workers. Pointing out the garbage lining the paths, one woman told me that she would not mind paying for an entrance ticket if she felt that she got something in return. Similarly, a man in his forties held that if visitors were given something tangible, like a small, informative map or even a complementary bottle of water when they bought their ticket, they would not feel cheated the way they did now. I found that many people resented having to pay to get access to the mountain, and, moreover, that local visitors to the mountain dodged the ticket booths as a matter of course. The antagonism between local townspeople and the reserve administration became evident one Saturday afternoon in December 2005 when a local friend and I took one of our weekly walks up the mountain slope.

Confrontation at Qingyuan Mountain

It was just past noon when Fang and I met at the foot of Qingyuan Mountain. We were planning to visit the Daoist priest in the temple on the mountain top, and to have some tea and vegetables at the nearby lake on our way down. Fang had been at work until noon and, for her, the trip to Qingyuan Mountain marked the start of the weekend, as it does for many people in Quanzhou. We decided to 'take the back path' (*zou houshan*) up the mountain, for two reasons: unlike most paths in the nature reserve, this path was unpaved and therefore popular among those who do not mind the strenuousness of walking a natural mountain path. Moreover, there was no ticket booth along the way, and the small gate barring the path at the top was easy to circumvent by a steep detour into the bush. For this reason the *houshan* path is especially popular with students and other young people who must spend their wages or pocket money carefully.

On a typical Saturday the *houshan* path will be crowded by groups of friends and colleagues making their way up the slope. About halfway up the mountain side vendors usually line the path, offering bottled water and fruit for sale. But this Saturday I was greeted by groups of murmuring hikers squatting along the path. 'You had better wait a while,' said one of the hikers as I approached. 'They are demanding tickets up there right now.' At this point, my friend Fang was already far ahead of me, so I kept going. When I got closer to the gate near the top I found that there were about 80 people, mostly teenagers and people in their early twenties, squatting along and beside the path, waiting for the ticket inspection to come to an end. There was a lot of frustration in the air. Behind the barred gates I saw four men displaying printed certificates and hostile attitudes. Fang was standing on a nearby hilltop shouting at the guards. She had failed to make her way through the shrubbery because the guards had smeared some kind of grease on the path and among the bushes to prevent people from sneaking past the gate. Fang, who had got greasy stains on her trousers, was furious with the guards, and a heated debate followed before she finally agreed to buy a ticket. We then passed through the gates and proceeded to the Daoist temple as planned.

174 *Contested leisure space*

Figure 8.3 Climbing the *houshan* path.

By the time we had settled down with the Daoist priest for a chat and a cup of tea, we heard people shouting and arguing. I rose to go out and take a look, but the priest smiled stiffly and insisted that it was 'only children playing'. I heard more shouts from outside, and then suddenly one of the four guards from the gate rushed in and asked to borrow the Daoist's cellular phone. The guard took

Contested leisure space 175

the phone and disappeared out of sight. Whether he called for backup or just reported the matter to someone in charge, I cannot say.

Coming down from the mountain and getting on the bus towards the city centre, Fang and I learned that there had indeed been more serious clashes at the gate that afternoon. A group of young people who recognized Fang and her foreign friend from the *houshan* path told us that after the two of us had paid our way, more and more people had gathered outside the gates – they estimated a total of around 300. Our fellow bus passengers had started arguing with the guards, and in the end three of them had been taken to the local police station for questioning.

Dodging fees and official regulations is a form of popular practice common in societies both past and present and in different parts of the world. What makes this incident interesting is the fact that local townspeople chose not only to evade the fees demanded by the management of the scenic area, they openly resisted the management's authority to govern the mountain area by sitting down in front of the guards, hoping to outwait them. The hikers interpreted the security personnel's methods for making the path impassable as overly confrontational. Moreover, the way the guards got into arguments with weary and disgruntled climbers indicates to me a confrontational line from the side of the management unit as well. The following analysis is an attempt to explain this level of antagonism between the different groups who lay claim to Qingyuan Mountain.

Reactions and rationalizations

The fact that we had all chosen the *houshan* path in order to evade the ticket office and were caught red-handed by the guards was not a topic for discussion among the passengers on the bus that afternoon. On the contrary, the hikers who approached us on the bus questioned the right of the Qingyuan Mountain management to charge for tickets in the first place. One of the young girls claimed that if what the guards really wanted was for visitors to pay the entrance fee, they should have barred the path at the foot of the mountain. She argued that checking tickets at the top of a strenuous climb was bound to make people angry. A man in his early twenties held that 'it does not make any sense to pay for a ticket if you climb *houshan*. This path was not made by the scenic area management; it has been there for ages.' Another youth said that he could not understand why he should buy a ticket, arguing that 'we did not look at any of their scenic spots. We just wanted to climb the mountain and sit down to have tea and a chat.'

The justification these young people gave for why they did not buy entrance tickets or use the paved paths restored and maintained by the scenic area administration reveals a conflict over symbolic ownership: by characterizing the tourist attractions and the main path as belonging to the scenic area administration, these youth rhetorically assigned the ownership of the *houshan* path to themselves, the local users. This claim was strengthened by their reference to the *houshan* path's historical legacy: 'it has been there for ages'. According to one of the residents who lives within the reserve, the history of the paved paths stretches back to long before the establishment of the scenic area. These paths were once the only access to the villages in the Qingyuan mountain range, and were used for travel and transport by local people. This may explain why some locals hold that these paths belong to the townspeople as a collective, and are not the legal property of the government-run scenic reserve.

A parallel rhetoric of 'people *versus* government' was invoked by my friend Fang, who regarded this sudden ticket inspection as an example of a more general trend of governmental misconduct. Employees in both state units and private enterprises expect to receive a considerable bonus to top up their yearly wages just before the holidays, and Fang firmly believed that the only reason there were guards at *houshan* that day was their need to increase the Qingyuan Mountain administration's revenue in time for the Chinese New Year. Fang interpreted the guards' actions in the light of popular narratives of corrupt officials who demand unreasonable and illegal fees (*luan shou fei*) from the people in order to boost their own incomes. To me, the reactions of these young people indicate a high level of distrust between the regular visitors to Qingyuan Mountain and the government unit charged with the area's management.

In the week that followed, I heard similar accounts of the incident at the mountain from other sources. A woman who worked in my neighbourhood and who had been on the *houshan* path that day told me that while squatting by the gate, she had called a journalist. By the time the journalist arrived, however, there was nothing left to report, she said. In the days after the incident I did not find any articles about the quarrels on the mountain in the local press or any references to people being taken in for questioning. Either the small crackdown on hikers that Saturday was too small to present as a propaganda victory in the local media, or the local government anticipated that by keeping quiet about the matter the whole thing would blow over. Surely, compared to the demonstrations and uprisings that have been carried out by peasant communities all over China during the last years to protest what local communities regard as unfair and unlawful government practices (Bernstein 2000; O'Brien and Li 2006), the incident at Qingyuan Mountain was of little significance to the authorities, even at a local level. For the individuals who took part in the spontaneous sit-down and ensuing argument, however, even an incident as small as this carried significant meaning. In their eyes, they had spoken out against unfair treatment. I argue that the act of evading the entrance fee to the Qingyuan Mountain is only one of several examples of the 'tactics', or ways of 'making do' (de Certeau 1988: 29–42), that ordinary people adopt in the face of official rules and regulations they hold to be unreasonable.

Quanzhou people's ways of 'making do'

In *The Practice of Everyday Life*, Michel de Certeau analyses the 'tactics' ordinary people use to circumvent or evade the 'strategies' of powerful agents such as a business, army, city or scientific institution (de Certeau 1988: 36).

Contested leisure space 177

Strategies, writes de Certeau, are used by power holders to 'produce, tabulate, and impose' the spaces they govern (de Certeau 1988: 30). The only opportunity left for 'others' (i.e. ordinary people) is to rely on tactics they play out 'within enemy territory' (de Certeau 1988: 37). Ordinary people's tactics can take a variety of forms:

> Dwelling, moving about, speaking, reading, shopping, and cooking are activities that seem to correspond to the characteristics of tactical ruses and surprises: clever tricks of the 'weak' within the order established by the 'strong,' an art of putting one over on the adversary on his own turf, hunter's tricks, maneuverable, polymorph mobilities, jubilant, poetic, and warlike discoveries.
>
> (de Certeau 1988: 40)

De Certeau describes these ways of making do as the 'art of the weak' (de Certeau 1988: 37), a form of counteraction in response to the dominant spaces imposed and produced by power holders. I argue that this is precisely what is happening when people in Quanzhou attempt to dodge the ticket booths on their way up the slopes of Qingyuan Mountain. De Certeau regards the spatial dimension as governed by the 'strong', while time and timing can be used by the 'weak' (de Certeau 1988: 26). So, whereas the Board governs the physical gates and ticket booths, townspeople utilize timing and clever tricks in order to evade the official ticket system. De Certeau uses examples as diverse as the South American Indians' reaction to Spanish rule and French workers' manipulation of time to illustrate 'making do' as a prevalent form of popular creativity (de Certeau 1988: xiii, 25). Consider the following variety of tactics employed by local people in their attempts to obtain free access to this leisure place, which they hold to be their own:

Mr Kong is employed in one of the cultural institutions in Quanzhou. He is a scholarly type of man, but also enjoys the outdoors. He usually bikes to work and he goes to Qingyuan Mountain once every week. Kong tells me that he knows of a small path that can take us to the main path up the mountain, but not via the ticket office. He himself has a yearly pass, but since his friends do not, they always use this back road up to Tianhu Lake. The cost of the entrance ticket may be one reason local people shun the ticket booths. The fact that the local authorities granted free access to the mountain area for Quanzhou's migrant labourers during the Spring Festival caused resentment among some locals and gave rise to sentiments similar to those among critics of international labour migration to Europe. One local woman put it like this: 'Nowadays, the local government takes better care of the migrants (*wailai de*) than the locals (*bendi ren*).' As discussed in Chapter 4, 30 *yuan* is a considerable sum to spend on leisure for many people in Quanzhou. I also found, however, that some interviewees exaggerated the ticket cost, claiming that the charge was 50 or even 80 *yuan* for one-time entry. This kind of misinformation may have contributed to the widespread idea that the ticket price at Qingyuan Mountain was unreasonably steep.

'It's very expensive,' said Mr Song, a scholar who had recently moved to Quanzhou. He had decided against taking the trip up the mountain because he found it far too expensive: 'I asked at the gate whether there was some time one could get in for free and they said "before five a.m. and after six p.m." – but who wants to go there at that hour?' In fact, the recreation areas by Tianhu Lake are very popular after nightfall. Although the official signs at the gates advise visitors not to stay in the scenic area between six in the evening and five in the morning, numerous people make their way up the slopes at night; most go either by motorbike or taxi, taking the mountain road past the villages on the eastern side of the mountain. On clear evenings, the view of the city from the reservoir wall is spectacular. Added to the opportunity to enter free of charge, this makes Qingyuan Mountain one of Quanzhou's most cherished leisure places on hot summer nights.

As mentioned in Chapter 4, the ability to procure free tickets, VIP memberships and special bargains for friends and connections is a type of resourcefulness people in Quanzhou appreciate. Similarly, the practice of evading the ticket booth at Qingyuan Mountain was something Quanzhou people talked about with great enthusiasm. I observed a typical example of this discourse during a trip to one of the strawberry farms at the foot of the mountain. I was there in the company of a group of employees from a nearby college. One of the women in the group bragged about her knowledge of the various 'secret' paths, pointing out numerous entry points for climbing the mountain without paying, each time exclaiming 'Here they don't charge you!' (*Bu shou piao!*). She assured her colleagues that no ticket would be needed to see any of the sights if they took the trip in her company. It was evident that she regarded her ability to evade the ticket booths as a form of resourcefulness, and that she wanted her colleagues to benefit from her special know-how.

Even among those who could well afford both a ticket and a yearly pass, the idea of paying to enter Qingyuan Mountain seemed almost unthinkable. Mr Yan, for instance, who held a good position in a local bank and earned enough to afford his own private car, employed his own customized form of tactics: he held a couple of certificates that identified him as being a journalist. These certificates gave free access to the mountain area for him and any accompanying passengers. Admittedly, Mr Yan did write articles now and again for an economic journal and a Party branch publication, but he was not a journalist by profession. This did not prevent him from exploiting the privileges that came with his press passes. Mr Yan's actions demonstrate that the evasion of the Qingyuan Mountain entrance fee is something that occurs even among the well-to-do. Moreover, it shows that the ticket inspection at the *houshan* path on the said Saturday targeted only those visitors who relied on physical strength as a way to dodge the ticket booths. These visitors did not have the sort of social capital that gave Mr Yan access to certificates and special agreements. I found a similar example in Ms Tian, who loved travelling and sightseeing but found this to be a rather costly hobby in the long run. She discovered that by taking a tourist guide exam in her native town, her license as tour guide would provide her with free access to numerous sites of cultural or historic significance all over China, Qingyuan Mountain included. Her peers commended Ms Tian on her ingenuity.

The activities undertaken by unlicensed vendors and drivers within the Qingyuan Mountain reserve also bear some resemblance to what de Certeau describes as ways of 'making do'. Villagers within the reserve area find ways to circumvent the regulations set up by the administration and open illicit businesses which provide them with a level of income which would be otherwise unattainable. Moreover, according to the regulations, inhabitants of the villages within the reserve have free access to the reserve, but they can also admit their own personal visitors free of charge. I heard many anecdotes about farmers who made money from letting people enter on their 'quota' at a cost of a few *yuan*.

I got further evidence of the general approval of such manoeuvres among people in Quanzhou when some of my contacts laid plans for a trip to the mountain around the time of the Spring Festival in 2007. Arrangements were made for me to make use of a yearly pass that had been left by a French student some weeks earlier. The argument was that the yearly pass was properly paid for and that despite the picture of a French woman on the issued pass, the clerks in the ticket booth would not be able to distinguish one foreigner from another. My initial scepticism was received with incredulity and laughter by my local friends, and it was made clear to me that I would be a fool not to seize this opportunity. When I finally used the borrowed pass, I discovered that not only was I waved past the ticket booth with no questions asked, but three additional visitors entered the park area for free together with me. In addition to my friend Fang, who was taken to be my personal tourist guide, a young couple who approached the gates together with us let the clerks understand that they also belonged to my party. There was apparently no end to the clever tricks people could employ in order to dodge the ticket fees at Qingyuan Mountain.

De Certeau describes popular tactics as ways of 'making do' in the here and now. They are not actions directed towards the goal of social change. In de Certeau's own words:

> [the] actual order of things is precisely what 'popular' tactics turn to their own ends, without any illusion that it will change any time soon.
> (de Certeau 1988: 26)

The examples listed above can be regarded as ordinary people's playful manipulation of the existing order. But to return to the quarrel that erupted at the top of the *houshan* path in December 2005, this incident was, I argue, of a different calibre. James C. Scott's theory of 'hidden transcripts' (1990) shows that the practices de Certeau describes as mere 'making do' make up a repertoire of actions subordinates can put to use in direct confrontations with power holders. I interpret the sit-down action and subsequent argument that took place on the mountain that afternoon as an example of how a hidden transcript becomes publicly declared.

Voicing a hidden transcript

Whereas de Certeau's theory of the 'art of the weak' analyses the playful counteractions of ordinary people, Scott's theory of 'hidden transcripts' provides a tool for the analysis of popular 'arts of resistance'. Scott describes the interaction between dominant forces in society (kings, elites, power holders at different levels) and their subordinates as a 'public transcript', where the expressions and actions of the subordinate 'with rare, but significant, exceptions [...] will [...] be shaped to appeal to the expectations of the powerful' (Scott 1990: 2). The backstage counter-narratives and counter-actions that tend to develop among subordinates are regarded by Scott as hidden transcripts, i.e. ways of acting or speaking that makes it possible for the weak to express their frustrations over unjust treatment without suffering reprimands from the power holders in a society. Traces of these hidden transcripts can be found in popular practices such as poaching, pilfering, tax evasion and foot-dragging (Scott 1990: 14). I find that these practices are similar to the dodging of ticket booths and manipulation with cards and certificates that the people of Quanzhou employ in their indirect resistance to the way the Qingyuan Mountain area is governed.

According to Scott, the hidden transcript is a 'collective cultural product' that functions as a supply of actions and roles on which subordinates can draw in those rare moments when 'public displays of deliberate insubordination' take place (Scott 1990: 9, 203). Thus the theory of hidden transcripts explains how it can happen that ordinary people seem to act in unison when they rise up against a dominant power. When hikers on the *houshan* path openly challenged the security guards that Saturday in December, they gave expression to the notion shared by many that the mountain area should be available to local townspeople free of charge. Added to this particular grudge, I argue that popular narratives concerning the corruption and misconduct among Chinese officials augmented the hikers' experiences of unfair treatment. This means that even if the sit-down action by the *houshan* path and the words that Fang and other hikers used in their quarrels with the guards were spontaneous, the prevalent discourse of unreasonable ticket prices and corruption provided a ready-to-use transcript for them to rely on in their display of resistance.

De Certeau's theory of ordinary people's small-scale insubordinations focuses on tactics and ways of making do. Scott takes his enquiry further and discusses the different strategies power holders can adopt when the indirect and hidden aspects of popular resistance surface within the domain of the public transcript. Power holders can choose to regard acts of insubordination as an overt challenge, they can attempt to reinterpret the actions of their subordinates by diminishing or ridiculing their actions, labelling them as acts of 'terrorism' or questioning the mental stability of the individuals involved, or they can overlook the whole incident and 'pretend they did not observe the insubordination' (Scott 1990: 205). In this case, local authorities chose to ignore the open resistance to the regulations of Qingyuan Mountain. Although some of the hikers were taken in for questioning by the police, this public declaration of a hidden transcript did not have an aftermath of any significance. When I returned to the area after a short field break, Fang had got news of yet another secret path we could take to the mountain. This was just one indication of the fact that, even if the incident blew over and status quo was maintained, the disapproval of the ticketing at Qingyuan Mountain remained strong among local townspeople. As Scott points out, 'the inevitability of domination does not necessarily make it just in [the subordinates'] eyes' (Scott 1990: 79). As expected, the next time I passed by the Daoist temple, the monks confirmed that the *houshan* path, where there had been a ticket inspection in December, was still in use by many of the regular visitors.

The antagonism between local visitors to Qingyuan Mountain and the administrative unit that governs the area has its roots in a disagreement over the way this popular mountain area is utilized. The problem is that the administrative unit lacks understanding of the significance Qingyuan Mountain has in the lives of local townspeople. Most people in Quanzhou Qingyuan perceive Mountain as a common good, and a place which therefore –some argue – should be made available to local visitors for free. The Managerial Board is in a position where they must balance the interests of preservation and commerce. The case study shows that, in its eagerness to satisfy standards of cultural and natural preservation while at the same time attracting the tourists to the city, the local administration and the management at the Qingyuan reserve fail to recognize and make plans that take into account the wishes of the local population.

My analysis of the activities that take place within the reserve leads me to conclude that preservation of the natural resources at Qingyuan Mountain is in the interest of all parties involved. I therefore argue that the antagonism that exists between local visitors to the mountain area and the Managerial Board stems not from a collision of interests but from colliding ideas concerning what sort of space the mountain is and should be. The case of Qingyuan Mountain is yet another example of the lack of correspondence between the envisioned leisure spaces administrative units and power holders seek to produce, and the actual leisure places and the activities practised there by real-life people (Lefebvre 1991: 37, 143). Moreover, the episode at the *houshan* path in December 2005 shows that some people are willing to challenge what in their eyes is an unreasonable form of control and regulation of a common leisure place. The right to access a place of leisure free of charge can rightfully be considered a minor cause, especially in the context of contemporary China, where peasants have in many cases braved local authorities and openly resisted unlawful taxation and the rigging of local elections (Bernstein 2000; O'Brien and Li 2006). Nevertheless, the fact that some hikers found it worthwhile to sit down and even to engage in an argument with government employees does indicate that the field of leisure can be an arena where popular arts of resistance are practised in public.

Director Hu held that, when it comes to Qingyuan Mountain, local people lack the necessary awareness. He identified this problem as a lack of propagation (*xuanchuan*) on the part of the administration. The kind of information dissemination called for by Director Hu may bring to people's attention the fact that their ticket fees contribute towards environmental protection and the restoration of cultural relics. But propaganda campaigns and the plans for a new tourist centre will not, I believe, cause the feelings of antagonism to disappear among local visitors who use the area as a leisure place. The main obstacle to getting the message of preservation across is not the general lack of awareness but the lack of a two-way communication between the administration and the people who are regular visitors to the area. The analysis of Qingyuan Mountain as a contested space gives an example of a general tendency in the relationship between people and government in China, namely that the government pays little attention to public needs and wants. This causes resentment among the general population, which therefore tends to resort to popular tactics and ways of making do. The one-way communication structure, sustained through the work units and neighbourhood committees on which Chinese authorities used to rely, has broken down. In a situation where diversity thrives in all aspects of life, top-down dissemination of the *xuanchuan* kind is no longer efficacious. Moreover, the development of an infrastructure for two-way communication in the public sphere in the form of a fully functioning civil society – or possibly an entirely new structure of people-to-government exchanges – has thus far been effectively curbed by the policies of the party-state. The case study thus serves as an illustration of a situation where the people have few opportunities to voice their demands, and the government is disinclined to consult them.

Conclusions

Commercial agents and authorities, be they government agencies or opinion makers, seek to influence the ways we lead our daily lives, including how we govern our leisure. The cases from Quanzhou tell us how in a local context authorities seek to influence the ways people spend their time and resources. At the same time, it is evident that individuals and groups in Quanzhou have room to manoeuvre within the locally defined leisure space. Moreover, the authorities tolerate certain kinds of transgression in the local leisure sphere, as long as they do not threaten the overall goal of social stability as defined by the party-state. These facts bear witness to the roles of both popular agency and governmental leniency in the negotiation of social space, not only in Quanzhou, but also in society more generally. The authorities' calls for healthier, more educational leisure practices, and ordinary people's continued love for simple fun constitutes an unresolved conflict which is observable in many societies and at different points in time. My aim here has been to demonstrate how the universal struggle for power over everyday life plays out in the context of a medium-sized Chinese city in a time of social transition.

Individuals and loosely organized groups may test the limits of the social space, and authorities will tolerate small-scale transgressions as long as these do not pose a (perceived) threat to social stability. This negotiation between official discourses and popular agency which the Quanzhou cases illustrate are emblematic of the relationship between the government and the governed, not only in the PRC but also in societies worldwide. What is particular in the case of the People's Republic is that the party-state exercises its power over the leisure sphere in a highly inconsistent manner. The leisure space is governed sometimes by subtle means (such as overly intricate procedures for the establishment of a popular organization) and sometimes through brute force (as in the examples of crackdowns on 'black' internet cafés or indeed the practices of *Falun Gong*). At the same time, the official PRC leisure ethic and its incessant calls for healthy leisure is not followed up with substantial plans for the facilitation of educational leisure. It seems that the development of a healthy leisure culture is less of a concern for the party-state than the efficacious control and surveillance of extant practices.

Nevertheless, as demonstrated in the chapters above, the official leisure ethic influences the practices of Quanzhou's inhabitants only to a limited degree. Few among my interviewees expressed any concern for the utility or waste of leisure as a national resource and the development of a healthy leisure culture. On the contrary, the opportunity to socialize with friends and family, watch the lively goings-on in the city streets, and enjoy different kinds of fun were the key concerns in most Quanzhou people's leisure lives. Some did, however, acknowledge the central metaphor of the leisure ethic, namely that leisure is a resource. These were mostly young white-collar employees who sought to increase their competence and skills through educational leisure activities. In these cases, however, the pursuit of educational leisure activities (i.e. self-study and extensive reading) was considered a means to further one's own personal development and career trajectory. This indicates that the call for Chinese individuals to make sacrifices on behalf of the national collective, a characteristic of Communist Party propaganda in both the past and present, falls on deaf ears in contemporary China.

I analyse the PRC leisure ethic as a dominant discourse produced by planners, technocrats and social engineers representing the party-state. I have considered this process in terms of a production of 'social space' (Lefebvre 1991). More specifically, I have analysed it as a process whereby government planners and legislators seek to project their visions of a 'healthy' leisure space onto Chinese society. The detailed analysis of people's leisure practices in the actual lived space supports Lefebvre's assertion that authorities 'cannot produce a space with a perfectly clear understanding of cause and effect, motive and implication' (Lefebrvre 1991: 37). In other words, government regulations and propaganda campaigns may seek to shape the forms popular leisure may take, but can never fully predict or prevent the tactical actions and counter-actions that ordinary people themselves produce through their actual practices (de Certeau 1988: 37). The way Quanzhou's inhabitants have embraced the square outside Mintaiyuan Museum as a place of leisure while other, designated, leisure places fail to appeal to them is a case in point. It is an indication of the power ordinary people actually have, not only as 'users' but also as co-producers of space as 'lived', not merely 'conceived' (Lefebrvre 1991: 40).

The failure of the official leisure discourse to dominate or alter people's leisure practices is an indication of the inefficiency of Party propaganda as a 'ruling technology'. The fact is that the government-sponsored museums, which present themselves as places of leisure, are hard-pressed to find an audience. Likewise, the number of readers who find their way to local public libraries is diminishing. At the same time, leisure places such as karaoke parlours, which the government treat as harbours of 'chaotic' activities, have gained popularity among a wide range of consumers. In more general terms, by studying leisure as a social field where power is exercised and negotiated it becomes clear that, in contemporary China, government propagation does not necessarily produce popular adherence. Moreover, as argued in Chapter 4, the fact that publications from local government units use the discourse of healthy leisure does not necessarily mean that the facilitation of healthy leisure activities is at the heart of the matter. As some interviewees in Quanzhou argued, if the local mayor really wanted to build museums and not just to make a display of the municipality's wealth, he would have provided the infrastructure and resources needed to attract visitors. This example suggests that the leisure ethic can also be used by the local government as a convenient excuse to pursue other agendas.

Consequently, as researchers we cannot simply limit our enquiries to the official discourses that inform government campaigns, legislative texts and information booklets. When studying the field of leisure in China, we must compare official publications with real-life practices. And in our calculations of the work-to-leisure ratio we must contrast the normative labour legislation with the amount of leisure that people actually enjoy. We must compare the official discourses with the lives lived. Only then can we estimate the real impact of official discourses on people's everyday lives.

The PRC leisure ethic promotes 'healthy' and 'rational' leisure activities, and cautions against the influence of 'chaotic' people and environments on the well-being of the general population. However, while these moralist sentiments guide the authorities' regulation of the leisure market, the leisure ethic does not cause local authorities to organize or in any way provide people with 'healthy' leisure alternatives. If, then, the concept of healthy leisure exists merely as an ideal and only at the level of discourse, why is it relevant to our understanding of leisure as practice? The policies of the reform era have meant that the provision and facilitation of urban leisure have gradually been transferred from work unit and neighbourhood committee to the leisure market and the individual. In the PRC, leisure has changed from the collective experiences of high socialism to individual experiences in the present. The fact that the choices of how and what to consume and which kinds of leisure to pursue is transferred from political authorities to the individual-as-consumer constitutes a radical break with the former Maoist organization of social life. From the point of view of the party-state, the leisure market now makes up an important part of the Chinese service sector. It contributes to the expansion of a national market where the salaried middle class can spend its earnings, which in turn stimulates the economy. At the same time, political authorities still worry about the possible negative consequences of city nightlife and luxury spending on the well-being and productivity of the national workforce. The fact that the government continues the propagation of 'healthy' leisure tells us that the political authorities in China seek to continue their influence over people's leisure practices, although to a lesser extent than before.

The diminishing power of political authorities to govern people's everyday lives means that Chinese individuals can, and also must, take possession of their own life choices. This exercise of choice does not necessarily mean more freedom for the individual. Chinese society is undergoing a process of 'individualization' (Bauman 2001; Beck and Beck-Gernsheim 2002), where the life trajectory of the individual is no longer a given but a result of choices the individual must make for him or herself (Bauman 2001: 7; Hansen and Svarverud 2010). Under these circumstances, the responsibility for failure and success is attributed to the individual, and his or her ability to make the right choices. While opportunities in terms of employment, leisure activities, lifestyles and consumption have become more diverse in China, people's actual choices are limited by increasing economic and social inequalities. In the contemporary PRC, social security and stable employment are no longer guaranteed for the urban population. Successful integration and socialization have consequently become the responsibility of the individual. It is the individual who must provide the income, the social networks and the cultural competence necessary to obtain and maintain the desired middle-class standard of living. This explains why young white-collar employees feel the need to 'recharge' their qualifications through various forms of self-study. In other words, their choice of educational, healthy forms of leisure is in fact no choice at all. The process of individualization means that people are forced to 'choose' their own fates. The insecurity caused by these social realities is significant, as the literature on individualization in Western societies demonstrates (Bauman 2001; Beck and Beck-Gernsheim 2002; Howard 2007).

This being said, in the case of contemporary China it is also important to recognize the value that people assign to making their own choices in matters where no choice used to be available. It is true that the labour market is fierce in China, but people also appreciate the chance to leave their present employment and search for opportunities elsewhere (Hansen and Pang 2008). As for leisure, it is true that many forms are expensive and therefore out of reach for a majority of the Chinese, but people still appreciate that the days of compulsory study sessions and politicized, government-initiated activities are now long gone. People can now pursue amateur photography or meet with friends for karaoke or a game of *majiang* without being suspected of 'wallowing in petty bourgeois amusements', as was the case in the 1960s (Shaoguang Wang 1995: 155). As this study from Quanzhou shows, middle-class citizens in urban China now participate in a range of activities without much interference from agents of the party-state. This conclusion concurs with Feng Chongyi's statement that 'everyday life no longer remains in thrall to a homogenous, abstract space of the state' (Feng Chongyi 2005: 148). What the present study also reveals, however, is that the Chinese leisure space has its limits. The rhetoric of 'healthy' and 'chaotic' leisure indicates that the party-state seeks to guide people towards the kinds of leisure that agree with the PRC leisure ethic. But whereas unregistered leisure associations may continue their activities undisturbed as long as they do not inspire social disorder, leisure businesses that are suspected of harbouring agents of chaos are held under close surveillance by the relevant local bureaus.

The reform policy, which allows some to 'get rich first', has meant a considerable increase in the standard of living among the urban middle classes. The legitimacy of the current regime rests in part on the preservation of social order and, as long as the government ensures social stability, it is unlikely that the urban middle class will feel a need for radical political change. In the urban context, young, uneducated, male migrant labourers are most frequently regarded – by the authorities and urban middle class alike – as potential agents of social disorder. These young men also make up the typical clientele of urban Internet cafés. I therefore argue that the substantial media coverage of government 'crack downs' on illegal conduct in Quanzhou's Internet bars is published partly to demonstrate to the urban middle classes the efficacy of the government in its handling of the urban 'others'. Thus, it reinforces prejudice among the urban middle classes against migrant workers as agents of chaos. To the outside observer, however, the prevalence of such reports in the media can lead to the erroneous assumption that the government's strict regulation of this part of the Chinese leisure market is indicative of how the party-state regulates leisure activities in general. What this study demonstrates, however, is the considerable leniency with which local authorities manage the field of leisure, commercial and otherwise.

Consumption and leisure are closely linked in the material analysed in this study. One of the findings is that, in their discourse, members of the cultured middle class in Quanzhou discriminate between the cultural and the commercial, with the former being 'clean' and the latter 'tainted'. In their consumer practices, however, the cultured middle class tend to be 'omnivores' who sample from a diverse cultural menu, ranging from 'popular' and 'commercial' to the fine arts. Moreover, in spite of their critique of lavish consumption, members of the cultured middle class are not afraid to spend their income on the kinds of leisure and consumer items they themselves, as cultured consumers, consider valuable. This attitude among the cultured middle class echoes the official PRC attitude towards consumption, which proposes that ordinary people are liable to be lead astray by the attractions of the commercial leisure market. This outlook is evident in articles in local Party-dominated media as well as in Chinese scholarly writing. Here, businesses in the commercial leisure market are portrayed as facilitators of squandering, binge drinking and prostitution, and accused of jeopardizing the mental and physical health of the general population. There is nothing inherently 'Chinese' in this sentiment. As argued in the opening chapters, the moralizing critique of popular culture and the commercial culture industry has been, and still is, expressed in a variety of forms. It is evident in the Protestant work ethic, in writings by conservatives in the US, among neo-Marxists inspired by the Frankfurter school, and among those Asef Bayat calls Islamic 'anti-fun-damentalists'. What these moralist approaches have in common is that they are all examples of how elites seek to impose their cultural values on the wider population, and thereby lay down guiding principles for the 'proper' forms of leisure.

Some scholars have argued that in China, cultural consumption is used by the political authorities as a means to pacify the population (Jing Wang 2001a; 2001b; Tomba 2004: 3; Croll 2006: 30–1). While my analysis suggests that the party-state seeks to influence the realm of leisure and consumption, Jing Wang and others suggest that the party-state effectively dominates the leisure market. It is against this background that Wang expresses her wish that 'the Chinese consumer public will start its own theoretical quest for a notion of leisure that is free from market rule' (Jing Wang 2001b: 82). I did not detect any such theoretical quest for alternative leisure outside the market or outside party domination among my interviewees in Quanzhou. What I found, however, were practices which in themselves defy the description of the Chinese leisure sphere as dominated by the hegemony of state and market. I argue that the existence of independent leisure associations such as Quanzhou's Happy Outdoor network and the Professional English Club means that the party-state's dominance of the Chinese leisure space is far from total. As for the leisure market, commercial leisure venues play an increasingly important role as facilitators of leisure activities. But this does not lead to the conclusion that the leisure activities of ordinary Chinese are governed by exploitive market forces.

In the analysis of leisure we must proceed beyond the study of institutions – be they state or market – and their representations of reality. Rather, we must seek answers in the places where people actually practice their leisure activities. If we focus solely on leisure as exchanges in a market or on how consumer needs are created and exploited, we lose sight of the variety of practices that take place in commercial leisure venues. So rather than lamenting the decline in library loans, we must seek out readers in bookshops and book cafés, and observe leisure reading where it actually takes place. And rather than criticizing the uniformity of China's commercial nightlife, we must observe in detail the function of the karaoke parlour as a social space, and analyse the variety of ways in which people entertain themselves in the karaoke setting. In other words, we must not let ourselves be blinded by the image of the commercial as something inherently repressive. And conversely, we must not let our analysis of actual, observable practices be clouded by an idea(l) of leisure as a non-commercial realm of authentic popular participation. In this study I have sought to demonstrate that the Chinese leisure space stretches further than official legislation and the discourse of 'healthy' leisure suggest. By studying in detail some of the leisure activities in which people engage, it becomes clear that in addition to (and sometimes in direct relation to) the officially defined leisure space, there is also room for people to transgress and redefine the leisure space through their own practices.

It is evident from the cases analysed in this study that leisure is a social field where power is exercised. Leisure is also a field where power is tested, as the case study of popular resistance towards the management of Qingyuan Mountain confirms. The leisure sphere is not, however, a seedbed for a budding civil society, and leisure practices only rarely make up the base from which substantial resistance can be launched. In the Chinese case, the cost of openly articulated resistance can be dear, as recent confrontations in Tibet and Xinjiang testify. In light of these and other incidents in Chinese history where social protest has been met with brute force, the fact that people have both the courage and the agency to dispute the regulations they find to be unreasonable is noteworthy. I interpret this as a sign of the latitude that characterizes the space that exists between the party-state and the Chinese population, both as individuals and as loosely organized collectives. I do not, however, propose that this space will necessarily expand with time, or even maintain its present scope. This, I believe, depends on whether or not the Chinese party-state manages to retain its legitimacy among the majority of the population as a guarantor of stability and an increased standard of living.

Glossary

ai pin cai hui ying	爱拼才会赢
ai wan	爱玩
anjing	安静
anning	安宁
Anxi	安溪
Anxi tie guanyin	安溪铁观音
Ba rong ba chi	八荣八耻
baohu	保护
Beijing	北京
bendi ren	本地人
benshen ai shu	本身爱书
bijiao xiuxian de shudian	比较休闲的书店
bieshu	别墅
bu jiankang	不健康
buliang	不良
bu shi fulixing de difang	不是福利性的地方
Bu shou piao	不售票
butie	补贴
bu zizai	不自在
cha'e bokuan	差额拨款
chanye hua	产业化
chenmi	沉迷
chi he wan le	吃喝玩乐
chi ku	吃苦
chi xian fan	吃闲饭
chongdian	充电
Chuxi	除夕
chuyi	初一
chuande hen xiuxian	穿地很休闲
chuantong xiaofei wenhua	传统消费文化
dasha	大厦
da wan	大玩
dazhong wenhua	大众文化

daixin jie-jiari	带薪节假日
daixin jie-xiujia	带薪节休假
danti	单体
danwei	单位
dangguande	当官的
daode	道德
digua qiang	地瓜腔
dianzi yuelanshi	电子阅览室
Ding	丁
diu mianzi	丢面子
Dongnan Zaobao	东南早报
dubo	赌博
dui naozi de touzi	对脑子的投资
erhu	二胡
fadu	法度
Falun Gong	法轮功
Fengze	丰泽
fubai	腐败
Fujian	福建
Fujian ribao	福建日报
Fuwenmiao	府文庙
Fuwenmiao guangchang	府文庙广场
Fuwenmiao guwan shichang	府文庙古玩市场
Fuzhou	福州
gaige kaifang	改革开放
ganbu	干部
geti laodongzhe	个体劳动者
Gongqingtuan	共青团
Gongren wenhuagong	工人文化宫
guanxi	关系
guan xianshi	管闲事
guang chaoshi	逛超市
guangjie	逛街
guang yixia	逛一下
Guangzhou	广州
Guo	郭
Guoji xiaofeizhe quanyi baohu ri	国际消费者权益保护日
Guojia zhongdian fengjing mingsheng qu	国家重点风景名胜区
guomin	国民
Haishang sichouzhilu de qi dian	海上丝绸之路的起点
Haixia dushibao	海峡都市报
Han	汉
haohua	好话
haowan	好玩
heli	合理

hei wangba	黑网吧
hen duo he cha de ren meiyou wenhua	很多喝茶的人没有文化
houshan	后山
huairen	坏人
Hui	回
Hui'an	惠安
Hui'an nü	惠安女
huodong	活动
jiankang	健康
jiankang, anquan, you yiyi	健康, 安全, 有意义
jiankang fazhan	健康发展
jiankang majiang	健康麻将
jiankang shangwang yuanli wangyin	健康上网远离网瘾
jiefang	解放
jin	斤
Jinjiang	晋江
jingji xiaoyi	经济效益
jingshen wenming	精神文明
jujinghuishende wanzhe	聚精会神地玩着
kaifa qu	开发区
kaifang jingshen	开放精神
kan dianshi, qu chi fan, guangguangjie, dengdeng	看电视, 去吃饭, 逛逛街, 等等
kan renao	看热闹
kexue	科学
keyi ziyou zhipei de shijian	可以自由支配的时间
langdang gong	浪荡工
langfeile hen duo shijian	浪费了很多时间　浪费了很多时间
laobaixing	老百姓
laoban	老板
Laojun	老君
lao shizhang	老市长
laowai	老外
Laozi	老子
Lei Feng youxi	雷锋游戏
Licheng	鲤城
lingdao shuo 'nali', jiu nali	领导说'那里', 就那里
louxi	陋习
luan	乱
luan shoufei	乱收费
Luojiang qu	洛江区
lüse wangba	绿色网吧
lüyou qu	旅游区
majiang	麻将

Meiyou shenme ziyou shijian	没有什么自由时间
milian	迷恋
minjian shetuan	民间社团
Minnan	闽南
Minnan ban	闽南版
Minnan hua	闽南话
Mintaiyuan bowuguan	闽台缘博物馆
minying shudian laoban	民营书店老板
minying tushuguan	民营图书馆
Minzheng ju	民政局
Ming	明
Nanjing	南京
nanqu	南曲
nanyin	南音
Ni qu nali wan?	你去哪里 玩?
nianhuo	年货
pashan	爬山
pao wangba	泡网吧
peiyang xingqing	培养性情
qiyejia	企业家
qiaoxiang	侨乡
qinfan yinsi	侵犯隐私
Qing lai women bangongshi wan	请来我们办公室玩
Qing lai women jia wan	请来我们家玩
Qingmingjie	清明节
Qingnian zhiyuanzhe xiehui	青年志愿者协会
Qingshaonian wenhuagong	青少年文化宫
Qingyuanshan fengjing mingsheng qu guanweihui	清源山风景名胜区管委会
Qingyuanshan fengjing mingsheng qu	清源山风景名胜区
Qingyuanshan youke zhongxin	清源山游客中心
qu	区
qu changge	去唱歌
qu guangjie	去逛街
qu K	去K
qu K ge	去K歌
qu KTV	去KTV
qu shudian kanshu	去书店看书
qu wan	去玩
qu xijiao	去洗脚
quan'e bokuan	全额拨款
quanguo shou jia zuida de minying tushuguan	全国首家最大的民营图书馆
quannian yue you bannian xiu	全年约有半年休
Quanzhou	泉州
Quanzhou bowuguan	泉州博物馆

Quanzhou wenhua	泉州文化
renao	热闹
san dajian	三大件
san ge huangjinzhou	三个黄金周
san, luan, cha, xiao	散,乱,差,小
Shanghai	上海
shangpinhua	商品化
shangwang	上网
shehui hunluan	社会混乱
shehui xiaoyi	社会效益
shehui ziyuan	社会资源
shenqing zhuanzhu	神情专注
shengcun zhuangtai	生存状态
shengtai xing tingchechang	生态型停车场
sheng xian qi	生闲气
shi	市
Shi caizhengju	市财政局
shijian	时间
shimin	市民
shuba	书吧
shuangxiu	双休
suzhi	素质
suzhi gao	素质高
taijiquan	太极拳
tai meiyou yinsi le	太没有隐私了
taoye qingcao	陶冶情操
tiaowu ting	跳舞厅
Tie Guanyin	铁观音
Tongfo si	铜佛寺
waidi ren	外地人
wailai de	外来的
wan	玩
wanju	玩具
wan QQ	玩 QQ
wan xiaoche	玩小车
wangba	网吧
Wangluo wenming	网络文明
wenbao	温饱
wenhua jingji	文化经济
wenhua shichang	文化市场
Wenhua shichang si	文化市场司
wenhua suzhi	文化素质
wenhua xiaofei	文化消费
wenhua xiuxian changsuo	文化休闲场所
wenming	文明

wenren	文人
Wenxue yishujie lianhehui	文学艺术界联合会
wo xiaofei, gu wo zai	我消费，故我在
women kao shehui	我们靠社会
Wuhan	武汉
wuzhi wenming	物质文明
Xia ke yihou ni pingshi zuo shenme?	下课以后你平时做什么？
Xiamen	厦门
xian page 21	县
xian page 50	闲
xianche	闲扯
xianchou	闲愁
xian fuqilai	先富起来
xianguang	闲逛
xianhua	闲话
xianjing	娴静
xianshi	闲事
xianshua	闲耍
xianwan	闲玩
xianxia	闲暇
xianzhi	限制
xiaofei louxi	消费陋习
xiaokang	小康
xiaokang shehui	小康社会
xiaoqian	消遣
xiaoqu	小区
xiehui	协会
xie xianwen	写闲文
xin chengshi zhongxin	新城市中心
Xinhua	新华
xin nongcun jianshe	新农村建设
xingxiang gongcheng	形象工程
xiu	休
xiuxian	休闲
xiuxian fuzhuang	休闲服装
Xiuxian guangchang, jinzhi tingche	休闲广场 禁止停车
xiuxian jiaoyu	休闲教育
xiuxian jingji shidai	休闲经济时代
xiuxian jingpin	休闲精品
xiuxian qu	休闲区
xiuxian shehui	休闲社会
xiuxian shijian	休闲时间
xiuxian shijian ziyuan	休闲时间资源
xiuxian wenhua	休闲文化
xiuxian zhongxin	休闲中心

xiuxian zige	休闲资格
xuanchuan	宣传
xuezhe	学者
yasui qian	压岁钱
yangchun baixue	阳春白雪
yecan	夜餐
Yi jiankufendou wei rong, yijiaosheyinyi wei chi	以艰苦奋斗为荣以骄奢淫逸为耻
yiqian	以前
yi she chong jian	抑奢崇俭
yiwu	义务
yiwu gongzuo	义务工作
Yi xinqin laodong wei rong, yi haoyiwulao wei chi	以辛勤劳动为荣 以好逸恶劳为耻
yindao	引导
yinsi	隐私
youke	游客
you wenhua	有文化
you wenhua suzhi	有文化素质
yule xiaoqian	娱乐消遣
yule xiuxi	娱乐休息
yuan	元
yueshu	约束
Zan dang bing de ren	咱当兵的人
Zhangzhou	漳州
zhengshi	正事
zhili fazhan	智力发展
zhishi fenzi	知识分子
Zhongguo shuzi tushuguan	中国数字图书馆
zhuan qian	赚钱
zishen wangluo youxi wanjia	资深网络游戏玩家
ziyou shijian	自由时间
ziyuan baohu	资源保护
zizhuquan	自主权
zongjiao bumen	宗教部门
zou houshan	走后山
zuji	祖籍
Zuijin you mei you qu FB?	最近有没有去FB?
zuyu dian	足浴店
zuo guanli	作管理

Notes

Orthography, reference style, and abbreviations

1 Data from *economagic.com*. Available at: www.economagic.com/em-cgi/data.exe/scratch/66–249–67–79!fedstl_exchus [accessed 14 August 2010].

Introduction

1 Publisher's original translation.
2 The expression 'leisure ethic' has also been used by William A. Gleason in his 1999 study of American writers' discussions of work and leisure in the US at the turn of the nineteenth century.
3 A Taiwanese pop song in the *Minnan* dialect has probably contributed to the lasting popularity of this local saying. The song is a cherished karaoke number in Quanzhou, and several performances of the song, both professional and otherwise, can be found on Internet services such as YouTube.
4 My use of the term 'middle class' in this study is discussed in more detail in Chapter 1.
5 In *The Exemplary Society*, Børge Bakken describes how the concept of 'quality' (*suzhi*) has been applied in the drive for modernization and reform in Chinese politics since the 1980s, and how the 'quality' discourse also includes arguments inspired by eugenics. Bakken refers to a critique of the one-child policy from 1989, where the practise of letting rural and minority populations give birth to more than one child was considered to cause an increase in the relative number of backward individuals (2000: 66–72). According to *Yingyong Hanyu Cidian*, '*suzhi*' refers not only to a person's innate abilities but also to abilities acquired through cultivation (Guo Liangfu 2000: 1199). Stig Thøgersen refers to suggestion made by Chinese scholars that '*suzhi*' should be translated into English 'competence' (2003: 214), and since I am here discussing *suzhi* in relation to an overall discourse of civilization and civility (*wenming*), I translate *suzhi* as 'cultural competence', unless otherwise indicated in the text.
6 De Certeau's perspective is applied also by Dutton in his analyses of everyday life in urban China in *Streetlife China* (2000).
7 The *erhu* is a traditional Chinese string instrument. *Nanyin*, or *nanqu*, is part of the local opera tradition in the *Minnan* area.
8 For examples, see Articles in Davis *et al.* 1995; and Chen *et al.* 2001. See also Mayfair Yang 2004; Jing Wang 2005a; Latham 2007. For more historical perspectives on the significance of the urban space, see Di Wang 2003 and Bray 2005. For the most recent, comprehensive analyses of consumption in China, see Croll 2006 and Latham *et al.* 2006.
9 Shaoguang Wang's article in Davis 1995 and the article from 2006 by Paul E. Festa are two important exceptions to this trend. Wu and Murphy's *Handbook of Chinese*

Popular Culture (1994) treats popular culture as a generic category and offer descriptions of a range of old and new popular leisure activities in China. Latham's *Pop Culture China!* (2007) provides an updated overview of Chinese leisure activities, and also introduces into his presentation the importance of space and sociality in both cultural production and cultural consumption.

10 Not all discourse analyses take the strict social constructivist stance that there is no reality prior to or 'behind' the level of discourse. For example, Laclau and Mouffe, who do regard discourses as constitutive of our reality, stress that even in their approach, '[w]hat is denied is not that [...] objects exist externally to thought, but the rather different assertion that they could constitute themselves as objects outside of any discursive condition of emergence'. See Laclau and Mouffe 1985: 108 in Neumann 2002: 63. The focus on language and representation in discourse analysis does, however, often result in a worldview where real-life practices are regarded as produced by discourses, or in some cases as a mere social frame.

11 I am grateful to my one of my anonymous reviewers for bringing my attention to this argument.

1 Locating leisure in a medium-sized Chinese city

1 A local guidebook from 2003 gives an estimate of 953,000 inhabitants for Quanzhou city proper (Lin Zhifeng 2003: 14).

2 This international competition, now renamed LiveCom Awards, is supported by the United Nations Environment Programme, and rewards best practice in the field of 'liveable communities'. In 2003, Quanzhou won the gold award for cities of an average daytime population between 200,000 and one million.

3 The five counties include the disputed island county of Jinmen in the Taiwan Strait.

4 According to the 2004 Quanzhou yearbook, the central city area of Quanzhou had 7.86 million residents in 2003 (Quanzhou shi difangzhi bianzuan weiyuanhui 2004b: 226).

The fifth national census, conducted in 2001, estimated a total of 7.28 million inhabitants in Quanzhou municipality, of which roughly 690,000 lived in the central city districts (Quanzhou shi tongji ju. 25 May 2001). The sixth national census was conducted in January 2008, but I have not been able to locate official reports from the last census.

5 Official numbers from 2007 (Quanzhou shi renmin zhengfu, 28 August 2008).

6 Numbers from 2006. *Fujian Statistical Yearbook 2007* quoted in Hong Kong Trade Development Council (Xianggang maofa ju).

7 The first teaching materials instructing middle school students in spoken *Minnan* dialect were published in Xiamen during the time of my field research.

8 This argument is also made in Tsai 2006.

9 In addition to the eight key informants mentioned above, I met repeatedly with more than 30 contacts throughout the field periods of 2005, 2006 and 2007. During this time span I made 33 semi-structured interviews with 25 informants, each with duration of one and a half hours. I spent roughly 270 days in the field, and recorded somewhere between two and ten informal conversations each day.

10 In one interview situation where the interviewee spoke little Mandarin, I brought both an interpreter and my recorder to make sure that as little as possible got lost in translation.

11 *Dongnan Zaobao* (*DNZB*) is published in Quanzhou. *Haixia Dushibao* (*HXDSB*), which was sold in Quanzhou, is the daily Minnan edition (*Minnan ban*) of the paper of the same name, published by Fujian Daily (*Fujian Ribao*, *FJRB*) in the provincial capital, Fuzhou.

2 What is leisure – in China and beyond?

1 Ma presents a similar tripartite division of leisure as time (*shijian*), activity (*huodong*) and state of being (*shengcun zhuangtai*) (Ma Huidi 2004a: Ch. 1). For my discussion of definitions of leisure, I am indebted to Fang Xuhong at Huaqiao Univeristy for his many suggestions for and challenging comments on my project.
2 The same amount of flexibility is certainly not enjoyed by the many factory workers in Quanzhou, who often work long hours under strict supervision.
3 Haworth and Veal (2004: Part 1 especially) offer detailed presentations of the state of the field, while Stebbins (2004) reassesses the significance of work through an in-depth study of occupational devotees.
4 The term '*yiwu*' means 'duty or obligation'; thus, the expression '*yiwu gongzuo*' literally means obligatory work. However, in the context of Chinese volunteering, the term '义务' translates as 'volunteer' in English. '*Yiwu gongzuo*' was the term used by the first volunteer organizations in the Pearl River Delta, established with assistance from volunteer organizations in Hong Kong in the late 1980s (Tan Jianguang et al. 2002: 51–2).
5 In this survey by Wang Yalin et al. (2004), engaging in trade, trading stocks, giving lectures, and consulting are listed together with activities such as window-shopping, playing games, playing an instrument, dancing, reading etc. under the joint heading 'leisure time' (*xiuxian shijian*).
6 See chapters by Henderson and Shaw; Harahousou; and Freysinger and Harris respectively, all in Rojek et al. 2006.
7 Here, Wang quotes two articles in *Zhongguo qingnian* in 1956: Guo Lin (1956) 'Weishenmo [sic.] yiding yao qiangqiu yizhi (Why do we have to impose rigid uniformity)' no. 12: 30–1; and Shang Qi (1956) 'Guanche ziyuan yuanzhe, gengjia fengfu duocai kaizhan kewei [sic] huodong' (Implement the principle of freedom and develop a more colourful program for extracurricular activities)' no. 17: 8–9. Wang's translation.
8 Wang Di's sources convey a different picture of tea houses in Guangzhou, however, in which patronising tea houses was strictly reserved for the well-to-do (Wang Di 2003: 44–5).
9 For the rural perspective, see Song Shuyang and Wu Xingwu 2002: 111; Jun Liping and Li Jing 2002: 27.
10 Surveys from Shanghai quoted in Davis 2000: 19.
11 Thøgersen stresses that he relies on a simplified version of Basil Bernstein's concept of language codes, and that he uses the codes more as a 'heuristic device meant to draw attention to socio-political aspects of Chinese language use' (2006: 112, 124 note 2).
12 As I have pointed out in the introduction, my formal and informal interviews were conducted in Mandarin. An assessment of the influence of the local *Minnan* dialect on the choice of leisure-related terms in Quanzhou people's everyday speech is, regrettably, beyond my expertise.
13 A widely used Chinese online chat site.

3 The utility of leisure and the dangers of idleness

1 As pointed out by Seabrook, labour-intensive industrial and agricultural production characterizes the working lives of the majority of the population in the less-privileged 'South'. This global division of labour – and leisure – has generally been overlooked in academic writing on leisure (Seabrook 1988: 17). In their edited volume, Rojek *et al.* (2006) include some global perspectives, particularly in Bhattachatya's chapter on leisure in India, but conditions in Europe and the US are still the main focus of both analyses and data collection (Bhattacharya 2006).

2 Gleason's analysis shows that the same worries over the proper guidance of ordinary people at work and play were present among social commentators in the US in the 1920s (Gleason 1999: 307).
3 Shaoguang Wang's translation.
4 For more examples, see Wang Yalin 2003: 4; Liao Qi 2004; Ma Huidi 2004c: 94; Xia Yiran 2004: 79; Chen Yong and Feng Lan 2006: 215–16; Fan Xiaoxian and Kong Linghua 2006: 88; Chang Qinyi *et al.* 2007: 123.
5 Wang Yalin's study is an exception to this general trend. In his introduction, Wang comments on the complex relationship between work and leisure.
6 Public servants, researchers, professionals and employees in foreign enterprises are entitled to an additional ten days of paid leave per year (*daixin jie-jiari* or *daixin jie-xiujia*).
7 For examples, see among others Wang Yihong 2005: 123; Ma Huidi and Zhang Jing'an 2004b: 5; Wang Yalin 2003: 4, 42. Also, Luigi Tomba writes, with reference to Wang Yalin's study, that urban employees now enjoy 115 days of rest. See Tomba 2004: 10.
8 For a similar observation, see Sun in Beck and Beck-Gernsheim 2002: 1.
9 For a fruitful discussion of the consequences of the reform policies, see articles from 'China and socialism roundtable' in *Critical Asian Studies* vol. 37, no. 3, September 2005.
10 I am here referring to the kind of scholar activism practised by He and others who promote a New Rural Reconstruction (*xin nongcun jianshe*) for the Chinese countryside.
11 Interestingly, Wang Yalin offers no policy recommendation in his 2004 study. The fact that his research was funded by the Ford Foundation may explain this deviation from the genre code.

4 Leisure in the Quanzhou cityscape

1 The cost of a taxi ride to any destination within the city centre is approximately eight to ten *yuan*.
2 Unless otherwise noted, data about the history of the Quanzhou cityscape can be found in Huang Meiyu 2007, pp. 1–22 especially, and in Quanzhou Municipal Gazetteer, Quanzhou shi difangzhi bianzuan weiyuanhui, ed. 2004a.

5 'Healthy leisure' in transition

1 The expression *minjian shetuan* suggests that the organization in question has risen from among the people. In the Chinese case, 'popular organizations' are in fact mass organizations initiated by the political elite. I will therefore retain the inverted commas when referring to such 'popular' organizations.
2 Data from 1996, 1997 and 2001.
3 '*Quanguo shou jia zuida de minying tushuguan*'. Beijing already had a *minying tushuguan* at the time, but the Quanzhou manager claimed that his is the first *big* private library since the one in Beijing is 'only a very small one'.
4 Lit. 'of high quality'.
5 Two interviewees claimed that the library closes at nine in the evening during summer, which I have not been able to confirm. The library employees I interviewed and the official signs at the libraries' entrances listed opening hours as quoted here.
6 While I heard the idiom used in reference to self-study on several occasions, I only once heard it used to describe a kind of recuperation.
7 Henderson and Cohen have written a study of an urban work unit (*danwei*) in 1979. Although significant social reforms were initiated at this point, Henderson and Cohen's descriptions of *danwei* life show that many aspects of the collective organization structure remained intact.

8 The continued existence of this system of approval was also confirmed during interviews in the field.
9 The choir has 80 official members, but at rehearsals and performances the number of participants varied from 20 to 50.
10 See for example Saich 2000; Zhang Ye 2003; Yang Guobin 2003; and Feng Chongyi 2005. For an historical perspective, see Rankin 1993.
11 The term the interviewees used here refers to industrialization, but in this context it was used to describe what they saw as a commercial trend in local popular culture.

6 Bad people in bad places?

1 I do not count the local culture bureau's funding of national and international tours for local professional and semi-professional performance troupes as investments in local leisure culture. The local troupes seldom perform in Quanzhou itself, and when they do, tickets are only distributed through the system of work units.
2 KTV, writes James Farrer, is short for 'karaoke television'. The abbreviation was first used in Taiwan in the 1980s to describe the parlours where you can rent a room and sing karaoke in private (Farrer 2002: 344, note 12).
3 As mentioned above, my data concerns legal leisure activities only. As a consequence, a discussion of the sex market with its high-end 'escorts' and lower-end sex workers will not be included into this analysis of leisure and social status.
4 Since the time of Deng' earliest reforms, one of the strategies in the development of the Chinese 'well-off society' (*xiaokang shehui*) has been to let one part of the population become rich first (*xian fuqilai*). This policy has increased the economic inequality between the urban coastal region and the predominantly rural hinterland.
5 I first saw this poster in Xiamen in October 2005. The image reprinted here is from a government web page, authorized by Xiangshan county office for the popularization of the law (Xiangshan xian pufa ban, 18 January 2006). Internet cafés and video game arcades are treated with the same level of suspicion in propaganda texts and the news media. I have therefore chosen to treat attitudes towards these two leisure places as examples of one and the same phenomenon.
6 Lit. 'as fresh as a flower'.
7 In the mid 1990s there were government campaigns against KTV parlours all over China, due to suspicion of prostitution and illegal conduct. See Jeffreys 1997: 49.
8 CNNIC is operated by the Chinese Academy of Sciences. The centre is responsible for the registration and approval of Chinese domain names and IP addresses, and conducts research at the request of the Ministry of Information Industry. For more information, see www.cnnic.cn/ [accessed 14 August 2010].
9 Defined by CNNIC as Chinese residents of age six and above who used Internet within a period of six months.
10 Numbers from www.internetworldstats.com/asia.htm [accessed 20 August 2010].
11 For Macao the corresponding numbers are 93 per cent and 3 per cent respectively (CNNIC 2008: 71).
12 The 2007 report from CNNIC even has a special chapter focusing on Internet use among 'young students', defined as students 'age 6–24' (CNNIC 2007: 52–9).
13 Series of ten propaganda posters outside the Quanzhou municipal library in February 2007, instructing young people in practical measures against Internet addiction and promoting 'civilized Internet use' (*wangluo wenming*). *Reuters* (Beijing) reported in March 2007 that according to the government think-tank China National Children's Centre, '13 per cent of China's 18 million Internet users under 18 were Internet addicts'.
14 Johansson and Götestam (2004: 45) argue that the number of hours spent online does not increase the likelihood of developing Internet addiction. The authors did, however, find a correlation between Internet addiction and a range of social factors such as level of academic achievement, financial and work-related problems etc.

15 Here the CNNIC report distinguishes between students in general (*vs.* non-students) with no reference to age or education level. Johansson and Götestam report an average of 4.3 online hours per week among Norwegian youth aged 12 to 18 (2004: 223).
16 For references to similar attitudes concerning youth and self control, see Bakken 2000: 328.
17 First printed in *Beijing Times*.
18 See also article from *Beijing Times* 'Lei Feng…' printed in *HXDSB* 16 March, A33.
19 In the *Far Eastern Economic Review*'s annual review of the Chinese economic elite in 1998, 60 per cent of the respondents 'enjoyed karaoke sessions' (quoted in Croll 2006: 94).
20 One exception here is the Professional English Club, which sometimes met in a local karaoke parlour and the purpose of which was to bring together English-proficient strangers in a 'friendly and relaxed environment'.
21 Earlier, only the Department of Reconstruction and Commerce (*Gongshangbu*) had this authority. The plans for a joint municipal platform for the handling of leisure market surveillance are also described in the Bureau of Culture's plans for 2006 (*QZSWHJ* 2005: 9).
22 In 2008 the Norwegian Data Inspectorate (Datatilsynet) revealed that several bars and restaurants had installed illegal surveillance equipment in order to keep an eye on the actions of both customers and their own employees. The restaurateurs explained this as a service for the protection of guests' security. Norwegian News Agency (NTB) in VG nett: www.vg.no/nyheter/innenriks/artikkel.php?artid=510409 [accessed 20 August 2010].
23 The Chinese term literally translates as 'personal secrecy', but I follow Yan's translation of *yinsi* as 'privacy (Yunxiang Yan 2003: 134–35).
24 See Chapter 1 for a more thorough discussion of the definition of middle class.

7 Consumption as a form of leisure

1 The cost of a non-brand sweater in Quanzhou would be approximately one hundred *yuan*.
2 My emphasis.
3 For a similar argument in the case of the US, see Ewen 2000: 190.
4 For a description of the new 'apartment craze', see Siu 2005: 72–91.
5 In one of her 2001 articles Wang comments on the need for further studies of how state discourses are implemented at a local level (Jing Wang 2001b: 91). This study is an answer to this call.
6 International Consumer's Day is celebrated on 15 March.
7 The term '*guang chaoshi*' is used for window-shopping in malls or supermarkets.
8 A Taiwanese beverage of sweetened tea and milk with tiny pearls of tapioca.
9 China Central Television, China's main television broadcaster.
10 See the following for a discussion of the term 'cultured middle class'.
11 The price was about two to three thousand *yuan* per half-kilo (*jin*).
12 In his article on the importance of sociolinguistic language codes in China, Stig Thøgersen discusses how a term like 'office-holder' (*dangguande*) can be used as a derogatory term in everyday speech (2006: 117). I believe this is also the case with '*zuo guanli*' in this sentence.
13 The impact of consumption on the natural environment is mentioned in several of the Chinese scholarly articles referred to in this study. See for example Wang Yalin 2003: 5; Wang Zhongwu 2005: 125; Fan Xiaoxian and Kong Linghua 2006: 88; Chen Pingyi and Zheng Yangfu 2007: 151. However, even when ecological philosophy is taken as a point of departure, as the case is in studies by Fan Xiaoxian and Kong Linghua (2006) as well as in Ma Huidi (2004a), the general message is still that increased consumption is the solution to China's social and economic challenges.

8 Contested leisure space

1 The term *xuanchuan* can refer to both propaganda and publicity. In this context, Director Hu communicates both that his work unit does too little to make the multiple responsibilities of the reserve known to the local population, and that this situation can be alleviated via propaganda.

Bibliography

'3.15 you dai, ni dui putaojiu de liaojie you duoshao?' [March 15 is here again. What do you know about wine?], *Haixia dushi bao* (HXDSB) 15 March 2006, A5.

Anagnost, A. (1997) *National Past-times: narrative, representation, and power*, Durham: Duke University Press.

Bailey, C.A. (1996) *A Guide to Field Research*, California: Pine Forge Press.

Bakken, B. (2000) *The Exemplary Society: human improvement, social control and the dangers of modernity in China*, New York: Oxford University Press.

Balsdon, J.P.V.D. (1969) *Life and Leisure in Ancient Rome*, London: The Bodley Head.

Bauman, Z. (1998) *Work, Consumerism and the New Poor*, Buckingham: Open University Press.

Bauman, Z. (2001) *The Individualized Society*, Oxford: Blackwell/Polity Press.

Bhattacharya, K. (2006) 'Non-western traditions: leisure in China', in C. Rojek *et al.* (eds) *A Handbook of Leisure Studies*, Basingstoke: Palgrave Macmillan, pp. 75–89.

Bayat, A. (2007) 'Islamism and the politics of fun', *Public Culture*, 19, 3: 433–59.

Beals, R.L., Hoijer, H. and Beals, A.R. (1977) *An Introduction to Anthropology*, 5th edition, New York: Macmillan Publishing.

Beck, U. and Beck-Gernsheim E. (2002) *Individualization: institutionalized individualism and its social and political consequences*, London: Sage Publications.

Borchgrevink, A. (2003) 'Silencing language: of anthropologists and interpreters', *Ethnography*, 4.1: 95–121.

Bourdieu, P. (1986 [1984]) *Distinction: a social critique of the judgement of taste*, trans. Richard Nice, London: Routledge & Kegan Paul.

Bourdieu, P. (2006 [1983]) 'Kapitalens former' [The Forms of Capital], *Agora: Journal for Metafysisk Spekulasjon* [Agora: Journal of Metaphysical Speculation], 24, 1–2: 5–26.

Bray, D. (2005) *Social Space and Governance in Urban China*, Stanford: Stanford University Press.

Burgess, R.G. (1991) 'Sponsors, gatekeepers, members and friends: access in educational settings', in W.B. Shaffir and R.A. Stebbins (eds) *Experiencing Fieldwork: an inside view of qualitative research*, London: Sage Publications, pp. 43–52.

Burke, P. (1995) 'The invention of leisure in early modern Europe', *Past and Present*, 146: 136–50.

Campbell, C. (2000 [1989]) 'The puzzle of modern consumerism', in M.J. Lee (ed.) *The Consumer Society Reader*, Oxford: Blackwell Publishing, pp. 48–71.

Cartier, C. (2005) 'Regional transformations and transnational urbanism in South China', in Jing Wang (ed.) *Locating China: space, place and popular culture*, New York: Routledge, pp. 52–71.

Ceng Xiaoqin, 'Haizi bu ai xuexi ai wan youxi?'[(Your) child does not like studying and loves to play games?], HXDSB 15 March 2006, A13.
Certeau, M.d. (1988 [1984]) *The Practice of Everyday Life*, Berkeley: University of California Press.
Chan, A., Madsen, R. and Unger, J. (1992) *Chen Village under Mao and Deng*, Berkeley: University of California Press.
Chan, A. (1997) 'Chinese *danwei* reforms: convergence with the Japanese model?', in Lü Xiaobo and E. J. Perry (eds) Danwei: *the changing Chinese workplace in historical and comparative perspective*, New York: M.E. Sharpe, pp. 91–113.
Chang Qinyi, Jin Yi, Lai Lifei and Chen Zhuanfeng (2007) 'Chengshihua jincheng zhong xin jumin wenhua xiaofei ji qi shenmei xinli de diaocha yanjiu' [An investigation of the culture consumption and aesthetics of new residents in a process of urbanisation], *Xueshu jiaoliu* [Academic Exchange], 160, 7: 122–5.
Chen Lengleng, 'Jiena weichengnianren liang jia wangba zao cha' [Two Internet cafés that admit underage customers meet with inspection), HXDSB 26 January 2007, A7.
Chen, N.N. *et al.* (eds) (2001) *China Urban: ethnographies of contemporary culture*, Durham: Duke University Press.
Chen Pingyi and Zheng Yangfu (2007) 'Xiaofei wenhua de gongneng fenxi' [An analysis of the function of consumer culture], *Heilongjiang shehui kexue* [Heilongjiang Social Sciences] 102, 3: 149–52.
Chen Xiangmu, 'Zu tu: "Haisi guangchang" diaosu liangxiang' [Picture series: the 'Maritime Silk Road Square' statues strike a pose], *Quanzhou wang* (Quanzhou web) 14 April 2006. Online. Available HTTP: www.qzwb.com/gb/content/2006-04/14/content_2050867.htm [accessed 13 April 2007].
Chen Yong and Feng Lan (2006) 'Geti gongshang hu qunti xianxia shenghuo zhuangkuang: laizi Hubei sheng Wuhan shi de diaocha' [An Exploration of the leisure lives of the self-employed: a survey from Wuhan Municipality, Hubei Province], *Shangchang xiandaihua* [Market modernisation], 478: 215–16.
Chick, G. (2006) 'Anthropology/pre-history of leisure', in C. Rojek *et al.* (eds) *A Handbook of Leisure Studies*, Basingstoke: Palgrave Macmillan, pp. 41–54.
China Internet Network Information Services (CNNIC) (July 2007) 'The 20th statistical survey report on the Internet development in China', English version. Online. Available HTTP: www.cnnic.net.cn/download/2007/20thCNNICreport-en.pdf [accessed 14 August 2010].
China Internet Network Information Services (January 2008) 'Zhongguo hulian wangluo fazhan zhuangkuang tongjibao gao' [(The 21st) statistical survey report on the Internet development in China]. Online. Available at: www.cnnic.cn/uploadfiles/pdf/2008/1/17/104156.pdf [accessed 14 August 2010].
Chinfit Real Estate, prospectus for Chinfit Mountain Villas, acquired in Quanzhou 2005, 44 unnumbered pages.
'Citonghua tushu cheng' [Zaitun flower book city] *Kaijuan wenzhai* [Open book digest], 79, 2007: 59–62.
Clark, H.R. (1991) *Community, Trade and Networks: southern Fujian Province from the third to the thirteenth century*. New York: Cambridge University Press.
Croll, E. (1997) 'Desires and destinies: consumption and the spirit of Confucianism', inaugural lecture, School of Oriental and African Studies (SOAS) of the University of London., 22 numbered pages.
Croll, E. (2006) *China's New Consumers: social development and domestic demand*, New York: Routledge.

Csikszentmihalyi, M. and LeFevre, J. (1989) 'Optimal experience in work and Leisure', *Journal of personality and social psychology*, 56, 5: 815–22.
Daily, G. and Ellison, K. (2002) *The New Economy of Nature: the quest to make conservation profitable*, Washington: Island Press.
Davis, D.S. et al. (eds) (1995) *Urban Spaces in Contemporary China: the potential for autonomy and community in post-Mao China*, Cambridge: Cambridge University Press.
Davis, D.S. (2000) 'Introduction: a revolution in consumption', in D.S. Davis (ed.) *The Consumer Revolution in Urban China*, Berkeley: University of California Press, pp. 1–22.
Davis D.S. and Sensenbrenner, J.S. (2000) 'Commercializing childhood: parental purchases for Shanghai's only child', in D.S. Davis (ed.) *The Consumer Revolution in Urban China*, Berkeley: University of California Press, 54–79.
Dikötter, F. (2006) *Exotic Commodities: modern objects and everyday life in China*, New York: Columbia University Press.
Donnelly, P. (1988) 'Sport as a site for "popular" resistance', in R. Gruneau (ed.) *Popular Cultures and Political Practices*, Toronto: Garamond Press, pp. 69–82.
Dutton, M. (2000 [1998]) *Streetlife China*, Cambridge: Cambridge University Press.
economagic.com (no date). Online. Available at: www.economagic.com/em-cgi/data.exe/scratch/66-249-67-79!fedstl_exchus [accessed 14 August 2010].
Evans, H. (2006) 'Fashions and feminine consumption', in K. Latham, S. Thompson and J. Klein (eds) *Consuming China: approaches to cultural change in contemporary China*, New York: Routledge, pp. 173–89.
Ewen, S. (2000 [1976]), 'Assembling a new world of facts', in M.J. Lee (ed.) *The Consumer Society Reader*, Oxford: Blackwell Publishing, pp. 186–91.
Fackler, M. (18 November 2007) 'In Korea, boot camp cure for web obsession', *New York Times*. Online. Available at: www.nytimes.com/2007/11/18/technology/18rehab.html?_r=1&oref=slogin&ref=asia&pagewanted=all [accessed 22 August 2010].
Fan Xiaoxian and Kong Linghua (2006) 'Guanyu xiaofei wenhua de yixie sikao' [Some reflections on consumer culture], *Journal of the Party School of CPC of Changchun Municipal Committee*, 101, 6: 87–8.
Fangen, K. (2004) *Deltakende observasjon* [Participant observation], Bergen: Fagbokforlaget.
Farquhar, J. (2002) *Appetites: food and sex in post-socialist China*, London: Duke University Press.
Farquhar, J. and Qicheng Zhang (2005) 'Biopolitical Beijing: pleasure, sovereignty, and self-cultivation in China's capital', *Cultural Anthropology*, 20, 3: 303–27.
Farrer, J. (2002) *Opening Up: youth sex culture and market reform in Shanghai*, Chicago: The University of Chicago Press.
Feng Chongyi. (2005) 'From barrooms to teahouses: commercial nightlife in Hainan since 1988', in Jing Wang (ed.) *Locating China: space, place and popular culture*, New York: Routledge, 133–49.
Festa, P.E. (2006) 'Mahjong politics in contemporary China: civility, chineseness, and mass culture', *Positions*, 1, 14: 7–35.
Fewsmith, J. (2007) 'The political implications of China's growing middle class', *China Leadership Monitor*, 21: 1–8.
Freysinger, V.J. and Harris, O. (2006) 'Race and leisure', in C. Rojek, S.M. Shaw and A.J. Veal (eds) *A Handbook of Leisure Studies*, Basingstoke: Palgrave Macmillan, pp. 250–70.

Friedman, S.L. (2006). *Intimate Politics: marriage, the market, and state power in southeastern China*. Cambridge: Harvard University Press.
Fu Jian, 'Gege meimei zheng "hi" jingcha congtianerjiang' [Police appeared out of the blue as boys and girls were getting 'High'], HXDSB 18 November 2006, A5.
Fujian Jinwei jituan, prospectus for Kingwei Waterside Villas, acquired in Quanzhou 2005, 20 unnumbered pages.
Galbraith, J.K. (2000 [1987]) 'The dependence effect', excerpt from *The Affluent Society*, in M.J. Lee (ed.) *The Consumer Society Reader*, Oxford: Blackwell Publishing, pp. 217–22.
Gans, H.J. (1974) *Popular Culture and High Culture: an analysis and evaluation of taste*, New York: Harper & Collins.
Gardiner, M.E. (2000) *Critiques of Everyday Life*, London: Routledge.
Gershuny, J. (1992) 'Are we running out of time?', *Futures*, 24, 2: 3–22.
Gleason, W.A. (1999) *The Leisure Ethic: work and play in American literature 1840–1940*, Stanford: Stanford University Press.
Goldstein, B. and Eichhorn, R.L. (1961) 'The changing protestant ethic: rural patterns in health, work, and leisure', *American Sociological Review*, 4: 557–65.
Gong Gao 'Wenhua bu guanyuan jiedu "yule changsuo guanli tiaoli" jiuba wangba liang dian hou reng ke yingye' [Ministry of culture official deciphers the 'Leisure Place Regulations': bars and Internet cafés can continue business as before], *Beijing times*, printed in HXDSB 17 February 2006, A30.
Goodman, D.S.G. (2001) 'Contending the popular: party-state and culture', *Positions*, 9, 1: 245–52.
Gross, E.F., Juvonen J. and Gable, S.L. (2002) 'Internet use and well-being in adolescence', *Journal of Social Issues*, 51, 1: 75–90.
Gu Cuo tea culture company, *Gu cuo chaguan* [Guo Cuo tea house], booklet acquired 2006, 28 unnumbered pages.
Gu, Xiaojia 'Muslims of Quanzhou', *New Statesman* 18 December 2006. Online. Available at: www.newstatesman.com/200612180062 [accessed 22 August 2010].
Guo Liangfu (2000) *Yingyong Hanyu cidian* [Dictionary of applied Chinese], Beijing: Shangwu yinshuguan.
'"Haisi" diaosu shi ri qi yu shimin jianmian' [On 10 April, the Maritime Silk Road sculptures will be revealed to the citizenry] *Dongnan zaobao* (DNZB) 10 April 2006, original source *Quanzhou wang*, online. Available at: http://info.gift.hc360.com/2006/04/10085319857.shtml [accessed 20 August 2010].
'Hanjia: jiu gai zheyang jiankang you kuaile' [Winter holiday: it should be as healthy and joyful as this], HXDSB 31 January 2007, B3.
Hansen, M.H. (2007) 'Organising the old: senior authority and the political significance of a rural Chinese "non-governmental organisation"', *Modern Asian Studies*, 42,5: 1057–78.
Hansen, M.H. and Pang Cuiming (2008) 'Me – and my family. Perceptions of individual and collective among young rural Chinese', *European Journal of East Asian Studies*, 7,1: 75–99.
Harahousou, Y. (2006) 'Leisure and ageing', in C. Rojek, S.M. Shaw and A.J. Veal (eds) *A Handbook of Leisure Studies*, Basingstoke: Palgrave Macmillan, pp. 231–49.
Haworth, J.T. and A.J. Veal (ed.) (2004) *Work and Leisure*, East Sussex: Routledge.
He Baogang (2004) 'Chinese intellectuals facing the challenges of the new century', in E. Gu and M. Goldman (eds) *Chinese intellectuals between state and market*, London: Routledge Curzon, pp. 263–79.

Heintz, M. (2002) 'Changes in work ethic in postsocialist Romania', unpublished thesis, University of Cambridge. Online. Available at: http://monica.heintz.free.fr/ [accessed 22 August 2010].
Henderson, G. and Cohen, M.S. (1984) *The Chinese Hospital: a socialist work unit*. New Haven: Yale University Press.
Henderson, K.A. and Shaw, S.M. (2006) 'Leisure and gender: challenges and opportunities for feminist research', in C. Rojek, S.M. Shaw and A.J. Veal (eds) *A Handbook of Leisure Studies*, Basingstoke: Palgrave Macmillan, pp. 216–30.
Highmore, B. (2002) *Everyday Life and Cultural Theory: an introduction*, New York: Routledge.
Hong Kong Trade Development Council [Xianggang maofa ju]. Online. Available at: www.hktdc.com/mktprof/china/mpfuj.htm [accessed 19 June 2008].
Hong Ming and Wang Hongli (2002) 'Jiating jiaoyu shiwu daozhi zhongxiaoxuesheng kaoshi jiaolü de fenxi yu duice' [Faults in family education that cause exam anxiety among primary and middle school students: evaluation and countermeasures], *Xinli kexue* [Psychological Science], 25, 6: 753–4.
Howard, C. (ed.) (2007) *Contested Individualization: debates about contemporary personhood*, Basingstoke: Palgrave Macmillan.
Huang Heqing (2001) 'Lun jiating jiaoyu yu xuexiao jiaoyu de hezuo' [Regarding the collaboration of family and school education], *Jiaoyu pinglun* [Education Review], 4: 24–7.
Huang Meiyu (2007) *Quanzhou gucheng jiefang zhi tan* [Quanzhou's ancient city and neighbourhood], Xiamen: Xiamen daxue chubanshe.
Huang, P.C.C. (1990) *The Peasant Family and Rural Development in the Yangzi Delta, 1350–1988*, Stanford: Stanford University Press.
Huang Shuikan (2005) *Quanzhou Wehua Guji* [The culture (sic.) and historic sites of Quanzhou], Beijing: Zhongguo wenlian chubanshe.
Huang Shumin (1989) *The Spiral Road: change in a Chinese village through the eyes of a Communist Party leader*, Boulder: Westview Press.
Huang Zuyang, 'Zhongguo xiuxian jingpin mingcheng' [City of top quality Chinese leisure goods], DNZB 23 February 2006, A6.
Hwang, A., 'Number of Internet users in China second only to US at the end of December 2007', press release *DIGITIMES Taiwan* 18 January 2008.
Hyde, S.T. (2001) 'Sex tourism practices on the periphery: eroticizing ethnicity and pathologizing sex on the Lancang', in N.N. Chen *et al*. (eds) *China Urban: ethnographies of contemporary culture*, Durham: Duke University Press, pp. 143–62.
Internet world stats. Online. Available at: www.internetworldstats.com/asia.htm [accessed 20 August 2010].
Jeffreys, E. (1997). '"Dangerous Amusements": prostitution and karaoke halls in contemporary China', *Asian Studies Review*, 20, 3: 43–54.
Jeffreys, E. (2004) *China, Sex and Prostitution*, London: Routledge Curzon.
Johansson, A. and Götestam K.G. (2004) 'Internet addiction: characteristics of a questionnaire and prevalence in Norwegian youth (12–18 years)', *Scandinavian Journal of Psychology*, 45: 223–9.
Johnson, J.C. (1990) *Selecting Ethnographic Informants*, qualitative research methods series 22, London: Sage Publications.
Johnson, S. (24 April 2005) 'Watching TV Makes You Smarter', *New York Times Magazine*. Online. Available at: www.nytimes.com/2005/04/24/magazine/24TV.html [accessed 14 August 2010].

Jun Liping and Li Jing (2002) 'Wo guo xiaofei yaoqiu bu zu de yuanyin ji duice yanjiu' [Enquiry into the reasons for insufficient consumer demands in our country, and how to resolve this], *Qiandong nan minzu shifan gaodeng zhuanke xuexiao xuebao* [Journal of Southeastern Guizhou National Teacher's College], 20, 4: 27–28.

'Just how big is China's book market?' *Beijing Review* 3 March, 2005. Online. Available at: www.bjreview.com.cn/books/txt/2006–12/16/content_51119.htm [accessed 14 August 2010].

Jørgensen, M.W. and Phillips, L. (1999) *Diskursanalyse som Teori og Metode* [Discourse analysis as theory and method], Frederiksberg: Roskilde Universitetsforlag.

Kleiber, D.A. (1999) *Leisure Experience and Human Development: a dialectical interpretation*, New York: Basic Books.

Lakoff, G. and Johnson, M. (1980) *Metaphors We Live By*, Chicago: The University of Chicago Press.

Larsen, B. and Pedersen, K.M. (2002) 'Diskursanalyse – for tabere og teenagere' [Discourse analysis for loosers and teenagers], in B. Larsen and K.M. Pedersen (eds) *Diskursanalysen til debat: kritiske perpektiver på en populær teoriretning* [Debating discourse analysis: critical perspectives on a popular theory], Frederiksberg: Nyt Fra Samfundsvidenskaberne, pp, 15–86.

Latham, K. (2006a) 'Introduction: consumption and cultural change in contemporary China', in K. Latham, S. Thompson and J. Klein (eds) *Consuming China: approaches to cultural change in contemporary China*, New York: Routledge, pp. 1–21.

Latham, K. (2006b) 'Afterword', in K. Latham, S. Thompson and J. Klein (eds) *Consuming China: approaches to cultural change in contemporary China*, New York: Routledge, pp. 231–6.

Latham, K. (2007) *Pop Culture China! Media, Arts, and Lifestyle*, Santa Barbara, Calif.: ABC-CLIO.

Latham, K., Thompson, S. and Klein, J. (eds) (2006) *Consuming China: approaches to cultural change in contemporary China*, New York: Routledge.

Lefebvre, H. (1991 [1974]) *The Production of Space*, Malden: Blackwell Publishing.

'Lei Feng chen wangluo youxi zhujue: Yao xiang shengji buduan zuo haoshi' [Lei Feng becomes an online game protagonist: you must unceasingly do good deeds in order to rise], *Beijing Times*, printed in *Haixia dushi bao* (HXDSB), 16 March 2006, A33.

Li Guangnian (1995) 'Nongcun xuexiao huodong kecheng jiaoxue xianzhuang ji duice' [In-school activities on the curriculum in rural schools, status quo and policy recommendations], *Lianyungang jiaoyu xueyuan xue bao*, 2: 86–7.

Li Xin (2005) 'Inspection report from Qingyuan Mountain and Wuyi Mountain Scenic Areas', Fengjing mingsheng chu [Office for scenic areas], Beijing: Shoudu yuanlin lühua zhengwu [Beijing Municipal Bureau of Landscape and Forestry]. Online. Available at: http://yfs.bjyl.gov.cn/cn/tabs/showdetail.aspx?iid=6303&ReadGuid=b94fa535-98a2-4f35-9117-2ee7455751cf&nav=0&tabID=300006 [accessed 11 March 2008].

Li Yisun (2007) 'Shi "xiaofei shidai", haishi "wenhua jingji" shidai?' [Is it a 'consumer era' or an era of 'cultural economy'?], *Journal of Langfang Teachers' College*, 23, 2: 1–3.

Lian Yuji (2006) 'Weichengnianren fanzui si yaosu: xueye shibai, buliang xixing, gemen yiqi, wuli jianguan' [Four factors that cause juvenile delinquency: failing at school, harmful habits, brotherhoods, and lenient supervision], HXDSB 28 November, C4.

'Liansuo wangba danti wangba paizhao fangkai caixiang' [Guesses concerning the release of Internet café licenses] *Information Times* [Xinxi shibao], printed in DNZB 7 April 2006, A2.

Liao Qi (2004) 'Xiuxian shijian: yi zhong shijian xingtai cunzai de shehui ziyuan' [Leisure time: a social resource that exists in the form of time]. Online. Available at: www.chineseleisure.org/jiyao.htm [accessed 22 August 2010].

Lin Fulong (2006) 'Qingyuanshan xia jian youke zhongxin, zongtouzi yue 1350 wan' [Tourist centre is being built at the foot of Qingyuan Mountain; a total investment of approximately thirteen million five-hundred thousand yuan], DNZB online. Available at: www.qzwb.com/gb/content/2006–03/26/content_2025387.htm [accessed 22 August 2010].

Lin Fulong, Yao Binghui, Jiang Haiping and Cai Lanchun (2006) 'Zhengfu chuqian chuli wei qiye qing gongren' [The government spends money and makes an effort in order to attract workers to local enterprises], DNZB 1 March, A4.

Lin Jiahua (2006) 'Qingyuan shan fachu Qingming jinhuo ling: Jieyan qu jinzhi yewai huoyuan, Qiyun lu, Beishan lu yao jioatong guanzhi' [Fire prohibition at Qingyuan Mountain during Qingming festival: open-air fires will be prohibited, traffic will be restricted on Qiyun and Beishan roads], DNZB 22 March, A3.

Lin Zhifeng (2003) *Guoji Huanyuan Chengshi: Quanzhou lüyou xiuxian shouce* [Garden cities of the world: a guide for travel and leisure in Quanzhou], Fuzhou: Fujian sheng ditu chubanshe.

Linhart, S. (1988) 'From industrial to post-industrial society: changes in Japanese leisure-related values and behavior', *Journal of Japanese Studies*, 14, 2: 271–307.

Link, P., Madsen, R. and Pickowicz, P.G. (2002) 'Introduction', in P. Link *et al.* (eds) *Popular China: unofficial culture in a globalizing society*, Lanham, Md.: Rowman and Littlefield, pp. 1–8.

Lippit, V.D. (2005) 'The political economy of China's economic reform: observations on China and socialism', China and socialism roundtable, *Critical Asian Studies*, 37, 3: 441–62.

Liu Yuanli (2004) 'Development of the rural health insurance system in China', *Health Policy and Planning*, 19, 3: 159–65.

Lu Hanlong (2000) 'To be relatively comfortable in an egalitarian society', in D.S. Davis (ed.) *The Consumer Revolution in Urban China*, Berkeley: University of California Press, pp. 124–41.

Luo Jiaming *et al.* (2004) 'Leshan shi gongzhong xianxia shijian liyong xianzhuang de Diaocha' [Survey of the spending of public leisure time in Leshan], in Ma Huidi and Zhang Jing'an (eds) *Zhongguo gongzhong xiuxian zhuangkuang diaocha* [Survey studies of the state of (*sic*) leisure life among the Chinese public], Beijing: Zhongguo jingji chubanshe, pp. 160–81.

Lü Xiaobo and Perry, E.J. (1997) Danwei: *the changing Chinese workplace in historical and comparative perspective*, New York: M.E. Sharpe.

Ma Feifeng (2002) 'Henansheng chengzhen jumin xiaofei jiegou wenti yanjiu' [A study of consumption patterns among city and township residents in Henan Province], *Zhengzhou jingji guanli ganbu xueyuan xuebao* [Journal of Zhengzhou economic management institute], 17, 1: 13–15.

Ma Huidi (2004a) *Zouxiang renwen guanhuai de xiuxian jingji* [Towards a leisure economy with humanistic concerns], Beijing: Zhongguo jingji chubanshe.

Ma Huidi (2004b) *Xiuxian: Renlei meili de jingshen huayuan* [Leisure: the making of (sic.) beautiful home for the human spirit], Beijing: Zhongguo jingji chubanshe.

Ma Huidi (2004c) '21 shiji yu xiuxian jingji, xiuxian chanye, xiuxian wenhua' [21st century and the leisure economy, leisure industry, and leisure culture], *Xinxi kongjian* [Information times], July 21: 89–94.

Ma Huidi and Zhang Jing'an (2004a) *Zhongguo gongzhong xiuxian zhuangkuang diaocha* [Survey studies of the state of (sic.) leisure life among the Chinese public], Beijing: Zhongguo jingji chubanshe.
Ma Huidi and Zhang Jing'an (2004b) 'Dao yan' [(Introductory Remarks) in Ma Huidi and Zhang Jing'an (eds) *Zhongguo gongzhong xiuxian zhuangkuang diaocha* [Survey studies of the state of (sic.) leisure life among the Chinese public], Beijing: Zhongguo jingji chubanshe, pp. 1–6.
Madsen, R. (1984) *Morality and Power in a Chinese Village*, Berkeley: University of California Press.
Madsen, R. (2000) 'Epilogue: the second liberation', in D.S. Davis (ed.) *The Consumer Revolution in Urban China*, Berkeley: University of California Press, pp. 312–19.
Marfany, J-L. (1997) 'The invention of leisure in early modern Europe', *Past and Present*, 156: 174–91.
McNay, L. (1994) *Foucault: a critical introduction*, Cambridge: Polity Press.
McNeill, D. (no date) 'The power of economic categories: "it's all capital now"', unpublished manuscript, 16 pages.
Meng Lei (2007) 'Zhongchan jieceng de xiaofei yu shenghuo' [The life and consumption of the middle class), *Lingdao wen cui*, 9: 22–6.
Meyer, M. (13 March 2005) 'The world's biggest book market', *New York Times*. Online. Available at: www.nytimes.com/2005/03/13/books/review/013MEYERL.html [accessed 22 August 2010].
Miller, D. (2001) *The Dialectics of Shopping*. Chicago: Chicago University Press.
Miller, L.J. (1999).'Shopping for community: the transformation of the bookstore into a vital community institution', *Media, Culture & Society*, 21: 385–407.
Morrison, H. and Eberhard, W. (1974) *Hua Shan; The taoist sacred mountain in West China, its scenery, monasteries and monks*, Hong Kong: Vecht and Lee.
Mort, F. (2000 [1989]) 'The Politics of Consumption', in M. J. Lee (ed.) *The Consumer Society Reader*, Oxford: Blackwell Publishing, pp. 271–81.
Mutula, S.M. (2003) 'Cyber café industry in Africa', *Journal of Information Science*, 29, 6: 489–97.
Neumann, I.B. (2002) *Mening, Materialitet, Makt: en innføring i diskursanalyse* [Meaning, materiality, power: an introduction to discourse analysis], Bergen: Fagbokforlaget.
Ng, B.D. and Wiemer-Hastings, P. (2005) 'Addiction to the Internet and online gaming', *CyberPsychology and Behavior*, 8, 2: 110–13.
Ni Ching-Ching, 'Game aims to make vintage communism a hit with children', *Los Angeles Times* 5 November 2005. Online. Available at: www.concordmonitor.com/apps/pbcs.dll/article?AID=/20051106/REPOSITOR/511060370/1037/NEWS04 [accessed 17 September 2010].
Norwegian News Agency (NTB) (2 February 2008) 'Utesteder fulle av ulovlige kameraer' [Numerous illegal cameras installed in restaurants and bars]. Online. Available at: www.vg.no/nyheter/innenriks/artikkel.php?artid=510409 [accessed 17 September 2010].
O'Brien, K. and Li, L. (2006) *Rightful Resistance in Rural China*, Cambridge: Cambridge University Press.
Ogden, S. (2004) 'From patronage to profits: the changing relationship of Chinese intellectuals with the Party-state', in E. Gu and M. Goldman (eds) *Chinese Intellectuals Between State and Market*, London: Routledge Curzon, pp. 111–37.
Oxford University Press (2010) *Oxford English Dictionary*. Online. Available at: http://dictionary.oed.com/ [accessed 14 August 2010].

Pan Deng (2006) 'Quanzhou wangluo wanjia zaoyu wei quan mangdian' [Quanzhou online gamer encounters a blind spot in (consumer) rights], DNZB 15 March, A13.
Peterson, R.A. (1992) 'Understanding audience segmentation: from elite and mass to omnivore and univore', *Poetics*, 21: 243–58.
Pieper, J. (1952) *Leisure: the basis of culture*, trans. Alexander Dru, London: Faber and Faber.
van der Poel, H. (2006) 'Sociology and cultural studies', in C. Rojek, S.M. Shaw and A.J. Veal (eds) *A Handbook of Leisure Studies*, Basingstoke: Palgrave Macmillan, pp. 93–108.
'Quanguo wangba nianchanzhi 250 duo yi yuan' [Total annual value of production for Internet cafés in China is more than 25 billion], DNZB 7 April 2006, A2.
Quanzhou bowuguan (2005) 'Jian jie' [Synopsis of Quanzhou museum]. Information booklet.
Quanzhou shi difangzhi bianzuan weiyuanhui (ed.) (2004a) *Quanzhou shi difangzhi* [Quanzhou gazetteer], volumes I–IV, Beijing: Zhongguo shehui kexue chubanshe.
Quanzhou shi difangzhi bianzuan weiyuanhui (ed.) (2004b) *Quanzhou nianjian 2004* [Quanzhou yearbook 2004], Beijing: Fangzhi chubanshe.
Quanzhou shi gongcheng zixun gongsi (2002). *Quanzhou shi tushuguan xin guan gongcheng: Yu ke xing yanjiu baogao* [The project to build a new building for the Quanzhou municipal library: preliminary feasibility study], internal report.
Quanzhou shi renmin zhengfu [Quanzhou municipal people's government], '07 nian Quanzhou shi renkou qingkuang' [The population of Quanzhou municipality as of –07]. *Zhongguo Quanzhou* 28 August 2008. Online. Available at: www.fjqz.gov.cn/07 CFEE1887BCDB2FD3DF0E26FDA13AB8/2007–10–06/BFE8F50D8F05FA9AB-774C7541B002AA2.htm [accessed 14 August 2010].
Quanzhou shi tongji ju, 'Quanzhou shi di wu ci quanguo renkou pucha zhuyao shuju gongbao' [Bulletin of data pertaining to Quanzhou municipality from the fifth nation-wide census] *Quanzhou statistical network* [Quanzhou tongji xinxiwang] 25 May 2001. Online. Available at: www.qztj.gov.cn/outweb/View.asp?NewsID=679 [accessed 14 August 2010].
Quanzhou shi tushuguan (1991) *Quanzhou shi tushuguan duzhe shouce* [Quanzhou municipal library readers' handbook], 2nd edition.
Quanzhou shi wenhua ju (QZSWHJ) (2005) 'Quanzhou shi wenhua ju 2005 nian gongzuo zongjie ji 2006 nian gongzuo yaodian' [Summary of the work of Quanzhou municipal bureau of culture in 2005 and main points for the work in 2006], internal report.
Rankin, M.B. (1993)'Some observations on a Chinese public sphere', *Modern Asia*, 19, 2: 158–82.
Roberts, K. (1999) *Leisure in Contemporary Society*, Oxon: CABI Publishing.
Roberts, K. (2002) 'Are long or unsocial hours of work bad for leisure?' in G. Crow and S. Heath (eds) *Social Conceptions of Time: structure and process in work and every-day life*, New York: Palgrave Macmillan, pp. 165–78.
Rojek, C. (1985) *Capitalism and Leisure Theory*, London: Tavistock Publications.
Rojek, C. (2006) 'Leisure, culture and civilization', in C. Rojek, S.M. Shaw and A.J. Veal (eds) *A Handbook of Leisure Studies*, Basingstoke: Palgrave Macmillan, pp. 25–40.
Rojek, Chris, S.M. Shaw and A.J. Veal (eds) (2006) *A Handbook of Leisure Studies*, Basingstoke: Palgrave Macmillan.
Rolandsen, U.M.H. (2004) 'In pursuit of education: attitudes towards education in a rural Chinese township', unpublished MA thesis, University of Oslo.
Rolandsen, U.M.H. (2010) 'A collective of their own: young volunteers at the fringes of

the Party realm', in M.H. Hansen and R. Svarverud (eds) *iChina: the rise of the individual in modern Chinese society*, Copenhagen: NIAS Press, pp. 132–63.

Rong An (1995) 'Dui kewai huodong hanyi de zai sikao' [Reflections on the contents of in-school activities], *Journal of Yuling Teachers College*, 16, 2: 89–92.

Saich, T. (2000) 'Negotiating the state: the development of social organisations in China', *The China Quarterly*, 161: 124–41.

Scott, J.C. (1990) *Dominance and the Arts of Resistance: hidden transcripts*, New Haven: Yale University Press.

Seabrook, J. (1988) *The Leisure Society*, Oxford: Basil Blackwell.

Shangwu yinshuguan (2003) *Xinhua xinciyu cidian* [Xinhua dictionary of neologisms], Beijing: Shangwu yinshuguan.

Siu, H.F. (2005) 'The cultural landscape of luxury housing in South China – a regional history', in Jing Wang (ed.) *Locating China: space, place and popular culture*, New York: Routledge, pp. 72–91.

Song Shuyang and Wu Xingwu (2002) 'Chuzhong xianxia jiaoyu xianzhuang diaocha yanjiu [Research survey into the status quo of junior middle school leisure education], *Jinghua zhiye jishu xueyuan xuebao*, 3: 110–12.

Stebbins, R.A. (2004) *Between Work and Leisure: the common ground between two worlds*, London: Transaction Publishers.

Stewart, J. (2000) 'Cafematics: the cyber café and the community', in M. Gurstein (ed.) *Community Informatics: enabling communities with information and communications technologies*, London: Idea Group Publishing, 320–38. Online. Available at: http://books.google.com/books?id=SZuV30B4XwYC&hl=no [accessed 17 September 2010].

Sun Hui and Wang Shujuan (2003) 'Guanzhu xuesheng chengzhang tianbu jiating jiaoyu de zhenkong: dui fumu wu guding zhiye, wu wending shouru jiating xuesheng de jiaoyu yanjiu' [Pay attention to students' development, fill the gaps in family education. A study of the education of students from families without regular employment or stable incomes], *Xiandai zhongxiaoxue jiaoyu* [Modern Primary and Secondary Education], 4: 58–9.

Sun Xiaoli (2004) 'Jianli kexue, jiankang, wenming de shenghuo fangshi' [Establishing a scientific, healthy, and civilised lifestyle], in Ma Huidi and Zhang Jing'an (eds) *Zhongguo gongzhong xiuxian zhuangkuang diaocha* [Survey studies of the state of (sic.) leisure life among the Chinese public], Beijing: Zhongguo jingji chubanshe, pp. 73–90.

Sæther, E. (2006) 'Field work as coping and learning', in M. Heimer and S. Thøgersen (eds) *Doing Fieldwork in China*, Copenhagen: NIAS Press, pp. 42–57.

Tai Rongli (1995) 'Zhongxiaoxue kewai huodong xianzhuang ji guanli sikao' [Thoughts on the state of affairs and the management of in-school activities in primary and secondary schools], *Qian dongnan minzu shi zhuan xue bao*,13, 1: 85–7.

Tan Jianguang, He Guosen and Liu Shan (2002) 'Zhong xiao chengzhen qingnian zhiyuan fuwu fazhan moshi chutan' [Development modes of youth voluntary service in small to medium towns], *Guangdong qingnian ganbu xueyuan xuebao*, 48, 2: 36–41.

Tang Qirong and Weng Hongxiang, 'Cunzai xiaofang yinhuan "hei wangba" bei chafeng' ['Black' Internet cafés sealed because of hidden fire hazards], DNZB 6 April 2006, A8.

Teslik, A. (18 September 2007) 'Eight honors, Eight disgraces', *China Government Watch*. Online blog post. Available at: http://cngovwatch.blogspot.com/2007_09_01_archive.html [accessed 14 August 2010].

Tian Cuiqin and Qi Xin (2005) *Nongcun xianxia* [Rural leisure], Beijing: Shehui kexue wenxian chubanshe.

Thompson, E.P. (1967) 'Time, work discipline and industrial capitalism', *Past and Present*, 38: 56–97.

Thøgersen, S. (2000) 'Cultural life and cultural control in rural China: where is the Party?', *The China Journal*, 44: 129–41.
Thøgersen, S. (2003) 'Parasites or civilizers: the legitimacy of the Chinese Communist Party in Rural Areas', *China: An International Journal*, 1, 2: 200–23.
Thøgersen, S. (2006) 'Beyond official Chinese: language codes' in M. Heimer and S. Thøgersen (eds) *Doing Fieldwork in China*, Copenhagen: NIAS Press, pp. 110–26.
Tomba, L. (2004) 'Creating an urban middle class: social engineering in Beijing', *The China Journal*, 51: 1–26.
Tsai, L.C.-T. (2006) 'The influence of Confucianism on women's leisure in Taiwan', *Leisure Studies*, 25, 4: 469–76.
Wang, D. (2003) *Streetlife Chengdu: public space, urban commoners, and local politics 1870–1930*, Stanford: Stanford University Press.
Wang, J. (2001a) 'The state question in Chinese popular culture studies', *Inter-Asia Cultural Studies*, 2, 1: 35–52.
Wang, J. (2001b) 'Culture as leisure and culture as capital', *Positions* 9, 1: 69–104.
Wang, J. (2005a) (ed.) *Locating China: space, place and popular culture*, New York: Routledge.
Wang, J. (2005b) 'Introduction: the politics and production of scales in China', in J. Wang (ed.) *Locating China: space, place and popular culture*, New York: Routledge, pp. 1–30.
Wang Mingming (1993) 'Flowers of the state, grasses of the people: yearly rites and aesthetics of power in Quanzhou in the southeastern macro-region of China', unpublished thesis, University of London.
Wang Qiting, Li Xin and Shi Lei (2004) 'Beijing shi jumin xianxia shijian liyong diaocha yu Yanjiu' [Survey and research into the spending of leisure time among citizens in Beijing municipality], in Ma Huidi and Zhang Jing'an (eds) *Zhongguo gongzhong xiuxian zhuangkuang diaocha* [Survey studies of the state of leisure life among the Chinese public], Beijing: Zhongguo jingji chubanshe, pp. 144–59.
Wang, S. (1995) 'The politics of private time: changing leisure patterns in urban China', in D. Davis *et al.* (eds) *Urban Spaces in Contemporary China: the potential for autonomy and community in post-Mao China*, Cambridge: Cambridge University Press, pp. 149–72.
Wang, S., Davis, D. and Bian Yanjie (2006) 'The uneven distribution of cultural capital: book reading in urban China', *Modern China*, 32, 3: 315–48.
Wang Yalin (ed.) (2003) *Chengshi xiuxian: Shanghai, Tianjin, Haerbin shi jumin shijian fenpei de kaocha* [Urban leisure: time distribution study among the inhabitants of Shanghai, Tianjin and Haerbin], Beijing: Shehui kexue wenxian chubanshe.
Wang Yalin, Xu Liya and Liu Er (2004) 'Zaiyezhe xianxia shijian fenpei zhuangkuang de diaocha: Dui Haerbin shi de diaocha' [Survey of leisure time distribution among employees: an investigation of Haerbin municipality], in Ma Huidi and Zhang Jing'an (eds) *Zhongguo gongzhong xiuxian zhuangkuang diaocha* [Survey studies of the state of (sic.) leisure life among the Chinese public], Beijing: Zhongguo jingji chubanshe, pp. 104–17.
Wang Yihong (2005) 'Diwei biaoqian yu xiuxian shenghuo' [Status markers and leisure life], in Zhou Xiaohong (ed.) *Zhongguo zhongchan jieceng diaocha* [Survey of the Chinese middle stratum], Beijing: Social Sciences Academic Press, pp. 111–51.
Wang Zhongwu (2005) 'Xiaofei wenhua yu Zhongguo xiandaihua' [Consumer culture and the modernisation of China], *Xuexi yu tansuo* [Study and exploration] 161, 6: 123–26.

Wenlin Institute (2002) *Wenlin Software for Learning Chinese*, version 3.0. Software.
'Worried China bans new Internet cafés for a year', Reuters (Beijing) 7 March 2007. Online. Available at: www.reuters.com/article/internetNews/idUSPEK24407720070307 [accessed 17 September 2010].
Wu Dingbo and Murphy, P.D. (1994) *Handbook of Chinese Popular Culture*, Westport, Conn.: Greenwood Press.
Xia Yiran (2004) 'Wailai wugongzhe de xiuxian shenghuo zhuangkuang yanjiu–Laizi Wenzhou Lucheng gongyequ de diaocha' [The study of leisure lives of migrant workers: a survey from Lucheng industry district in Wenzhou], unpublished thesis, Xiamen University.
Xiangshan xian pufa ban [Xiangshan county office for the popularization of the law], 'Ta tanlian youxiji er fanzui' [Clinging to video games made him a criminal], *Xiangshan pufa wang* 18 January 2006. Online. Available at: http://xspf.nbxs.gov.cn/Article/ArticleShow.asp?ArticleID=106 [accessed 14 August 2010].
Xie Weiduan (2006) 'Xianchang: wangba nei jiman le haizi [On the spot: internet cafés crowded with children], DNZB, 22 March, A5.
'Xin "san dajian" jinru Zhongguo xunchang baixing' [The new "three big items" enter ordinary people's homes] xinhuanet.com 25 September 2005. Online. Available at: http://news.xinhuanet.com/politics/2005-09/25/content_3539533.htm [accessed 17 September 2010].
Xiu Sheng, 'Xue Lei Feng youxi: xin ping dai jiu jiu?' [The Study Lei Feng Game: old wine in new bottles?], HXDSB, 16 March 2006, A4.
Yan Peng, Xie Weiduan, Huang Yifen and Wang Xiaolin 'KTV yao "dong da Shoushu" le?' [Are KTVs in for 'major surgery'?], DNZB, 15 February 2006, A8.
Yan, Yunxiang (1999) 'Rural youth culture in North China', *Culture, Medicine and Psychiatry*, 23: 75–97.
Yan, Yunxiang (2000) 'Of hamburger and social space: consuming McDonald's in Beijing', in D.S. Davis (ed.) *The Consumer Revolution in Urban China*, Berkeley: University of California Press, pp. 201–25.
Yan, Yunxiang (2003) *Private life under socialism: love, intimacy, and family change in a Chinese village*, Stanford: Stanford University Press.
Yang Guobin (2003) 'The Cc-evolution of the Internet and civil society in China', *Asian Survey*, 43, 3: 405–22.
Yang, Mayfair Mei-hui (2004) 'Spatial struggles: postcolonial complex, state disenchantment, and popular reappropriation of space in rural Southeast China', *The Journal of Asian Studies*, 63, 3: 719–55.
Yu Guangyuan (2004) 'Xu yi' [Preface], in Ma Huidi, Zhouxiang renwen guanhuai de xiuxian jingji [Towards a leisure economy with humanistic concerns], Beijing: Zhongguo jingji chubanshe, 1–2.
Yu Guangyuan and Ma Huidi (2006) 'Guannyu "xianxia" yu "xiuxian" liang ge guannian de duihua lu' [Record of a dialogue on the concepts 'xianxia' and 'xiuxian'], Ziran bianzheng fa yanjiu [Studies in the Dialectics of Nature], 22, 9: 86–92.
Zhang Jian (2004) 'Qianshaonian xianxia shijian liyong zhuangkuang duice yanjiu' [How young students make use of their leisure time. Research and countermeasures], in Ma Huidi and Zhang Jing'an (eds) Zhongguo gongzhong xiuxian zhuangkuang diaocha [Survey studies of the state of leisure life among the Chinese public], Beijing: Zhongguo jingji chubanshe, pp. 208–23.
Zhang Taiyuan (2007) 'Ershi shijie jiushi niandai Zhongguo chengshi jumin de wenhua xiaofei: Yi Beijing wei lie' [Cultural consumption of the Chinese urban residents in the

1990s: taking Beijing as an example], *Contemporary China History Studies*, 14, 1: 102–10.

Zhang Xiaofeng and Fan Guorui (2002) 'Chengshihua shijiao xia nongcun jiaoyu de wenti yu duice: Yi Henan sheng Shenqiu xian wei li' [Policies and problems in rural education seen from the angle of modernisation: the case of Shenqiu County in Henan Province], *Journal of Xinzhou Teachers University*, 18, 1: 50–3.

Zhang Ye (2003) 'China's emerging civil society'. Online. Available at: www.brookings-institute.org/fp/cnaps/papers/ye2003.pdf [accessed 24 September, 2010].

Zhang Zujun (1997) 'Dui shuangxiu ri de yixie sikao' [Some thoughts about weekends], Longyan shishuan xuebao [Journal of Longyan Teachers' College] 15, 1: 65–6.

Zhao Jicheng, 'Wangba paizhao jiejin, yi fang jiu luan?' [Do Internet cafés become chaotic as soon as license restrictions are lifted?], HXDSB 7 Apri l2006, A4.

Zhou Xiaohong (2005) 'Daoyan: Zhongguo zhongchan jieceng de lishi yu xianzhuang' [Introduction: The history and current situation of the Chinese middle class], in Zhou Xiaohong (ed.) Zhongguo zhongchan jieceng diaocha [Survey of the Chinese middle stratum], Beijing: Social Sciences Academic Press, pp. 1–28.

Zhu Huangnian (2007) 'Puxie xin pianzhang – Zai zhu xin huihuang. Di si jie chengshi sheyin dahui zongjie baogao' [Writing a new chapter, casting brilliance once again: final report from the fourth Urban Photo Conference], Quanzhou: Di si jie chengshi sheyin dahui zuweihui, report, March 15, 3 unnumbered pages.

Index

Please note: locators in **bold** type indicate figures or illustrations, those in *italics* indicate tables.

administrative elite, leisure practices of the 130
agency 12, 44, 71, 138, 143, 145, 147, 160
ai pin cai hui ying (you can only succeed if you exert yourself) 5
alcohol abuse: binge drinking 109, 127; excessive drinking 67, 130, 132–3
Anagnost, A. 14, 57, 65, 67, 125, 134, 141
Analects, The 51
ancient Rome 45
anthropological analysis, value of local terms and concepts for 49
Anxi tie guanyin tea 24
Appetites (Farquhar) 151

Bailey, C.A. 31
Baixingese 49–53
Bakken, B. 60, 111, 125–6
Bauman, Z. 55
Bayat, A. 56
Beck, Ulrich 185, 186, 199
Beck-Gernsheim, Elisabeth 185, 186, 199
Beijing: fear of chaos among elderly people in 110; propagation of 'leisure culture' in 144–5
binge drinking 109, 127
birth planning 141
book cafés/bookshops: accessibility 92; cultured consumption 157–8; and educational leisure 93–6; increasing popularity 93; layout 88; loan services 90–1; opening times 92; as place of study 90; pleasant surroundings 92; in the US 88; user interviews 89–90
Book of Changes 51
Bourdieu, Pierre 72, 148
'bread and circuses' 160

Britain, Roberts' study of leisure in 48
bu jiankang see unhealthy leisure
burial rites 159
Burke, P. 45
business transactions, leisure places as site for 40

cadres: leisure time 130; spare time 49; use of leisure spaces 109
Cartier, C. 72
censorship, Internet 115
de Certeau, M. 6, 9, 13, 41, 162, 176–7, 180
chaotic leisure *see luan* (chaotic leisure)
charging the batteries (*chongdian*) 93–6
chi ku (hardship) 5
Chinese authorities, regulatory practices 83
Chinese Hero Registry (government-sponsored online game) 123
Chinese leisure, earliest research 3
Chinese middle class, Zhou's survey 26
Chinese New Year 79, 85, 124, 137, 152–3, 176
Chinese Scholars' Leisure Research (Ma) 51
chongdian (charging the batteries) 93–6
civil society 10, 64, 104, 182
civility (*wenming*) 57, 60, 84, 95–6, 123, 154–5
civilization 14, 57, 60, 65, 67, 95, 138, 159
Civilized Internet Use, posters 35
clothing, use of colour in 139–40
CNNIC (China Internet Network Information Centre) 118–19, 122
code-switching 49–50, 52
Cohen, M.S. 8

the collective: and official leisure discourse 2, 5–6, 47, 57–8, 61, 65; sociologists' preoccupation with the duties of the individual towards 58
commercial leisure places, role of 106–7
computer games: engagement and stimulation 56; government initiatives 123; media portrayal 120; as unhealthy leisure 54, 124; in the workplace 47, 78
Confucius Temple and Square 24, 80–1, 142
conspicuous consumption 154–6, 159–60
consumer habits, examples of bad 159
consumer rights: awareness 147; and the media 145; as a substitute for democracy 146–7
consumerism: anti- 140; concerns about the detrimental effects of 141; Latham on 143
Consumers' Day 120, 145–6
Consuming China (Latham) 143
consumption: acceptability 140, 142; across the generation gap 151–3; children and 150; and clothing styles 139–40; Communist Party's mixed messages 159; consumers and advertisers as agents in the market 145–8; contradictory attitudes towards 4, 10, 14–15, 26, 28, 33–4, 39, 47, 49, 60, 63, 65, 67, 89, 129–30, 132, 136–60, 166; Davis and Sensenbrenner's study 150; indicators of the Chinese government's interest in boosting private 145; media's role 145; migrant worker with a taste for middle class-style **136**; positive side effects 147; of 'rational recreation' 144; in real-estate advertisements 141–2; 'revolution' in 137–8; scope of cultural 142–3; separating culture from commerce 157–60; shopping as a meaningful leisure activity 148–53; and social engineering 143–5; 'three big items' 140; traditional concept 138–9; under Maoist collectivism 140; Wang's analyses 15, 138, 142–8, 153
cricket 48
Critiques of Everyday Life (Gardiner) 6
Croll, E. 137–8, 141, 143, 145, 149
Csikszentmihalyi, M. and LeFevre, H. 41
cultivation 10, 14
cultural capital 49, 72–3, 83, 107, 125, 143, 148, 154
cultural competence: and consumption 144, 155, 160; and the health of leisure activities 134; increased focus on 57; of the Internet café customer 124–5; and the PRC leisure ethic 63–4, 66, 93; raising levels of 5, 57, 95, 107, 158–9
cultural phenomenon, leisure as a 46–8
cultured middle classes: anti-commercialist values 158, 160; contradictory attitudes towards consumption 155–6; definition 154; 'obscured consumption' strategies 160; and official leisure ethic 159; types of leisure spending 155

Daily, G. and Ellison, K. 169
Davis, D.S. 10, 97; and Sensenbrenner, J.S. 47, 150
defining leisure 38–9, 45
definitions of leisure: as experience 41–3; as practice 43–4; as 'spare' time 39–41
democracy, consumer rights as a substitute for 146–7
Dikötter, F. 139
discourse analysis 11
discourse of civility 60, 65, 84, 134
discourse of class 57, 134
discourse of healthy leisure 13, 71
discourse of leisure 2, 5, 11, 67, 83
discourses of morality 10
Dongnan Zaobao (newspaper) 34
drinking: binge 109, 127; excessive 67, 130, 132–3
drug abuse 109, 126, 129–30, 132, 134

East Lake Park **1**, 110
education: and chaotic leisure practices 133; healthy leisure and 109; and upward social mobility 95
educational leisure 14, 57, 71, 73, 93–6, 107
Elderly People's Day 43
English language practice, as leisure pursuit 101, 103
'entertainment market', role of the authorities 116
entertainment places, regulations for the supervision of 129
everyday life: analyses of 6; and city planning 83; conditions of 27; consumption's place 143, 154; dullness of under collectivism 9; hiking's place in 82; insights into 10; lack of information about 8; speed of 63; state control 2; tea culture's place 24; work and leisure's coexistence as an aspect of 48; as worthy of scholarly attention 55

Everything Bad Is Good for You (Johnson) 56
excessive drinking 67, 130, 132–3
Exemplary Society, The (Bakken) 125
Exotic Commodities (Dikötter) 139

Falun Gong 183
Fangen, K. 31
Farquhar, J. 151, 153; and Qicheng Zhang 110
'FB' 35, 52
Federation of Literature and Art Circles 99, 104
Feng Chongyi 10, 104–5
Festa, P.E. 11, 67
Fewsmith, J. 26, 146
food scandals 147
foot massage 20, 25, 43, 51, 127, 148
Foucault, M. 13
Frankfurter school 15, 54
'free-riding' 47
free time 7, 38–9, 41, 50, 56, 59, 63, 160
free time (*ziyou shijian*) 38, 50, 59
freedom: agency and 44; leisure as 39, 41, 43–4, 94
Friedman, S.L. 11, 67, 114
friendship ties 114
Fujian 5, 20–1, 23, 28, 34, 36, 50, 80–1, 100, 102, 114, 140, 142
Fujian Ribao (newspaper) 34
fun *see wan*

gambling 67, 108, 112
Ganbunese 49–50, 52–3
Gans, H. 55, 67
Gardiner, M. 6
gender separation, in Friedman's analysis 114
geti laodongzhe (self-employed workers) 49
Glorious Bookshop 124
Great Leap Forward 151
guanxi (social network) 79
Gutting, G. 95

Haixia Dushibao (newspaper) 34
Happy Outdoors 101–5, 164
hardship (*chi ku*) 5
having fun (*wan*) 35, 51–3, 64, 75, 91, 95, 148
He Xuefeng 64
healthy leisure: 'charging the batteries' 93–6; criteria 4; the decline of the library and the rise of the book café 86; and education 109; examples 85–6; local government's contribution 108; state promotion 12, 85–6; towards a public sphere with Chinese characteristics 104–7; typical activities 86; vs unhealthy 60; unofficial leisure organizations 101–4
hedonism 4, 155, 160
Heintz, M. 47
Henderson, G.E. and Cohen, M.S. 8–9
'hidden transcripts', Scott's theory of 162, 179–80, 182
history of leisure 44–6
Huang, P.C.C. 47
Hui'an women, Friedman's monograph 11
human capital 63, 65–6

idleness: authorities' fear 60; in Chinese scholars' writing 64; fear of the consequences of 60; negative connotations 47, 50–1, 64; and poverty 55; Puritan perspective 55
individual: concern for 6; denial of under collectivism 140; development opportunities for 42; and the leisure ethic 63–5, 107; and the power of consumption 147; significance of leisure for the well-being of 41; sociologists' preoccupation with the duties of towards the collective 58; and the spread of chaos 111, 114
individual choice 44
individualization 185–6
industrial revolution, leisure as a product of the 45
informal interviews 29–32, 150, 155–6
informed consent, of interviewees 32
intellectuals (*wenren*) 156
International Consumers' Day 145
International Women's Day 35
Internet: censorship 115; civilized use (*Wangluo wenming*) 35; home accessibility 118–19; information centre (CNNIC) 118–19, 122; parental regulation 118; penetration rate in China 116
Internet addiction: Johansson and Götestam's study 119; official statistics 119; in South Korea 122; treatment 122
Internet bars, regulations for the management of 4
Internet cafés: annual production value 116; 'black' 116–17, 119–20; as chaotic leisure places 124–6, 134; Glorious

Bookshop's facilities 124; 'green' 123; guidance and self-governance 121–4; and income level 123; justifications for government monitoring 118; market regulation 115–18; media portrayal 120–1, 125–6; middle-class attitudes 133–4; nationwide chains 117; propaganda posters 115, 119–20, 122–3; and public security 118; regulation 115; as threat to moral order 122
interviewee identification strategies, Quanzhou study 29–30

Japan, Linhart's study of leisure values and activities 46–7
Jeffreys, E. 129
jiankang see healthy leisure
Jinjiang 23, 117
Johansson, A. and Götestam, K.G. 119
Johnson, S. 56
juvenile delinquency 59, 122

karaoke: acceptability 130; ambiguous reputation 126; as chaotic leisure practice 132–3; costs 127; in Friedman's analysis 114–15; media portrayal 126, 132, 134; middle-class attitudes 126–7, 132, 134; multiple meanings 127–9; and privacy 128–31; supervision regulations 129–31
key informants 27
kite-flying 74, 75, **76**, 83
Kleiber, D. 41

langdang gong (loitering work) 47
language codes 49–50
Latham, K. 143
Lefebvre, H. 6, 9, 12–13, 69, 72–3, 114, 171
Lei Feng youxi (Party produced computer game) 123
leisure: Chinese scholars' studies of 48–9; cultural perspective 46–8; defining 38–9, 45; etymology 39; historical perspective 44–6; paradoxes in scholars' descriptions and analyses of 4; pioneering studies of in China 59; rhetoric of useful and goal-oriented 71
leisure activities, decisive indicators 49
leisure consumption: as a form of 'bread and circuses' 160; party-state's message 67
'leisure culture', guiding principles for 144
leisure duty 43

leisure establishments, local cadres' attitudes towards 109
leisure ethic 4–6, 10, 12–14, 16, 49, 53–4, 57–9, 63–7, 71, 83–6, 93–6, 103, 107–9, 115, 122, 130, 133–5, 144, 154–5, 158–9
leisure organizations, unofficial 101–4
leisure place 13–14, 25, 73, 77–80, 82, 90–2, 121, 128, 144, 161, 164, 177, 181–2
leisure space 3, 12–13, 16, 20, 69, 73, 83, 127, 144, 148, 161–82
leisure time, as wealth 64
Li Chunli 26
Li Chunling 146
Li Yisun 65
libraries, public *see* public libraries
Linhart, S. 46–7, 58
Lippit, V. 64
Little Huang 112, **113**, 114, 122
Locating China (Jing Wang) 10
loitering work (*langdang gong*) 47
luan (chaotic leisure) 4, 12, 14, 107, 109–11, 114–15, 117, 125–6, 133–4, 141

Ma Feifeng 65
Ma Huidi 41, 50–2, 59, 61, 64, 87, 93; and Zhang Jing'an 34
Madsen, R. 6, 8
majiang 10, 60, 67, **69**, 80, 164
making do 13, 171, 176–7, 179–80, 182
Mandarin 35–7, 49–50
Manell, R. 41
Maoism 2, 6–8, 58, 81, 96, 110, 137, 140
Maritime Silk Road Festival 99
'material civilization' 57
McNay, L. 13–14
McNeill, D. 63
Meng Lei 60, 153
metaphorical concept, leisure ethic's basis in 57
Mid-Autumn Festival 35
middle class consumer, media imagery 153
middle classes: and consumer policies 145; consumption of services 148; definition 154; Fewsmith's analysis of the relationship between the party-state and 146; interest in political participation 146; significance of shopping among 137
migrant worker with a taste for middle class-style consumption **136**
Miller, D. 147

Minnan area 21, 27, 36, 149
Minnan culture, chauvinism in 27
Minnan hua (dialect) 24, 36
Mintaiyuan Museum and Square 70–1, 73, 75, **76**
moonlighting 47
mountain climbing (*pashan*) 163–7
museums: audience 71; funding 72; location of in Quanzhou 70; public expectations 72; *see also* Mintaiyuan Museum and Square; Quanzhou Museum and Square

nanyin (song tradition) 7, 24, 80
Neumann, I.B. 66
newspapers 34

official leisure discourse *see* PRC leisure ethic
Ogden, S. 154
one-child policy 15
out-of-town workers (*waidi ren*) 110

pacification tools, consumer policies as 138
participant observation 12–13, 15, 31–3, 36, 131
party-state: administrative hierarchy 104; campaigns against 'superstitious' activities 110; clothing styles 139; encouragement of private consumption 159; Festa's analysis 10–11; Foucaldian perspective 6, 13; and healthy leisure 4, 10, 13, 57, 96, 106–7; justification for official leisure ethic 5; language codes 49; and leisure associations 97, 99–100, 103; 'leisure duty' 43; and the media 34, 105; mixed messages 67–8; official language 49; organized leisure activities 97; and PRC leisure ethic 57; relationship between middle classes and 146; social engineering attempts 138, 143–4; and unhealthy leisure 108–9, 115; use of leisure consumption as governing tool 15; Wang's analysis of attitudes to leisure of 7, 146, 148, 159–60; young people's attitude 105
party-state's attitudes 7, 146, 148, 159–60
pashan (mountain climbing) 163–7
personal development 59, 66
Photographers' Association 97, **98**, 99–100, 104, 106
piano lessons 43
Pieper, J. 41

playing cards **78**
Popular China (Link *et al.*) 10
popular culture: criticisms 54; development of new genres of 35; elitist denunciation 54–5; examples of 53, 61; influence 135; Johnson's defence of 56; and the PRC leisure ethic 49; restrictions on 56; scepticism towards 86; as 'unhealthy' 107
popular culture critique 5, 15, 54, 56, 58; Gans on 55, 67
practice, leisure as 43–5, 148
Practice of Everyday Life, The (de Certeau) 41, 176
PRC leisure ethic: in academic writing 59–68; central aim 86; characteristics 57–9; class and civility discourses 134; contradictions in Chinese scholars' analyses 61–3; disciplinary perspective 94–5; impact on local practices 5; influence 133; leisure and the fate of the nation 65–6; leisure as a resource 63–4; leisure practices of the privileged 155; leisure types 4; term analysis 5–6
predestination, Calvin's theory 55
privacy 131
problem drinking 67, 109, 127, 130, 132–3
production of space 12, 69, 72, 114, 143
Production of Space, The (Lefebvre) 72
Professional English Club 30, 101, 103–5, 128
propaganda campaigns 2, 5, 35, 67, 144–5, 182
propaganda posters 30, 112, **113**, 115, 119–20, 122–3, 125, 139
prostitution 108, 114, 129–30
Protestant work ethic 5, 42, 54–5, 65, 67
public funds, unlawful spending of 109
public libraries: accusations of money worship 157; criticisms 91; government investment 88; Internet provision 124–5; opening times 92; users 88
public sphere: Rankin's definition 105; towards a 104–7
public squares 20, 24, 69–75, **76, 77**, 79–81, 93, 142
Puritan ethics 55

Qingyuan Mountain: antagonism between locals and reserve administration 173–6, 181–2; climbing (*pashan*) 163–5; costs of restoration work 162; cultural relics 170–1; environmental protection 169–70, 182; family tombs 170–1; fire hazards 171; funding and management priorities 168–9; income generation 167–8; lunch on **165**; most popular leisure activities 163–4; official opening times 178; as a place of recreation 165–6; as a source of wellness 166–7; Tianhu Lake area 163–4, 167–9, 171, 177–8; ticket evasion 173, 177–8; ticket prices and sales 162; tourists and local visitors 171–3; ways of 'making do' 176–82

quality of life 6, 59, 139

quantitative studies 40

Quanzhou: analyses of the relationship between the official discourse of leisure and the leisure practices of people in 144; book cafés 85, 88, 90 (*see also* book cafés/bookshops); cadres' patronization of 'unhealthy' leisure places 109; centre of activities 81; changing practices in a changing cityscape 81–4; cinemas 25; code-switching 51–2; Confucius Temple and Square 24, 80–1, 142; contemporary architecture 23; cultural perspective 24–5; Culture Palaces 25, 80–1; design 81; dialect 24; dismantling of 'black' Internet cafés 117; East Lake Park **1**; elderly people enjoying a game of *majiang* at *Tongfo si* **69**; exercise areas 78–9; Fengze district and Square 75, **77**, 81; historical perspective 21–2; Internet cafés 123–4; key informants 27; leisure organizations with party connections 97–100; leisure trends 49; library location 82–3; local authority plans for a connected tourist area 70; location 21; Maritime Silk Road Square 77; middle-class leisure in 26–7; most common forms of local leisure 19–20; museum area 70–2, 83 (*see also* Mintaiyuan Museum and Square; Quanzhou Museum and Square); *nanyin* performances 80; 'new city centre' 81; plans for a new leisure area 80; recreation area plans 70–1; skyline **19**; tea culture 24; temple square 80; transport links 23–4; university campuses 25; use of *xiuxian* 51; villa living 142; West Lake Park **38**, 70, 74, 82

Quanzhou Book City 90, 93

Quanzhou Library: funding 87; location 87; number of visitors 88

Quanzhou Municipality: ethnic groups 21; structure 21

Quanzhou Museum and Square 70–3, 75, 79, 81

Quanzhou Photographers' Association 97–9

Quanzhou study: fieldwork language 35–7; gate openers and key informants 27–9; interviewee identification strategies 29–30; interviews, observation, participation 31–3; sources 34–5

Rankin, M. 104–5

reading 5, 20, 25, 33, 39–40, 52, **85**, 96; *see also* book cafés/bookshops; public libraries

'Regulations for the supervision of public entertainment places' 129

religious festivals 159

renao (lively activities) 75, **77**, 80, 150, 152

resistance 6–7, 12–14, 41, 47, 55, 73, 162, 171, 180–1

resource, leisure as a 63–4

Roberts, K. 45–6, 48

Rojek, C. 5; *et al* 44

Romania, work ethic 47

Rome 45

rural teenagers, field study of leisure among 50

'Rural youth culture in North China' (Yan) 152

Saich, T. 100

SARS outbreak 147

Sæther, E. 31

Scott, J.C. 13, 162, 180

self-censorship 44, 66

self-employed workers (*geti laodongzhe*) 49

semi-structured interview 32–3

Shaoguang Wang 48, 56, 107

Shenzhen, urban planning 72

Shishi 23

shopping, as a meaningful leisure activity 148–53

singing, as leisure pursuit (Quanzhou Municipal Choir) 32, 99–100, 104–5, 107, 128

SMS-greetings 35

social capital 178

social engineering 12, 15, 106, 138, 143, 143–5

social networks (*guanxi*) 79

social production of space 12, 69

socialization: Bakken's metaphor 125–6; basic principle of 111

space: Lefebvre's argument 114; the production of 12, 69, 72, 114, 143; as a social product 72–3
spare time 38–9, 41, 48–9, 55, 57–9, 62–3, 93–4
'spatial economy', Lefebvre's 73
Spiral Road, The (Huang Shumin) 151
'spiritual civilization' 14, 57, 65, 138, 159
sponsored housing 26
Spring Festival 35, 43
Stebbins, R.A. 42
strategy and tactics, de Certeau on popular 41, 47, 162, 176–7, 179–80
Streetlife Chengdu (Wang) 45
Sun Xiaoli 4, 64–5
'superstitious' activities: authorities' campaigns against 110; authorities' campaigns against 110
surveillance 108, 118, 129
Survey studies of the state of leisure life among the Chinese public (Sun) 4
suzhi see cultural competence

taijiquan 80
task oriented time 40
tea culture, in Quanzhou 24
tea houses 5, 19–20, 25, 40, 45–6, 90, 104, 127, 135, 156–8
Thøgersen, S. 49–50, 97, 116, 132, 156
Thompson, E.P. 40, 45, 55
Tiananmen protests 15
Tianhu Lake 163–4, 167–9, 171, 177–8
Tibetan protests 110
Tomba, L. 15, 143, 145
Tongfo si, elderly people enjoying a game of *majiang* **69**
town walls, demolition of 81

unhealthy leisure: examples of 108–9; and income level 107, 109, 132; Internet cafés as 125; karaoke parlours as places of 133–4; in official discourse 60, 109; policing and control 108; and social status 133
upward social mobility, and education 95

video games, propaganda poster warning against the menace of 30, 112, **113**, 115, 119–20, 122–3, 125, 139
video surveillance, use of in places of entertainment 129
villa living, in Quanzhou 142
vocational reading 93–4
vocational schools 125

Volunteer's Association 128

waidi ren (out-of-town workers) 110
walking in the park **1**
wan 1, 5, 9, 43, 50–2, 56, 61, 64, 75, 95–6, 112, 114–15, 134, 148–9, 172
wan (having fun) 35, 51–3, 64, 75, 91, 95, 148
Wang Di 40
Wang, Jing 83, 106, 138, 143, 145–8, 151, 153
Wang Shaoguang 2, 7, 10, 25, 44, 48, 56, 58, 60, 89, 97, 106, 107, 186, 196
Wang Yalin 34, 49, 59, 64, 93, 150
Wang Zhongwu 60, 65, 130, 139
Wangluo wenming (Civilized Internet Use) 35
watching TV, and choice of activities 48
ways of making do 13, 177, 180, 182
wenming (civility) 57, 60, 84, 95–6, 123, 154–5
wenren (intellectuals) 156
West Lake Park, Sunday leisure in **38**, 70
window-shopping 5, 9, 20, 52–3, 80, 90, 138, 142, 148–50, 153
women's leisure, chauvinistic expectations 27
work ethic, Romania's 47
Workers' Culture Palace 25, 80–1
workplace leisure practices 40–1, 78, 99
workplace management, French employees' resistance to 47

xian: in classical texts 51; term analysis 50–1
xianxia (leisure as a temporal resource) 38, 50
xiaoqian (idleness) 64
xiuxian (leisure as a spiritual good) 38, 42, 50–2, 64, 70

Yan, Yunxiang 9, 152
Yang, M. 73
Yu Guangyuan 41, 50–2, 59, 64; and Ma Huidi 59

Zhang Jian 59, 61
Zhang Xinjian 129–30
Zhongguo gongzhong xiuxian zhuangkuang diaocha (Survey studies of the state of leisure life among the Chinese public) (Sun) 4
Zhou Xiaohong 26
ziyou shijian (free time) 38, 50, 59